TAXOMETRICS

TAXOMETRICS

**Toward a New
Diagnostic Scheme for
Psychopathology**

Norman B. Schmidt
Roman Kotov
Thomas E. Joiner Jr.

American Psychological Association
Washington, DC

Published by
American Psychological Association
750 First Street, NE
Washington, DC 20002
www.apa.org

To order
APA Order Department
P.O. Box 92984
Washington, DC 20090-2984
Tel: (800) 374-2721; Direct: (202) 336-5510
Fax: (202) 336-5502; TDD/TTY: (202) 336-6123
Online: www.apa.org/books/
E-mail: order@apa.org

In the U.K., Europe, Africa, and the Middle East, copies may be ordered from
American Psychological Association
3 Henrietta Street
Covent Garden, London
WC2E 8LU England

Typeset in Goudy by Stephen McDougal, Mechanicsville, MD

Printer: Edwards Brothers, Inc., Ann Arbor, MI
Cover Designer: Naylor Design, Washington, DC
Technical/Production Editors: Casey Ann Reever and Tiffany L. Klaff

The opinions and statements published are the responsibility of the authors, and such opinions and statements do not necessarily represent the policies of the American Psychological Association.

Library of Congress Cataloging-in-Publication Data

Schmidt, Norman B.
    Taxometrics : toward a new diagnostic scheme for psychopathology / Norman B. Schmidt, Roman Kotov, Thomas E. Joiner.
        p. cm.
    Includes bibliographical references and index.
    ISBN 1-59147-142-7 (hardcover : alk. paper)
    1. Mental illness—Classification. 2. Mental illness—Diagnosis. I. Kotov, Roman. II. Joiner, Thomas E. III. Title.

RC455.2.C4S35 2004
616.89'075—dc22   2004000026

British Library Cataloguing-in-Publication Data
A CIP record is available from the British Library.

Printed in the United States of America
First Edition

For Kendall and Kaitlyn (Brad),
Anna Antipova (Roman),
To students, friends, and colleagues in the Florida State University
Department of Psychology (Thomas)

And dedicated to Paul Meehl, for his inspiration.

CONTENTS

INTRODUCTION: TAXOMETRICS CAN "DO DIAGNOSTICS RIGHT"

> Objective nature does exist, but we can converse with her only through the structure of our taxonomic systems.
>
> —Gould, 1996, p. 39

We have noted elsewhere (Joiner & Schmidt, 2002) that in 1980, the *Diagnostic and Statistical Manual of Mental Disorders* (3rd ed.; *DSM–III*; American Psychiatric Association, 1980) changed the way that mental health professionals and experimental psychopathologists conduct business. It is only a slight overstatement to say that one cannot get paid—either by insurance or by granting agencies—unless *DSM* diagnoses are assigned. The *DSM–III* revolution, carried on by the *DSM–III–R*, the *DSM–IV* (American Psychiatric Association, 1987, 1994), and beyond, has exerted a salutary effect in numerous ways. The *DSM* provides a shorthand with which professionals can efficiently communicate, has greatly enhanced the reliability of diagnoses, and has focused research efforts so that various researchers can be sure that they are studying the same thing.[1]

However, the *DSM* has gone as far as it can go, a point demonstrated by at least two sources of discontent with the *DSM*. The first is that the *DSM*'s categories and their particulars—the "same things" that scientists are studying—may not be "things" at all. That is, the categories and indicators are

---

[1]The general reference to *DSM* refers to the psychiatric nosology generally rather than one specific version of the manual.

ix

decided more by committee than by science. While it is true that the *DSM* committees pay careful attention to available psychopathology science, it is also true that the basic methodology of the *DSM* for inclusion and delineation of disorders is based on committee consensus, the pitfalls and gross errors of which can be substantial.

The second area of discontent with the *DSM* is its rote assumption that areas of psychopathology comprise categories, not dimensions. According to the *DSM*, either a person has a disorder or they do not; people differ by kind not by degree. This assumption in itself is not illogical and actually may be accurate for many disorders. The problem lies in the broad and empirically untested assumption that *all* areas of psychopathology represent classes or categories and not dimensions or continua. Regardless of whether a given syndrome is a category or not, a related area of confusion involves just what diagnostic criteria of the syndrome should be included and why.

Heated controversy exists about this fundamental question: Do psychopathological syndromes represent "all-or-none," "either-you-have-it-or-you don't" categories or are they graded, dimensional continua along which everybody can be placed, ranging from those with absent or minimal symptoms to those with very severe symptoms? The particulars of a post-*DSM* diagnostic manual hinge on this question.

Yet, regarding the vast majority of mental disorders, we do not know the answer. Take depression, as one example. Articles in *Psychological Bulletin* have capably and persuasively defended both positions (Coyne, 1994; Vredenburg, Flett, & Krames, 1993). It is interesting that psychologists tend to reflexively assume continua, whereas psychiatrists tend to assume categories; neither have definitive empirical evidence for their assumptions. Regarding psychologists' rote dimensional assumptions, Meehl (1999) stated, "There is a dogmatism among many American psychologists that no taxa exist, or could *possibly* [italics added] exist, in the realm of the mind. Are they unaware of the more than 150 Mendelizing mental deficiencies, to mention one obvious example?" (p. 165). Those who rotely assume a categorical approach fare similarly in Meehl's estimation:

> my main criticism of the DSM is the proliferation of taxa when the great majority of clients or patients do not belong to any taxon but are simply deviates in a hyperspace of biological, psychological and social dimensions, arousing clinical concern because their deviant pattern causes trouble. Further, for that minority of DSM rubrics that do denote real taxonic entities, the procedure for identifying them and the criteria for applying them lack an adequate scientific basis. (p. 166)

It is worth emphasizing that Meehl, who made remarkable contributions to the scientific study of psychiatric nosology including the use of taxometric procedures in the investigation of psychopathology, has indicated here and elsewhere (e.g., Meehl, 1997) that a probable minority of psychopathology syndromes represent categorical phenomena, with the rest representing dimensional continua.

What is needed, then, is an applied data-analytic tool that discerns categories from continua, and further, that establishes defining indicators of presumed categories. Moreover, this tool needs to be widely applied to various psychopathological syndromes. In our view, only this will allow the field to advance beyond the *DSM*. Fortunately, we believe there is a highly promising solution, represented by the work of Paul Meehl and colleagues on *taxometrics*.

The purpose of this book is to begin the ambitious task of "true diagnostics," standing on the shoulders of taxometric theory, by reviewing taxometric studies, analyzing several large new data sets, and trusting in the future cooperation and enterprise of psychologists and others who read this book. The book begins with a review of the nature of classification procedures by highlighting some of its main problems and controversies. In chapter 2, the evolution of our current diagnostic system—the *DSM*—is discussed and our central argument is advanced. We suggest that for the *DSM* to continue to advance, we must begin to scientifically determine the underlying nature of these diagnostic entities through the use of procedures such as taxometrics. Chapter 3 offers a detailed analytic primer on the nature of taxometrics. The primer is written in a user-friendly manner so clinicians and others not familiar with the underlying mathematics associated with taxometrics can gain a full understanding of the importance and utility of these procedures. Chapter 4 is specifically focused on outlining a method by which taxometric procedures can be applied to diagnostic entities within the *DSM*. The final two chapters provide a review of the current taxometrics literature and the degree to which it has been applied to specific psychopathological entities (e.g., schizophrenia spectrum, anxiety, eating disorders).

In summary, this book represents our "call to action" to revolutionize the diagnostic system. The point of this book is not that a diagnostic revolution has occurred; it is that it can and should occur and that, to a degree, it is occurring. Through this book, we hope to stimulate this enterprise by describing it, summarizing its initial progress, and contributing toward it. The enterprise, although difficult, is clearly feasible (within years not decades), if a core of psychological scientists join the fray. One of the main purposes of the book is to invite them to contribute to this cause. If Meehl is right (and we believe that the record shows he usually is), taxometrics should eventually revolutionize diagnostics. This book will serve as a clarion call for psychologists and scientists to take this mission seriously.

TAXOMETRICS

1

THE NATURE OF CLASSIFICATION

The greatest enemy of the truth is not the lie—deliberate, contrived, and dishonest, but the myth—persistent, pervasive and unrealistic.
—John F. Kennedy

The organization of information is a necessary and critical function, but it is also an intrinsically appealing and satisfying enterprise that is required to master our environs. The world is overwhelmingly complex. At a mundane level, obtaining understanding of these complexities is an automatic, essential, and basic process that is necessary for survival. As a scientific enterprise, attempting to determine order in the universe rests at the core of all endeavors.

The human brain is arguably the most miraculous result of evolution. Yet for all its potential, the brain's limitations are clear when it is given the task of unraveling the intricacies of the natural world. At any point in time, our brains must be highly selective in processing the vast amount of information that continuously assaults our perceptions. Moreover, the methods and organizational strategies for managing this information are countless.

We would suggest that the complex natural world and the limits of our perception lead to two potential problems regarding organization. First, the associations we make may be arbitrary. This contention is based on the premise that there is both an infinite array of elements that could be included in any reasonably complex organizational scheme, as well as countless ways of associating elements within the scheme. For example, in considering a mental illness, defining elements could be chosen from cognitive processes, physiology, and behaviors past and present. Second, the associations we make may be superficial. This contention is based on the idea that we intuitively seek simple and easy methods of association. Simple associations are easy to manage (e.g., simple main effects), but more complex organizations are troubling and difficult to understand (e.g., three- and four-way interactions). We do not presume that these two problems, arbitrariness and superficiality, are necessarily problems in all organization schemes. We highlight these as potential difficulties, especially when the elements constituting an organizational scheme are not well understood. Relative to other scientific fields, most would agree that mental illnesses are poorly understood. This brings us to the first of several questions we raise in this chapter: How do we know whether our organizational schemes make sense? In other words, is our organization nonarbitrary and meaningful in terms of accurately reflecting the natural world?

Clinical psychology and psychiatry are concerned with organization as it pertains to mental illnesses or psychiatric conditions. Most of these conditions are complex and elusive. In fact, some of them are so elusive that it is difficult to determine whether they are psychiatric conditions. Diagnostic classification is a method used to simplify and reduce complex phenomena to a more manageable state—that is, to systematically arrange these conditions according to similarities and differences. The theoretical side of classification involves deciding what constitutes a mental illness; the practical side of classification is determining whether any of these conditions exist in an individual.

This book is concerned with the theoretical side of psychiatric classification. As a starting point, we review the history of psychiatric classification during the past 50 years in the United States (see chap. 2). This brief review, along with a discussion of the current psychiatric classification system, is necessary to appreciate where we have come from as well as where we want to be. The current diagnostic system has great utility and has significantly advanced our knowledge and understanding of psychiatric conditions. Our current system, represented within the *Diagnostic and Statistical Manual of Mental Disorders* (DSM; American Psychiatric Association, 1994) was developed by well-meaning scientists and is based on the empirical study of psychiatric conditions. Our chief contention, however, is that despite the strengths of the DSM (including its empirical basis), there is reason to believe that this scientific basis is incomplete or possibly faulty.

The central tenet of this book is that the current diagnostic system is questionable because diagnostic entities have not received the type of empirical scrutiny that should be applied to them. Without further scrutiny there is a risk that psychiatric entities will attain "mythic" legitimacy, based largely on their codification within the DSM. This is not a small problem, and we would suggest that mental health researchers and practitioners be very concerned about this because we have quite possibly constructed a nosologic "house of cards."

WHY CLASSIFY?

We have noted that classification is a necessary process for understanding the world. There are also more specific outcomes achieved by developing a classification system. One such outcome is facilitation of information retrieval. Classification systems allow for chunking of information that can be more readily retrieved from memory. For example, master's level chess players can readily recall the positions of all playing pieces when they view a board of a game in progress, but their recall of randomly placed pieces will be no better than that of anyone else. Skilled chess players have learned to meaningfully chunk information (assuming meaningful information is present) on the basis of an organizational system. Similarly, symptomatology of patients can be more readily recalled in the context of an organizational system. Mental health professionals learn to chunk meaningful clinical features of particular types of patients on the basis of diagnostic criteria.

Classification also facilitates communication. A classification system represents the development of a common language that allows for consistency in communication. Clinicians can be confident that they are talking about the same thing when they use classification labels for disorders x, y, or z.

We would suggest, however, that one of the most important roles of classification is that it forms the basis for theory. Most believe that theory and classification are inextricably linked: The nature of the linkage between theory and classification was described by Cronbach and Meehl (1955). They argued that psychiatric disorders are open concepts. An open concept is one that is characterized by unclear or fuzzy boundaries, an absence of defining indicators, and an unknown inner nature (such as unknown etiology). The fuzziness surrounding psychiatric conditions suggests that classification based on a criterion-referenced approach will not work. A criterion-referenced approach would include linking a specific criterion for membership into a category. In the case of psychiatric categories, there are no clear-cut criteria available.

Instead, Cronbach and Meehl (1955) suggested that classification should be based on a construct validation approach. Construct validation involves developing a theory about a construct that is defined by a set of interconnected laws. These laws are ideas that relate constructs to one another as well as to observable behaviors. The set of constructs, laws, and observable behaviors is called a nomological network.

Construct validation follows a three-stage process. The first stage, theory formulation, involves specifying relationships among constructs and their relation to external variables (e.g., etiological factors). Disorder x is created by process y. For example, a theory about the construct "panic disorder" could specify that it is caused by the catastrophic misinterpretation of benign bodily cues (Clark, 1986) or by a faulty suffocation monitor (Klein, 1993). Internal validation is the second stage and involves operationalizing the constructs and examining internal properties of the theory (e.g., stability and internal consistency of the measures, interrater reliability). Disorder x should have its symptoms specified in the classification system. The internal validity of disorder x rests with the clustering of these symptoms over time. In the case of panic disorder, patients should consistently show panic attacks, elevated panic-related worry, and phobic avoidance. External validation is the final stage of construct validation and involves establishing relationships between the theory and other variables related to theory. If the theory suggests that disorder x is caused by ingesting too much caffeine, blood levels of caffeine should be related to the symptoms that characterize disorder x, drugs that affect caffeine use should affect the disorder, and so forth. In terms of panic disorder, changes in the tendency to catastrophically misinterpret bodily perturbations or changes in the deranged suffocation monitor would be expected to mediate the relationship between treatment of this disorder and outcome.

Construct validation suggests that classification is central to and inseparable from theory. Classification of a disorder forms a representation of the theoretical construct that is needed for the basis of elaboration and testing of the theory. A classification system like the *DSM* provides a means of translating or operationalizing abstract theoretical ideas into more concrete (often behavioral) definitions. Testing the theory (classification system) rests on tests of its internal and external validity. These tests inform us about the adequacy of both the classification system and the theory. It is conceivabe that theory and classification evolve together over time. Theory creates an initial classification scheme that is evaluated and, when refined, informs us about theory.

One important implication of the relationship between classification and theory is that classification systems define and propel research. Classification is a necessary starting point for the vast majority of research that takes place in mental health. Studies would not be funded or published if clinical populations were not first defined on the basis of diagnostic criteria. We are emphasizing that an inadequate classification scheme is likely to create a faulty starting point that results in considerable expense in terms of time, effort, and research dollars (not to mention the human costs in regard to delaying our ultimate understanding of these disorders).

WHAT IS A TAXON AND WHAT IS ITS RELATION TO CLASSIFICATION?

Definitions relevant to classification should be reviewed before we continue. The act of classification is typically defined as the process of making sense of entities. To be more precise, classification is concerned with forming classes of entities. Determining whether something is a mental illness or whether a mental illness can be meaningfully divided into subcategories, such as anxiety versus mood disorders, is an act of classification. A related enterprise involves assigning diagnoses. Giving an individual a psychiatric diagnosis consists of correctly placing that individual within the diagnostic system. The process of assigning diagnoses to the individual is referred to as identification (Simpson, 1961). In this book, we are more concerned with classification of disorders than with identification of diagnoses, although it should be pointed out that taxometrics also has much to say about identification. As described in chapter 3, taxometrics allows for the assignment of individuals to taxa.

The process of classification is typically based on systematically arranging entities on the basis of their similarities and differences. A bowl of fruit can be systematically arranged to have apples on one side and bananas on the other. Chemical elements can be systematically arranged into distinct "families" on the basis of their atomic structures. Classification of this sort is relatively easy and can be grounded on any number of relatively distinctive parameters or combinations of parameters, including color, size, shape, structure, taste, and so forth. We have already noted that psychiatric disorders are best characterized as open concepts. In open psychiatric concepts, overt, objective, and distinctive parameters are often less apparent, making their classification considerably more difficult.

Nosology is a specific branch of science that concerns itself with the classification of diseases. Although there may be some debate about conceptualizing mental illnesses as diseases, within psychiatry psychiatric conditions are considered to be diseases. Because we largely refer to the classification of mental illness, we use the terms nosology and classification interchangeably. Taxonomy sometimes refers to the study of classification as well as to the process of classification. Taxonomy may be considered a specific form of classification in that it is concerned with arranging entities into *natural categories* on the basis of similar features.

According to these definitions, we are distinguishing classification from taxonomy on the basis of whether the categories organized are *natural*. This distinction pertains to a fundamental issue of psychiatric classification. The issue is whether we believe that psychiatric classification is arbitrary or whether it reflects underlying, naturally occurring entities. It is important to recognize that methods of classification can vary in terms of whether they are arbitrary. I may classify people on the basis of their height and call them "tall" if they are over 5'11" or "short" if they are under 5'6". My classification system is arbitrary because I do not care whether "tall" and "short" accurately reflect true categories that occur in nature. There is nothing wrong with an arbitrary classification method as long as I am clear about the reasons for using this type of system and I explicitly recognize its arbitrary nature.

Psychiatric diagnostic systems appear to make the implicit assumption that diagnostic entities reflect natural categories. The DSM makes divisions among types of mental illness. For example, anorexia nervosa and bulimia nervosa are separate eating disorder diagnoses in the current *DSM–IV* (American Psychiatric Association, 1994). An individual can only receive one of these two diagnoses at any point in time. Classifying anorexia nervosa and bulimia nervosa as two separate eating disorders is based on the idea that these are two related (because they are both eating disorders) but meaningfully differentiated conditions that independently exist "in the real world." We consider this idea in more detail in chapter 2. Our purpose here is to illustrate that a classification system may or may not reflect "nature" or the "real world," and that an implicit assumption of the *DSM–IV* is that diagnostic categories are believed to reflect natural, nonarbitrary categories.

The term *taxon* is typically used to refer to these natural, nonarbitrary categories. Taxa are described by sets of objects like biological species or organic diseases but need not be biological in nature. Dogs, cats, or mice could be considered taxa, and so could surgeons or cathedrals. Taxa represent meaningful elements in nature that can be discriminated. In reference to Plato, if we could somehow successfully "carve nature at its joints," what we would be left with is a bunch of taxa. A taxon is something that naturally exists whether or not we are currently capable of accurately identifying it. Something is not a taxon when it is an arbitrary category or is dimensional. For example, many believe that *neuroticism* is a dimensional personality trait. If this is true, classifying individuals as *neurotic* or *not neurotic* would be arbitrary because there is no "real" underlying category of neurotic. Instead, some people simply show more or less of this trait. The term *neurotic* is used for the sake of convenience and is based on some arbitrary cutoff point on a dimensional measure of neuroticism.

How do taxa fit into the *DSM–IV* (American Psychiatric Association, 1994)? Authors of the *DSM–IV* have been careful to state that they believe these diagnostic categories are arbitrary. The introduction of the *DSM–IV* (American Psychiatric Association, 1994, p. xxii) contains a section entitled "Limitations of the Categorical Approach." In this section, the authors argue that a categorical approach is a useful method of classification, especially when members of the diagnostic category are relatively homogeneous, when the boundaries between different diagnoses are clear, and when inclusion into a category is mutually exclusive. Yet the authors state that there is no assumption in the *DSM–IV* that diagnostic entities are absolutely discrete from one another or are clearly differentiated from having no mental disorder. Recognition of the arbitrary nature of diagnostic classification seems prudent because there are undeniably arbitrary elements in this system. The most obvious example of arbitrariness is the use of *cutting scores* (i.e., requiring a certain number of available criteria for a diagnosis to be met). In a system that uses cutting scores, the individual displaying x criteria is assigned a diagnosis, whereas an individual with $x - 1$ criteria does not receive a diagnosis. The arbitrary issue is the assignment of the correct or best cutting score.

Does having necessarily arbitrary diagnostic boundaries mean that the entities underlying the diagnoses (i.e., the taxa) must also be arbitrary? If this is so, then the *DSM* diagnoses could not be representative of taxa that are, by definition, nonarbitrary categories. As we discuss, having "fuzzy boundaries" or arbitrary diagnostic criteria is not inconsistent with being taxonic. In fact, we have already noted that the *DSM*, consistent with other medically based nosologic systems, makes an implicit (if not explicit) assumption that each syndrome represents a taxon. It is fairly uncontroversial to argue that the process of psychiatic nosology involves the identification of nonarbitrary psychiatric entities. In other words, despite the *DSM*'s "recognition" of the arbitrary nature of its classification scheme, the division of diagnoses (e.g., bipolar disorder, panic disorder) is assumed to reflect our efforts at carving nature at its joints. The *DSM* reflects our current best guess about mental illness taxa. The *DSM* acknowledges that it might be wrong and that its diagnoses may not represent taxa. Instead, some mental illness might be thought of as dimensional traits rather than nonarbitrary categories. The *DSM* recommends that further evaluation of dimensional classification schemes is warranted in determining their utility for the classification of mental illnesses.

This discussion returns us to the central issue of this book. At issue is the fact that the *DSM* is a taxonomy that is implicitly interested in reflecting the taxa that represent mental illnesses. An important question is whether, or to what degree, the taxonicity of mental illnesses has been tested. We argue that despite the central nature of taxa to the *DSM*, the taxonicity of diagnostic entities has not been adequately assessed; thus, we are not currently in a position to know the degree to which the *DSM* accurately represents natural categories.

WHAT ARE WE CLASSIFYING?

Evaluation of diagnostic endeavors reveals two principal and interrelated functions of a classification system. First, diagnostic systems are used to determine what constitutes a disorder (psychiatric condition or not); second, diagnostic systems are used to discriminate among the identified psychiatric conditions. Therefore, in discussing classification, we must first ask what a mental disorder is (i.e., should x be considered a psychiatric condition?). If we answer affirmatively, we must then consider whether this disorder is unique from other disorders within the classification system. We briefly consider each of these issues next.

What Is a Mental Disorder?

A determination about what constitutes a mental disorder is a necessary preface to any discussion of what should be included in a diagnostic system. An answer to the question of what a mental disorder is has obvious relevance to diagnostic classification because our diagnostic enterprise first has to decide which elements it will include in its nosology. Our conceptualization of mental disorder has critical implications for classification. As we have already noted, concept and classification are inextricably linked.

Determining the division between normal and abnormal behavior has historically been a difficult task. Some of the more recently debated diagnoses include homosexuality (Spitzer, 1973), self-defeating personality disorder, sadistic personality disorder (Holden, 1986), and premenstrual syndrome (DeAngelis, 1993). Some have argued that these difficulties stem from a failure to adequately define mental illness (Gorenstein, 1984).

Definitions of mental illness tend to contain two aspects: a normative element and a functional element. Normative definitions delimit abnormal behavior in light of what is typical, usual, or the norm. Some degree of deviance from the norm is necessary for a behavior to be considered abnormal. Deviance alone, however, is never sufficient for a label of abnormality. High IQ is just as deviant as low IQ, but only mental retardation is labeled abnormal. This leads us to the functional element of the definition. Typically, the label of abnormality requires deviance plus maladaptation. Maladaptation suggests some diminished capacity to function relative to an average. For example, the *DSM* defines mental disorder as a syndrome that is associated with distress or impairment in functioning (American Psychiatric Association, 1994, pp. xxi–xxii).

The *DSM* is careful to recognize that culture also determines definitions of mental illness. In the *DSM*, unusual and distressing behaviors such as culturally sanctioned responses to the death of a loved one are excluded from diagnosis. Most current conceptualizations of mental illness recognize that societal values play an important role in establishing whether something is a mental disorder (Lilienfeld & Marino, 1995; Wakefield, 1992). The result is that the boundaries of mental illness are believed to shift as a function of culture, both across cultures and within cultures, over time. One important implication of cultural relativism is that definitions of mental illness will necessarily vary.

Evaluation of the concept of mental illness suggests that there are other aspects of its definition that create variability. Lilienfeld and Marino (1995) stated that there has always been great difficulty in establishing the boundary between mental illness and normalcy. These authors suggested that we need to accept this "fuzzy boundary" as a necessary condition of mental illness. They argued that mental illnesses should be considered "open concepts" (Meehl, 1977) or Roschian concepts (Rosch, 1973). A Roschian concept is essentially the same as the open concept we have already defined. It is a mental construction used to categorize natural entities that are characterized by fuzzy boundaries. Lilienfeld and Marino argued that this conception of mental illness implies that it is impossible to explicitly or scientifically define mental illnesses. Moreover, there has historically been little success in providing a scientific definition of mental illness, suggesting that mental illness is a nonscientific concept. As a result, there will always be controversy about whether something represents a mental illness because this question cannot be answered in a scientific manner.

The contentions of Lilienfeld and Marino (1995) further suggested that there will never be a consensus definition of mental illness. This obviously complicates the process of classification, but Lilienfeld and Marino qualified this issue in a manner important to our discussion. These authors highlighted the idea that determining whether the concept of mental illness is vague and cannot be scientifically defined is a separate issue from determining whether specific mental illnesses themselves can be scientifically defined. In other words, a mental illness can still be defined as an open concept that is characterized by fuzzy boundaries (Meehl, 1986). As we have noted, an open concept is not incompatible with the existence of a taxon that underlies the mental illness. Thus, a taxon can underlie an open concept. There are numerous examples of this idea from nonpsychiatric medicine, in which the symptomatic presentation of a disease is characterized by fuzzy boundaries but the inner nature or etiology of the disease can be known. As Meehl (1992) noted, the symptoms of meningitides overlap even though they possess distinctive etiologies. In essence, there are two separate questions: What makes something a mental disorder? and, Does this thing form a category?

The discussion of vagueness in definitions of mental illness brings us back to the importance of determining the taxonic nature of a proposed mental illness. Earlier, we argued that extant diagnoses should be scrutinized in regard to their taxonic basis. We would also suggest that this process could be important in decisions about abnormality. Determining the taxonic nature of a proposed mental illness should be helpful in the ultimate decision of whether to classify it as a mental illness. This should be particularly true in marginal examples of mental illness (e.g., self-defeating personality disorder), where the diagnostic status of these marginal illnesses is questionable. By marginal, we are implying that their status (as abnormal) is not as clear as for other disorders. For example, self-defeating personality disorder is likely to be considered a more marginal mental illness than schizophrenia.

We recognize that determination of the taxonic nature of something is not the most important piece of data impacting decisions regarding abnormality. Obviously, taxa can be nonclinical, nonpsychiatric entities. Marginal diagnoses, however, explicitly suggest abnormality. Determination of the structure of this entity is diagnostically compelling. For example, dissociation is a phenomenon believed to be relatively common. Markers or symptoms of dissociation include amnesia, absorption (i.e., becoming so involved in an activity that you are unaware of events going on around you), derealization, and depersonalization. The DSM dissociative disorders are premised on the idea that some people exhibit such high levels of dissociation that it causes significant distress and impairment. However, if dissociative experiences are common in the general population, it becomes difficult to determine whether a pathological level of dissociation exists. Moreover, if dissociation is a dimensional condition, establishing a cutoff for pathological levels becomes arbitrary.

However, if a taxon underlies extreme dissociative experiences it makes our classification process much easier because the existence of this taxon implies not only that there is a more severe form but also that there is a discrete form. The discreteness of this entity suggests there is a qualitative difference, perhaps with a different etiology, course, and treatment. These issues are unknown initially but form an important starting point for future work.

Can Mental Disorders (Diagnostic Entities) Be Discriminated?

Simultaneous to determining whether something should be considered part of a diagnostic system, we must also determine whether it is sufficiently unique from other elements within the system. This process of differentiation is manifest in a number of different ways within the current *DSM* system, including (a) separating disorder from disorder (e.g., anxiety disorders from somatiform disorders); (b) separating primary forms from an overarching diagnostic type (e.g., separating panic disorder from social phobia within the anxiety disorders); and (c) subtyping specific disorders (e.g., paranoid vs. nonparanoid schizophrenia).

The process of classification in terms of each method of discrimination among diagnostic entities rests on two assumptions. First, the diagnostic entity or subtype is presumed to be a mental disorder. Second, the diagnostic entity is presumed to be discriminable from other mental disorders on some basis. Evaluation of this first assumption returns us to the earlier discussion of what constitutes a mental illness, so we do not need to consider this further. The second assumption raises a new question relevant to classification. Is this condition significantly unique from all other diagnostic categories? An answer to this question should be empirically based, but the type of answer received may depend on the methods used to obtain the answer. Next, we consider different methods of classification.

Methods of Classification

Discussion of discrimination among mental illnesses must be augmented by a general discussion of the typical methods used in classification. There are a variety of different approaches for classification, including categorical versus dimensional and prototypic as well as monothetic versus polythetic. The dimensional scheme assumes that there are not dichotomies or qualitatively different types of behaviors being classified. Behaviors are typically viewed as continuous dimensions that reflect quantitative deviations from normal levels. A dimensional approach to anxiety is the view that anxiety pathology is a quantitatively (not qualitatively) greater manifestation of the symptom. According to this scheme, anxiety could be viewed as a normally distributed bell curve. Cutoff scores would be assigned along this curve to demarcate levels of psychopathology. For example, the Beck Anxiety Inventory (BAI; Beck, Epstein, Brown, & Steer, 1988) is a popular and well-validated measure of anxiety symptoms. Scores on the BAI represent varying levels of anxiety pathology. Clinical norms for the BAI are based on different cutoffs, so a certain score is indicative of *mild*, *moderate*, or *severe* anxiety. Of course, these demarcations have arbitrary qualities.

The categorical approach to classification is the dominant method used in psychiatric nosologies. In the categorical scheme, assignment to a given category is based on the presence of particular signs and symptoms that are believed to characterize the disease. Categorical classification involves defining a category by delineating its essential features and then comparing the observed features of objects to be classified with the formal criteria for the category. For example, panic disorder could be defined by the presence of various symptoms, including panic attacks, fear about additional panic attacks, and avoidance of situations in which panic is believed to occur. Individuals displaying these symptoms are believed to be different from people showing other types of symptoms (or just general symptoms of anxiety) and would be classified as having panic disorder.

Assigning a diagnosis (identification) in a categorical approach tends to be absolute. The person either has panic disorder or does not. In addition, items within the category are generally similar (all individuals with panic disorder) and different from those outside the category (people with panic disorder are different from people with social phobia). One consequence of this approach is that variation within a category is minimized relative to variation among categories. Symptomatic variation within panic disorder is considered less important in this system than symptom variation between panic disorder and other Axis I conditions. Subtyping within a disorder, however, is one method of highlighting the importance of within-category indicators. In the case of panic disorder, the level of phobic avoidance could become a marker that is pertinent for subtyping. In this case, individuals with high levels of avoidance could receive an additional diagnosis of agoraphobia, resulting in two panic disorder subtypes: with and without agoraphobia.

There are also differences in categorical classification methods. Prototypic classification is a method that suggests the indicators for inclusion and exclusion from a category are fallible rather than perfect. In a psychiatric classification system, the patient's assignment to a category is based on the similarity of that patient to the "most typical patient" for that disorder. A prototypical depressed patient may show symptoms of sadness, apathy, hopelessness, anhedonia, and so forth. A given patient would not be expected to show all of these symptoms but could be classified as depressed if he or she shows many of these symptoms. Each symptom of the prototypic exemplar is typically neither necessary nor sufficient for a diagnosis.

Implications of the prototypic classification method are that categories within the system will possess fuzzy boundaries. Individuals within a category will be somewhat heterogeneous and may not share any common features. In our depression example, a prototypic classification scheme may yield a diagnosis of depression in one patient who shows agitation, anhedonia, and suicidal ideation and the same diagnosis in another patient who shows sadness, fatigue, worthlessness, and decreased appetite.

The monothetic or classical categorical approach requires that all of the criteria for a category must be met for something to be included in that category. If panic disorder is defined by (a) persistent spontaneous panic attacks, (b) worry about additional panic attacks, and (c) having panic symptoms erupt within 10 minutes after onset, only individuals displaying these three essential symptoms could be given the diagnosis. In the monothetic approach, patients are required to meet a group of jointly necessary and sufficient characteristics. The result of a monothetic approach is that relatively few people will meet criteria for any given disorder, and these people will look very similar. Thus, there will be little overlap or covariation among disorders that will have distinct boundaries.

Polythetic (or prototypal) criteria sets refer to multithemes or variations in themes. The polythetic approach has the advantage of requiring fewer categories to capture the range of behavioral variation. For example, a polythetic system can consider depression to be a certain subset of symptoms within a larger range of symptom possibilities, with individual symptoms being necessary but none being sufficient for a diagnosis. A monothetic approach to depression divides depression into different forms (e.g., hopelessness, vegetative, interpersonal), with each of these subtypes requiring specific symptoms that differentiate it from other forms of depression.

It is not unusual for nosologic systems to adopt a mixed approach that contains both monothetic and polythetic elements. This type of system, which is used in the DSM, may require that certain diagnostic criteria are present. Other criteria for the disorder may be definitive but not necessary so that any combination of these latter criteria may be sufficient for the diagnosis. For example, panic attacks and some form of panic-related worry are both definitive and necessary criteria for panic disorder. However, any combination of 4 of the 13 symptoms constituting a panic attack is sufficient for this particular element in the diagnosis.

The principal implication of the continuous approach is the assumption of continuity across a trait that is indexed on a continuum. The primary implication of a categorical approach—whether it is monothetic, polythetic, or prototypal—is that disorders are discontinuous and that those with the disorder should be qualitatively different from those without the disorder.

Different methods of classification have various strengths and weaknesses. Their true strengths, however, should primarily rest with whether they adequately map onto the real world. Why has the *DSM* adopted a mixed, categorical approach? We would suggest that this decision is largely based on history and preference. Historically, psychiatric nosology grows out of a medical nosology that uses a categorical approach. For medical diseases, a categorical approach makes sense because medical diseases are "closed" concepts. This approach may also be applicable for psychiatric disorders. We would suggest, however, that it is not currently clear what type of classification method is best, as mental illnesses are open concepts that may or may not relate to real-world discrete entities. The preferential aspect that impinges on the classification system is that a categorical approach is simple, easy to use and understand, and facilitates communication. It is important, however, to consider that the classification preferences are arbitrary unless there is some empirical basis for them. In other words, different sorts of classification methods can be used to organize psychiatric entities. Decisions about which method is the correct one, meaning the method that provides the best scheme of representing the real world, often fail to be considered. We return again to the issue of taxa and would suggest that evaluation of the taxonic nature of diagnostic entities is an important step in determining whether the method of classification is an appropriate one. Evidence for a taxon suggests a categorical method of classification, whereas evidence against a taxon suggests that dimensional methods should be used.

SUMMARY

We have initiated our discussion of the role of taxometrics within psychiatric nosology with a broader consideration of methods of organizing information and classification. In this preliminary discussion, we have raised two basic issues critical to classification and therefore to our theory and understanding of mental illnesses. The first issue pertains to the adequacy of psychiatric nosology. This nosology attempts to map diagnoses onto the real world. We believe that an important piece of information about this process—namely, the taxonic nature of diagnostic entities—is missing. The second and related issue questions the choice of classification methodology used in the present diagnostic system. The degree to which dimensional and categorical methods of classification represent the real world is basically unknown. Once again, an understanding of taxometrics should be highly informational in this regard.

2

EVOLUTION OF CLASSIFICATION IN THE *DIAGNOSTIC AND STATISTICAL MANUAL OF MENTAL DISORDERS:* CURRENT PROBLEMS AND PROPOSED ALTERNATIVES

The beginning of health is to know the disease.
—Cervantes, *Don Quixote* (Pt. Ii, Ch. 60)

The *Diagnostic and Statistical Manual of Mental Disorders* (DSM) represents the most widely used psychiatric nosology in the United States. From a historical perspective, it appears that the major changes to the DSM have taken place to solve a few specific problems—particularly, problems with reliability. Over time, the DSM has done well in addressing problems related to reliability, but this evolution has raised many criticisms and has created additional problems. In this chapter, the history of the DSM is reviewed, along with the major criticisms that have been raised about its more recent versions. We also suggest taxometric analysis as one method that will prove useful in addressing many of the limitations of the current system.

The DSM is the codification of our nosologic thinking. When first published in 1952, it was a relatively brief manual, 130 pages long and containing fewer than 35,000 words. The first edition of the DSM (DSM–I; American Psychiatric Association, 1952) rapidly became the first widely used manual of mental disorders. However, the *DSM–I* was problematic in several important respects. First, the *DSM–I* explicitly advocated one theory to the exclusion of others: the authors of the *DSM–I* had adopted a psychoanalytic theoretical stance. Use of one particular theoretical stance hindered the acceptance and use of this system by clinicians and researchers who were not affiliated with the Freudian camp.

The second main problem with the *DSM–I* was that the disorders were vaguely described, and diagnostic criteria were ambiguous. As a result, there were reliability problems in the *DSM–I*. In particular, interrater reliability (agreement between two raters on the presence and absence of a diagnosis) was very low. Poor interrater reliability calls into question the validity of a diagnostic system if trained mental health practitioners cannot consistently agree on diagnoses.

The next revision of this system, the *DSM–II* (American Psychiatric Association, 1968), appeared 16 years later. This revision offered some expansion of the diagnostic categories but it was only four pages longer and had the same problems as the *DSM–I*. These problems included the continued adoption of psychoanalytic theory along with unacceptably low levels of interrater agreement on many diagnoses. An excerpt from the *DSM–II* illustrates the vagueness that resulted in poor reliability. In the *DSM–II*, schizophrenia is described as

> a group of disorders manifested by characteristic disturbances in thinking, mood and behavior. Disturbances in thinking are marked by alterations in concept formation, which may lead to misinterpretation of reality and sometimes to delusions and hallucinations, which appear psychologically self-protective. Corollary mood changes include ambivalent, constricted and inappropriate emotional responsiveness and loss of empathy with others. Behavior may be withdrawn, regressive, bizarre. (American Psychiatric Association, 1968, p. 33)

This terse and general description exemplifies the sort of information that was available to guide diagnosis.

Certain events appear to have shaped the later emphasis on addressing the *DSM–II*'s problem of interrater reliability. In 1973, a few years after the *DSM–II* was unveiled, David Rosenhan (1973) published in *Science* his now famous study. Rosenhan's study evaluated whether mental health professionals could correctly determine the presence of mental health among pseudopatients. These pseudopatients presented at mental hospitals feigning symptoms of mental illness. The fact that all of Rosenhan's pseudopatients (including himself) received a psychiatric diagnosis led him to conclude that the diagnostic system of that day was grossly inadequate and should be replaced by a descriptive system that included specific behavioral markers of illness.

Rosenhan's methodology and conclusions have been criticized on numerous grounds (Spitzer, 1975). One outspoken critic, Robert Spitzer, was highly influential in the development of the *DSM–III* (American Psychiatric Association, 1980) as well as later versions of the *DSM*. Despite his criticism, Spitzer appears to have adopted some of Rosenhan's suggestions. Whether influenced by Rosenhan's study or by the growing problems associated with an unreliable system, Spitzer and the other *DSM–III* collaborators developed a diagnostic system that was more behaviorally based and focused on improving interrater reliability. In effect, Spitzer appears to have wanted the next version of the *DSM* to provide explicit guidance to the clinician.

The *DSM–III* (American Psychiatric Association, 1980) is widely regarded as the most significant and important revision of this document. The structural changes that appeared with this revision have been retained through the current version of the *DSM*. In the *DSM–III*, a new emphasis on providing clear descriptions to increase interrater reliability is evident. In the introduction, the authors state that "The purpose of the *DSM–III* is to provide clear descriptions of diagnostic categories in order to enable clinicians and investigators to diagnose, communicate about, study, and treat various mental disorders" (American Psychiatric Association, 1980, p. 12).

The emphasis on clearly described diagnoses resulted in the introduction of explicit behavioral categories for each *DSM–III* (American Psychiatric Association, 1980) diagnosis. The difference in the length of the two versions attests to the more detailed descriptions found in the *DSM–III*. The *DSM–III* contains approximately 200 more pages than the *DSM–II* (American Psychiatric Association, 1968). The *DSM–II* covers schizophrenia and its subtypes in three half-pages. In contrast, the *DSM–III* uses 14 full pages to describe schizophrenia. Whereas the *DSM–II* offered single sentence descriptions of disturbances in thought, mood, and behavior in schizophrenia, the *DSM–III* provided several paragraphs or even pages of description for each category.

The detailed descriptions in the *DSM–III* were a marked departure from the vague, ill-defined descriptors provided in the *DSM–II*. Along with these descriptions came a mixed monothetic and polythetic categorical approach in which some diagnostic criteria were deemed essential for diagnosis and other criteria were considered associated but nonessential for diagnosis. In schizophrenia, for example, the *DSM–III* describes characteristic disturbances in areas such as content and form of thought, perception, and volition. It also specifies that individuals with schizophrenia may show associated features, including dysphoric mood, stereotypic behavior, and hypochondriacal concerns. Moreover, the *DSM–III* provided explicit inclusionary and exclusionary criteria for each diagnosis.

A variety of decision rules were also provided to further assist clinicians in the use of the *DSM–III* and, ultimately, to increase interrater reliability. These decision rules pertain to specific criteria as well as to differential diagnoses and are presented to give clinicians more guidance and allow for less leeway in making diagnostic decisions. The diagnostic process is effectively narrowed, so a diagnosis is made in a straightforward manner when the decision rules are painstakingly followed. In the case of schizophrenia, for example, if a depressive or manic syndrome is present, the *DSM–III* specifies that the mood syndrome must be separate from earlier psychotic symptoms or relatively minor in comparison to the psychotic symptoms.

The final and related change we will mention is that the *DSM–III* removed psychoanalytic jargon and was written as an atheoretical document, especially with regard to etiology. Although some have argued that the *DSM* continues to display an implicit disease-model theoretical stance, the *DSM–III* authors observe (American Psychiatric Association, 1980, p. 9) that they worked diligently to remove terms such as *neurotic* because evidence failed to be sufficiently supportive of psychoanalytic etiological theory (American Psychiatric Association, 1980, p. 7). In addition to increasing the appeal of the diagnostic system to a wider audience of mental health practitioners, another practical aspect of the change to an atheoretical document was to assist in increasing interrater reliability by eliminating vague analytic terminology. Large field trials confirmed that interrater reliability of the *DSM–III* Axis I disorders is good to excellent and the overall kappa value (chance-corrected level of agreement between clinicians) for the Axis I diagnoses was around .70 (Spitzer, Forman, & Nee, 1979; Williams, Hyler, & Spitzer, 1982).

The most recent revisions of the *DSM* (*DSM–III–R*; *DSM–IV*; *DSM–IV–TR*; American Psychiatric Association, 1987, 1994, 2000) might be considered a fine-tuning of the *DSM–III* (American Psychiatric Association, 1980). These versions have provided minor structural changes relative to the shift from the *DSM–II* to the *DSM–III*. The *DSM–IV* continues to use the same sort of explicit decision rules, along with utilization of diagnostic criteria based on reliably observed behaviors. This general approach seems unlikely to change drastically for *DSM–V* and beyond, although it is conceivable that some diagnostic criteria will become more and more influenced by advances in genetics and neurobiology. If so, it is important to note that the taxometric approach would only be strengthened. That is, taxometrics benefits from disorder indicators that come from different domains (e.g., biology as well as symptom phenomenology), and from different measurement approaches (e.g., clinician-ratings vs. self-reports).

CRITICISMS OF THE *DIAGNOSTIC AND STATISTICAL MANUAL OF MENTAL DISORDERS*

By many practical measures, the *DSM–III* (American Psychiatric Association, 1980) has been an immensely successful taxonomy. The energy that was focused on improving interrater reliability appears to have been successful. Compared with earlier versions, the *DSM–III* resulted in significantly higher interrater agreement for most psychiatric conditions. Conversion to an atheoretical approach has helped to consolidate widespread use of the DSM, so it is now the most widely used psychiatric taxonomy in the world (Maser, Kaelber, & Weise, 1991). In sum, the DSM was designed to solve several specific problems, particularly with respect to diagnostic reliability, and it appears to have accomplished its task. However, many have questioned whether the DSM has overlooked other problems and created new problems in its evolution. We outline some of the main criticisms that have been leveled at more recent versions of the DSM, starting with the DSM–III.

Diagnoses Lack Scientific Support

The inclusion of a number of diagnoses within the DSM has been criticized on the basis of a lack of empirical support for these diagnostic entities (Blashfield, Sprock, & Fuller, 1990). The Axis II Personality Disorders are prime examples of those that generally lack clear empirical support (one exception is Antisocial Personality Disorder). By and large, personality disorders are poorly researched. Moreover, studies of personality disorders frequently suggest low interrater reliability with kappa values ranging from *poor* to *fair* (.35–.50; Perry, 1992); high levels of diagnostic overlap among these disorders so individuals frequently receive multiple personality disorder diagnoses, with 85% of patients with personality disorder receiving more than one diagnosis (Widiger & Rogers, 1989); and questionable validity (i.e., a personality diagnosis does not predict performance on laboratory tasks, predict course or treatment response).

Others have suggested that in the rush to publish subsequent revisions to the DSM–III (American Psychiatric Association, 1980), there has been insufficient time between revisions to evaluate the adequacy of the extant diagnoses for a given version (Zimmerman, 1988). Evaluation of the appendix of the DSM–III–R (American Psychiatric Association, 1987) supports this contention, as it appears that only a minority of the changes from the DSM–III to the DSM–III–R were clearly based on newly acquired or accumulated research. The same criticism can be leveled at the DSM–IV (American Psychiatric Association, 1994), which closely followed the DSM–III–R; for example, only 3 of the 12 changes to the DSM–IV anxiety disorders section appear to be linked with a literature review or evidence acquired from field trials (pp. 782–783).

The Quest for Reliability Has Sacrificed Validity

Reliability is a fundamental prerequisite for a valid classification system. The level of reliability delimits validity and, as we have discussed, problems with reliability appear to have provided the main impetus for the evolution of the DSM. Can too much reliability be a good thing? Some have argued that the *DSM*'s quest for reliability has actually led to decreased validity (Carson, 1991).

The reason for the "double-edged" nature of reliability is that reliability is a necessary but not sufficient criterion for validity. It is necessary to make consistent assessments to have a valid system. However, it is possible that these reliable assessments measure something that is largely irrelevant to what is actually of interest. The quest for increasing interrater reliability has resulted in disassembling disorders into only those components that can be reliably assessed. However, some have suggested that some of the more essential behaviors (i.e., valid indicators of the diagnostic entity) that are less reliably assessed have been excluded.

How do you select the best basketball player for your team? Use of indices with extremely high reliability may not produce the best results. Height and vertical leaping ability are important qualities for basketball players, and they can be reliably assessed. Use of these criteria alone, however, would never result in the selection of Michael Jordan over other basketball players who are taller and have better physical leaping abilities. It is likely that less reliably assessed, psychological factors such as competitive drive and devotion to the game are more critical in separating great players like Michael Jordan from other very good players.

Similarly, some have argued that there are certain psychiatric diagnoses that have been modified to increase the importance of less central behavioral criteria. Changes in the diagnosis of psychopathy to antisocial behavior is an oft-cited example of this potential problem. In this case, some of the crucial Hare–Cleckley criteria for psychopathy, including "glibness" and "lack of empathy" have been removed in favor of criteria that can be more reliably assessed, such as the frequency of engaging in physical fights.

In dealing with psychiatric conditions, there are "open" concepts (meaning they lack firmly defined boundaries). It might be suggested that fuzzy boundaries are likely to produce some level of unreliability in diagnosis until a deeper understanding of the mental illness is achieved. In this regard, lower levels of unreliability should likely be tolerated if this involves the incorporation of diagnostic criteria that are more essential to the true nature of the disorder.

Ignores Course for State Psychopathology

Diagnostic criteria rely heavily on presenting features. Some have criticized the *DSM* as making diagnostic criteria too focused on presenting symptoms while ignoring the course of the disorder. Kraepelin (1899) distinguished manic depression from schizophrenia largely on the basis of differences in the course of illness. There are many developmentalists who would prefer longitudinal (vs. cross-sectional) analysis of psychopathology to be used in making diagnoses.

Evaluating diagnoses over time often yields findings that are markedly divergent from cross-sectional studies. In evaluating *DSM–III* (American Psychiatric Association, 1980) personality disorders, the stability of the disorders over time were found to be low (κ range = .2 – –.4) whereas interrater agreement is much higher at any given time point (κ range = .6–.7; van den Brink, Schoos, Hanhart, Rouwendael, & Koeter, 1986). Findings such as these, while raising questions about the validity of presumably stable pathological personality types, also raise questions about the adequacy of cross-sectional assessment. It is possible that some valid and useful information is lost when the course of psychopathology is not systematically incorporated in diagnostic criteria.

Categorical (Dichotomous) Nature of Diagnoses Is Arbitrary

In chapter 1, we discussed differences in classification strategies. The strengths and implications of the use of categorical versus dimensional methods of classification were reviewed. In the United States, there has historically been a strong bias toward dimensional typologies (Meehl, 1992). As would be expected, the *DSM* has been criticized by proponents of a dimensional approach (Carson, 1991). If certain forms of psychopathology are best viewed as dimensional phenomena, the current diagnostic dichotomies are arbitrary.

Similar criticisms of the *DSM*'s categorical syndromal approach to classification were made on practical grounds (Hayes, Wilson, Gifford, Follette, & Strosahl, 1996). The argument here is that the syndromal approach in psychiatry has historically led to little progress in the identification of underlying diseases, differences in course, or differential treatment. One possible reason that the syndromal approach has been disappointing is that the symptoms that constitute a syndrome may not adequately map onto an underlying disease process. The lack of isomorphism between syndromes and disease entities often arises because a single syndrome can map onto a wide variety of etiological factors, and a single etiological factor can produce an array of syndromes. Thus, the identification of syndromes may not correctly or completely identify the underlying entity.

Ignores Cross-Cultural Manifestations

The *DSM* was produced by the American Psychiatric Association primarily as a manual for American clinicians and has been largely guided by research on the U.S. population. As a result, the document reflects an "American" version of psychopathology that may not accurately describe psychopathology found in other cultures. Cross-cultural epidemiological studies suggest that certain disorders (e.g., anorexia nervosa, dissociative identity disturbance) exist mainly in industrialized countries and are rarely seen in other cultures. There is also evidence for a number of culture-specific disorders that exist in non-European cultures (e.g., Koro [McNally, 1994], Pibloktoq [Landy, 1985]) that are not represented in the DSM.

The DSM–IV (American Psychiatric Association, 1994) does describe 25 "culture-bound" syndromes, but these are included in an appendix. Many of these syndromes show similarities to DSM–IV diagnoses. It has been speculated that dissimilarities between the DSM diagnoses and "culture-bound" syndromes may be due to cultural differences that affect the expression of a common underlying disorder. For example, kayak angst afflicts only male Eskimos in West Greenland (Amering & Katschnig, 1990). This disorder appears to be similar to a panic attack but only occurs when the individual is alone in a kayak on a hunting trip. It has been speculated that this is a cultural variant of panic disorder—a disorder highly prevalent in the United States (McNally, 1994). The degree of overlap between "culture-bound" syndromes and existing DSM–IV categories, however, is largely unknown.

Structure of the Classification System Poorly Developed

Blashfield (1986) has argued that the structure of classification in the DSM is poorly developed. In comparison to other scientifically based classification systems, such as those used in biology, there has been relatively little work on psychiatric taxonomy. Blashfield suggests that the DSM's structure is so primitive that it more closely resembles nonempirically based "folk" classification systems. Several questions and problems are raised when the psychiatric taxonomy used in the DSM is juxtaposed with biological classification systems. In general, the DSM's mixed classification approach (monothetic and polythetic), its allowance for multiple diagnoses, and its hierarchical organization do not conform to the taxometric principles that are applied to biological classification systems (Blashfield, 1986). When the systems are compared, significant problems with the DSM system become evident.

Politics Affect Diagnoses

There has been some suggestion that the DSM may be influenced by the development of other classification systems, most notably by the *International Classification of Diseases* (ICD-10; World Health Organization, 1992) which is a widely used international diagnostic system. There are certainly examples in the DSM–III–R and DSM–IV (American Psychiatric Association, 1987, 1994) that clearly indicate that the DSM was changed simply to make it more compatible with an ICD diagnosis. For example, the DSM–IV added a new diagnosis termed Acute Stress Disorder "for compatibility with the ICD-10" (American Psychiatric Association, 1994, p. 783).

There are also suggestions that the structured, categorical nature of the *DSM* simply reflects the remedicalization of psychiatry (Carson, 1996). As such, the *DSM*'s taxonomy (based on the presentation of classical medical diseases) is not scientifically based but, rather, is designed to facilitate psychiatry's interest in realigning itself within medicine.

Diagnoses Are Based on *DSM* Committee Members' Preferences Rather Than Extant Literature

The *DSM* is constructed through a committee system that involves the participation of well-known researchers and scholars. In the *DSM–IV*, there were several hundred work group advisors, international advisors, and field trial investigators. The committee system, however, has been criticized by some who suggest that the decisions regarding the *DSM* are largely based on the findings and opinions of committee members, rather than on wider literature. Though the *DSM* revisions are partially based on literature reviews and field trials, the final decisions about the *DSM* are often based primarily on expert consensus rather than data (Spitzer, 1991). This contention has been fueled by a lack of documentation of the empirical support for nosologic decisions as well as evidence suggesting that *DSM* committees rely on the clinical judgment of members to fill gaps in the data (Zimmerman, 1988).

Lack of Theory of Pathogenesis

A cough might be a symptom of influenza or it might be an adaptive response to something caught in the throat. Ignoring the cause of the symptom may result in confusion as to what it represents. This is the sort of argument that has been raised by various camps. Psychoanalysts would like Freudian theory reinserted in the *DSM*. Biologically minded researchers and behavior geneticists would like it to reflect psychopharmacological and genetic perspectives, especially when there is substantial evidence for these factors in the pathogenesis of the disorder.

The *DSM*'s preoccupation with a descriptive, clustering-based system of psychopathology runs the risk of instituting diagnoses that lack meaning. Theory is needed to constrain groupings rather than have them based on simplistic overt patterns of similarity. For example, people judge white hair to be more similar to gray than to black hair, but they also judge gray clouds to be more similar to black than to white clouds (Medin & Shoben, 1988). This pattern of linkages indicates that groupings are based on theory, not on superficial similarities in color.

We discussed in chapter 1 that a necessary interplay exists between theory and classification. It has been suggested that an explicit theory is necessary for a classification system to be successful (Follette & Houts, 1996). Categories within a classification system will proliferate unless bounded by theory; eventually the classification system will become overly cumbersome and fail (Faust & Miner, 1986). Evaluation of the number of *DSM* diagnoses is consistent with this sort of analysis. For example, the number of *DSM* diagnoses has increased from approximately 250 in the *DSM–III* (American Psychiatric Association, 1980) to 350 in the *DSM–IV* (American Psychiatric Association, 1994). The *DSM* authors suggest that new diagnoses are based on empirical findings, but proliferation of categories is not a sign of traditional scientific progress, which typically results in fewer categories over time as more phenomena are brought together under general laws (Hempel, 1965). Historically, rapidly expanding taxonomies have tended to collapse under their own weight as the growth results from enumeration of symptoms with no organizing theory that provides simplification. Evaluation of the history of the rapidly expanding *DSM* categories suggests there is a considerable risk for the development of a simply descriptive, superficial system.

In a related vein, researchers have argued that theory based taxonomies are needed for research to progress. Theory is obviously useful in making the taxonomy testable. Explicit theory based models of mental illnesses can be compared with one another to allow us to determine which model is more consistent with available data. Failure to specify a theory may limit the pace of scientific progress.

In the face of ambiguous empirical evidence, a purely descriptive classification system (one that does not involve an explicit assumption of whether it reflects natural or arbitrary categories) is likely to respond by the generation of new categories and through the production of cosmetic repairs. This can be done with little difficulty because there are no underlying theoretical restrictions. Such a response to challenges, however, is not likely to lead to any kind of conceptual advancement. This process is potentially deceiving and may produce the impression of progress when, in actuality, there is an enduring stagnation. A purely descriptive system is, in a sense, nonfalsifiable. If there is no hypothesis, not even about the nature of the categories, the system is really nothing more than drawings in the sand. Currently, the *DSM* is very much a purely descriptive system, seemingly scientific, but only quasi-testable.

Perhaps it is time to move beyond simple description to start making explicit inferences, build and test theoretical connections, and advance our understanding of psychiatric "open" concepts until we achieve the closure. Arguably, we should start with inferences about relationships between *DSM* diagnoses and objective reality (i.e., whether diagnosis *x* refers to a natural category or not).

WHERE DO WE GO FROM HERE: TAXOMETRICS

This discussion clearly suggests that a wide array of potentially damning criticisms have been leveled at the *DSM*. Unlike some critics, however, we do not believe that the *DSM* should be disposed of (nor do we think it is reasonable to believe that the *DSM* will be readily replaced). In our view, the *DSM* should be considered a starting point for the development of a new taxonomy that may or may not resemble the current structure of the *DSM*.

The approach we advocate is relatively simple. Expose each of the current diagnostic entities within the *DSM* to a taxometric analysis as described in chapters 3 and 4. This line of research will yield an understanding of the taxonic nature of proposed diagnostic entities. Findings from these analyses will be important in directly or indirectly addressing many of the most telling criticisms that we have outlined. Taxometric analysis will be extremely helpful in addressing at least four key criticisms: (a) the lack of scientific support for diagnoses, (b) the questionable reliability and validity of diagnoses, (c) the lack of a theory of pathogenesis, and (d) the dimensional–categorical nature of diagnoses. We believe that taxometric analysis will indirectly affect other areas of criticism, including questions regarding state versus course, structure of the diagnostic system, cross-cultural manifestations, and political influences on the diagnostic system. Taxometric analysis has the capacity to influence these other areas by introducing greater scientific rigor that will create a better nosologic system.

One obvious area that taxometric research can address is the central question of whether it is reasonable to assume that diagnostic entities are best represented as categories or syndromes, rather than as dimensions. The categorical and mixed classification method of the *DSM* is not based on taxometric analysis. These symptom clusters may or may not accurately reflect taxa. It is interesting to note that many critics of the *DSM* suggest that what is wrong with the *DSM* is its categorical nature, which should be replaced with a dimensional system (Carson, 1991). Unfortunately, these proponents of a dimensional taxonomy focus on circumstantial arguments and fail to recognize that the objective nature of psychopathology can be *determined*. A taxometric analysis provides the means for evaluating whether a diagnostic entity is in fact a taxon or a dimensional phenomenon. It seems that taxometric analysis is such a natural and straightforward method for addressing the contentions about categories versus dimensions. Identifying the underlying nature of diagnostic entities is one area in which taxometrics can clearly advance our understanding and instruct us with regard to whether our nosology is sound or should be changed to reflect the true dimensional nature of some psychiatric phenomena.

Determination of categories is directly relevant to the determination of syndromes. The *DSM* has used a syndromal approach to classification that focuses on the identification of clusters of symptoms that are believed to co-occur with enough regularity that we may call them a syndrome. The authors of the *DSM* believe that identification of syndromes may reflect something important about etiology, course, and treatment. In other words, the *DSM* taxonomy is based on the idea that syndromes reflect something about their underlying nature. There is the implicit assumption (in the medical model that is the basis of the *DSM*) that disease entities underlie syndromes. Historically, there has been little evidence supporting a linkage between any psychiatric syndrome and some underlying disease. The fact that psychological or psychiatric diseases have not been identified has led to questions about their existence. A taxometric analysis would directly tell us whether the described symptoms do, in fact, define an entity. Obviously, identification of a taxon is not isomorphic with identifying a disease entity. However, failure to find a taxon would be suggestive that some underlying entity does not exist.

Determination of the taxonicity of diagnostic entities is critical for the scientific support of diagnoses. Confirming the existence of a taxon that underlies a diagnostic syndrome is an important step in establishing that this syndrome should be represented as a category. A lack of taxonicity may suggest that the phenomenon is dimensional and should be organized in this manner. Moreover, taxometric investigations can revolutionize our approach to diagnosing a single individual. Once we determine the boundaries of an underlying entity, we can construct measures that will allow for the best assessment (e.g., highest sensitivity, specificity, simplicity, brevity) of the taxon. Our current diagnostic assessment is extremely primitive. We developed (in a more or less scientific manner) a set of diagnostic criteria, but the assessment itself does not involve much more than subjective ratings made by clinicians, a process that has benefited little from empirical science. In the process underlying an empirical (taxometric) search for psychiatric taxa, we will not only discover better diagnostic criteria but also develop a set of standardized measures that in addition to clinician-ratings can include behavioral tasks, lab tests, and so forth, that will allow for much more efficient assessments. In addition, taxometric investigations will enable us to evaluate the accuracy of a diagnostic decision, that is, estimate the probability that the individual has disorder *x* given the results of the assessment (more details about this process are provided in chap. 3).

The issue of the reliability of *DSM* diagnoses and efforts to further increase the reliability of these diagnoses ignores the importance of the need to further our understanding of natural entities or taxa that underlie symptoms. As mentioned earlier, in the quest for high interrater reliability, the diagnostic elements may have failed to adequately cut nature at its joints. The syndrome may be missing some critically valid elements that have been excluded, or perhaps a "true" entity has been divided into many parts that are believed to be independent. If the criteria elements of a diagnosis are inaccurate— that is, they do not reflect the true boundaries of an underlying taxon—then our understanding of the diagnostic entity will be severely hampered. Taxometric analysis will provide a means to determine whether we have gone too far in dissecting behaviors (or perhaps not gone far enough). Taxometric analysis can also be used to evaluate the degree to which we have sacrificed validity, in terms of adequately measuring a diagnostic entity, in the pursuit of reliability.

In this chapter, we have suggested that the *DSM* has a number of deficiencies, many of which can be corrected through the application of appropriate statistical analyses. In the following chapters, we provide concrete examples of how taxometric analysis can revolutionize how nosologic entities are determined.

3

AN ANALYTIC PRIMER:
HOW DO YOU DO TAXOMETRICS?

Lacking a gold standard criterion, the only rational basis for inferring the existence of a taxonic entity, a real class, a nonarbitrary natural kind, must lie within the pattern displayed by the presumed indicators of the conjectured taxon.

—Meehl, 1995a

Taxometrics is much more than a family of statistical procedures; it is a complex approach to investigating structures of objective reality. Taxometric methodology can be decomposed into statistical and epistemological components. These components, of course, are intertwined: Statistical procedures stem from certain epistemological considerations, and epistemological principles are applied with the aid of statistical techniques. For illustrative purposes, discussion of taxometric methods in this chapter is divided into various sections. The "methodology" and "group assignment" sections focus on mathematical aspects, while "consistency testing" and "bootstrapping" sections focus on the epistemological aspects.

All current taxometric procedures are based on a single statistical method termed *Coherent Cut Kinetics* (CCK). We decipher the meaning of this term in the next section in the example of the MAXCOV-HITMAX (MAXCOV stands for MAXimal COVariance; the reason for this name will become clear in the next section) technique. However, we emphasize that it is not the shared statistical method that defines taxometrics. Adherence to a particular set of epistemological principles distinguishes taxometrics from other approaches. In other words, any analytic procedure that can identify taxa may be considered taxometric, as long as the investigation is faithful to the philosophical premises of taxometrics.

The computational complexity of taxometric procedures varies, and some of them require fairly sophisticated software. A few such software packages have been created and are now available on the Internet. These programs differ in the scope and details of their execution of taxometric principles. Because discussion of these principles is more fruitful when supplemented by concrete examples, we had to choose one package as the background for the more detailed explanations. Our choice was a set of programs published by Dr. Neils Waller on his Taxometrics Home Page (Waller, 2004; http://peabody.vanderbilt.edu/depts/psych_and_hd/faculty/wallern/tx.html). There are several reasons for this choice. Waller's package has been tested in more simulation studies (e.g., Meehl & Yonce, 1994, 1996), it has been used in more empirical studies (e.g., Blanchard, Gangestad, Brown, & Horan, 2000; Gleaves, Lowe, Snow, Green, & Murphy-Eberenz, 2000; Waller & Ross, 1997), and it appears to receive the most attention (on the basis of the hit counter on the Taxometrics Home Page).

MAXCOV-HITMAX

Let us begin by describing the logic and technique behind the most prominent taxometric analytic procedure, MAXCOV-HITMAX (Meehl & Yonce, 1996), to which we refer as MAXCOV. MAXCOV is by far the oldest taxometric procedure. For example, the mathematical basis for MAXCOV was established in 1965 (Meehl), and the original version of the technique was described in 1973 (Meehl). Learning the principles employed by this classic method can facilitate understanding of the newer procedures, which are described later in the chapter.

MAXCOV Methodology

The first step in understanding MAXCOV methodology is to understand its *general* logic. It is instructive to do this with an example. Consider biological gender, which most would agree is a true categorical phenomenon (i.e., it is a taxon, not a continuum). More specifically, let's consider male gender and two valid but imperfect indicators of male gender—height and baldness. Height and baldness are not perfect indicators of male gender, but as will be shown, the approach works despite this. If you measured the height and baldness of the next 100 people you see (men and women alike), you will certainly find that height and baldness are correlated. This is true because the taller people you meet (in whom men are over-represented) are more likely than the shorter ones (among whom women are over-represented) to be bald. But *why* are height and baldness correlated? The answer to this ques-

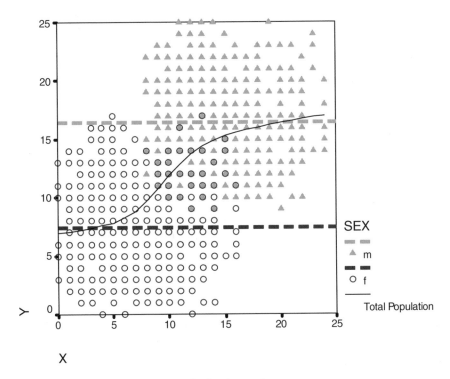

Figure 3.1. Correlations in pure and mixed samples.

tion goes to the key idea of the MAXCOV method. Height and baldness, like any good indicators of a taxon, correlate precisely and only *because* they differentiate men from women.

To understand this, consider the correlation of height and baldness among "pure" samples of men, or among "pure" samples of women. *Within* both pure samples—that is, within the two latent classes—where there are only men or only women, height and baldness are negligibly correlated. Within the male class, one's height says little about whether one is bald; the same is true for the female class. But within a mixed sample of men and women, taller people are more likely to be bald than shorter people. Figure 3.1 illustrates this idea.

On the figure, triangles represent males and circles represent females; dashed lines are regression lines for the subgroups; and the solid line is the overall regression line. As can be seen, indicators X and Y are completely uncorrelated in subgroups, but there is a correlation in the overall sample, and it is highest at the boundary between the groups.

In sum, this is how ideal indicators of taxa behave—they intercorrelate in samples where taxon members and nonmembers are mixed, and they do *not* correlate in pure samples of taxon members or in pure samples of nontaxon members. This behavior of taxon markers is captured by a reduced General Covariance Mixture Theorem (GCMT; for the derivation of the theorem see Meehl & Yonce, 1996, Appendix A), which provides the mathematical basis of MAXCOV.

To understand this idea better, consider the following. Suppose that a certain dimension (a spectrum, a trait) is truly continuous, and we have two ways to measure it. These measures should correlate about the same, whether the correlation is calculated at the low, middle, or high end of the spectrum. For example, if we were to study a correlation between vocabulary and matrixes subtests of the Wechsler Adult Intelligence Scale (Wechsler, 1997), we would expect to find that the correlation is about the same for people with borderline, average, and superior intelligence. In other words, if a dimension is truly continuous, there is no reason for the correlation to be significantly elevated at any point along the spectrum. If such an elevation is observed, however, the continuum is broken. The idea reflected by GCMT is that latent discontinuity is marked by a significant elevation in correlations at a certain part of a spectrum.

The basic strategy in using taxometric procedures is to presume a taxon—for example, depression. Next, we are required to conjecture the presumed taxon's indicators—sadness, anhedonia, and suicidality. Presume and conjecture based on what? Clinical experience, intuition, past theory and research . . . it really does not matter. The presuming and conjecturing take place in what Popper (1959) called the "context of discovery," where ideas, theories, and hypotheses are developed from any source. The empirical evaluation of these ideas, however, takes place in Popper's "context of justification"; when the question is a taxometric one, the context of justification involves taxometric analyses.

We have presumed a taxon and some indicators. Next, we take one of these indicators and assign scores to a group of individuals on each indicator (e.g., everyone gets a score from 1 to 7 on sadness, anhedonia, and suicidality), much as one does with the Beck Depression Inventory and similar self-report scales. Finally, we examine the pairwise intercorrelations of the indicators at all possible values of all other indicators. In the depression example, we would examine the correlation of sadness and anhedonia for those who score 1 on suicidality, those who score 2 on suicidality, and so forth, up the scale to those who score 7 on suicidality. Similarly, we would examine the correlation of sadness and suicidality for those who score 1 on anhedonia, those who score 2 on anhedonia, and so forth. This would be continued for all possible combinations of indicators.

If depression is a taxon, two indicators (e.g., sadness and anhedonia) would correlate negligibly at the low end of the third indicator (e.g., among those who score one on suicidality), where the majority of taxon nonmembers would be. The two indicators would correlate more highly as the midrange of the third indicator is approached, where the mixture of taxon members and nonmembers is close to equal proportions. Finally, the indicators would correlate negligibly at the high end of the third indicator, where the majority of taxon members would be. If depression is not a taxon but a dimensional continuum, the intercorrelation of any two indicators would not systematically vary as a function of a third indicator. This is a brief review of the procedural part of MAXCOV.

To clarify this further, let us go back through the depression example but in greater detail. Assume we have a reason to *conjecture* a depression taxon (again, the reason does not matter; this is Popper's [1959] context of discovery, not context of justification). Similarly, assume we have other reasons to conjecture valid indicators of this presumed taxon (sadness, anhedonia, and suicidality).

Assume $N = 10,000$; indicators are on a 1–7 scale. Let us single out anhedonia for a moment, and slice up the sample based on anhedonia scores, which for now we call the input variable (meaning that it was sliced), as follows:

Anhedonia = 1; n = 4,000
Anhedonia = 2; n = 2,000
Anhedonia = 3; n = 1,000
Anhedonia = 4; n = 1,000
Anhedonia = 5; n = 800
Anhedonia = 6; n = 700
Anhedonia = 7; n = 500

Next, in each anhedonia interval we compute the covariance between the other two indicators, sadness and suicidality, which we now call output variables (meaning that their covariance was calculated), as follows:

Anhedonia = 1; n = 4,000—COVsad.suic = ?
Anhedonia = 2; n = 2,000—COVsad.suic = ?
Anhedonia = 3; n = 1,000—COVsad.suic = ?
Anhedonia = 4; n = 1,000—COVsad.suic = ?
Anhedonia = 5; n = 800—COVsad.suic = ?
Anhedonia = 6; n = 700—COVsad.suic = ?
Anhedonia = 7; n = 500—COVsad.suic = ?

Assume the results are as follows:

Anhedonia = 1; n = 4,000—COVsad.suic = .0012
Anhedonia = 2; n = 2,000—COVsad.suic = .0089
Anhedonia = 3; n = 1,000—COVsad.suic = .067
Anhedonia = 4; n = 1,000—COVsad.suic = .098
Anhedonia = 5; n = 800—COVsad.suic = .131
Anhedonia = 6; n = 700—COVsad.suic = .399
Anhedonia = 7; n = 500—COVsad.suic = .0014

In Figure 3.2, the same results were rotated and graphed. Additional results using different input and output indicators can be seen in Figure 3.3.

With three indicators, three such graphs are possible. With = 3 indicators (i), the number of possible graphs = i × (i–1) × (i–2)/2; that is, 12 graphs

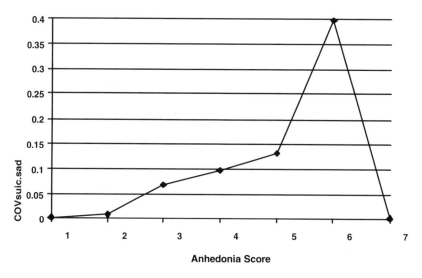

Figure 3.2. Taxonic MAXCOV plot (anhedonia).

are possible with 4 indicators, 30 graphs are possible with 5 indicators, etc. We will call a *subanalysis* the process of plotting one of these graphs and doing related calculations. For example, construction of a MAXCOV graph with anhedonia as the input variable and sadness and suicidality as the output variables constitutes one subanalysis; construction of a MAXCOV graph with sadness as the input variable and anhedonia and suicidality as the output variables constitutes another subanalysis.

What to do with these graphs? If the underlying structure is taxonic, graphs of the conditional covariances generated by MAXCOV tend to be peaked (Meehl & Yonce, 1996). A series of peaked graphs indicates taxonicity; a series of flat graphs indicates dimensionality. In Figure 3.4, the graph has no clear peak, and would be inconsistent with the conjecture of a depression taxon. The determination of whether a graph is peaked or not is done the old-fashioned way—by visual inspection. In response to the concern that visual inspection lacks the clarity that a statistical test would provide, Meehl and Yonce (1996) had five people of varying degrees of statistical sophistication sort 90 MAXCOV outputs, each containing 12 graphs, as taxonic or nontaxonic. Outputs came from analyzing nontaxonic and taxonic simulated data sets with various underlying distributions. Accuracy of the sorting was perfect for all five people! On the other hand, these simulated data were idealized, which can enhance the clarity of the MAXCOV plots. Analyses of real data can produce less obvious curves. Moreover, taxometricians recently became more interested in evaluating the taxonic status of individual graphs rather than of the entire panel; although research on this topic is very limited, there is some evidence that individual plot ratings may have modest reliability. Data from our lab suggests that even after extensive training, rat-

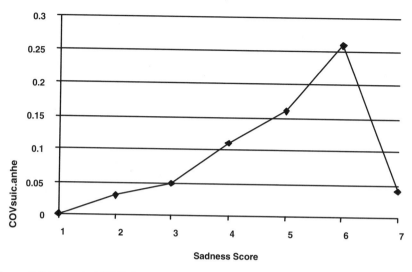

Figure 3.3. Taxonic MAXCOV plot (sadness).

ers do not agree perfectly. We recommend that researchers develop a rating scheme with examples drawn from simulated data (e.g., the data sets that Meehl and Yonce have created) to serve as a guide for raters, and to evaluate interrater agreement quantitatively (e.g., with kappa, or interclass correlations) on a sufficiently large subset of the plots.

Usually MAXCOV graphs do not look as clear as those we have created for this example, especially if the sample size is modest. Such curves are difficult to interpret, and taxometricians often smooth the plots to remove random noise and to make the patterns clearer. The most common choice of a smoother is Tukey's (1977) median-of-three repeated twice procedure. We are generally sympathetic to the notion of smoothing, but this procedure can be problematic. Smoothing removes noise from the data, but it can also minimize true differences. Hence, smoothed taxonic plots may appear relatively flat and may be mistakenly judged as nontaxonic. Smoothing may distort the precise positions of the peaks and lead to inaccurate estimation of parameters of the underlying distributions, such as the taxon base rate (discussed later in this section). To the best of our knowledge these issues have not yet been empirically tested, so at present it is unclear which approach is more advantageous. We recommend starting with "raw" graphs since they are more "natural" and applying a smoother if the plots appear too noisy. However, the best solution to the noise issue is to increase the sample size.

The location of a graph's peak (if there is one) depends on the base rate of the taxon; that is, the proportion of taxon members in the overall sample. A base rate of .50 (half of individuals are taxon members) produces a centered peak; low base rates (common in psychopathology research) produce right-shifted peaks, such as those in the depression example. Conversely,

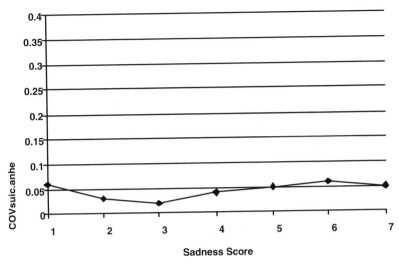

Figure 3.4. Nontaxonic MAXCOV plots.

taxa with high base rates produce left-shifted peaks. Importantly, peaks can be shifted so much that they appear to be "shifted off" the graph. For example, Figure 3.5 could be interpreted as being consistent with the taxonic conjecture (as if it is peaked).

The main problem with upward slopes that do not result in a peak is that such plots can provide an upper boundary for estimates of taxon base rate, but there is no telling how small the base rate really is. In our depression example, the upward slope suggests that the taxon base rate is anywhere between three percent and zero. Another potential problem with low base rate situations is that relatively few subjects fall in the final interval, which can make computation of covariance in that interval tenuous. In the depression example, if the sample size was 150, rather than the admittedly optimistic 10,000, only eight people would have scored seven on sadness. In general, the minimum recommended n for an interval is 15, with higher numbers always being desirable. Waller's MAXCOV program allows researchers to ensure there are enough participants in each interval. This is done by setting the MRIN (minimal required interval n) parameter at a certain value, and excluding all intervals that have fewer cases than MRIN from the analysis. However, a large sample is the only satisfactory solution to the problem of low base rate taxa.

Sample Size

How large is large? The recommended sample-wide minimum N is 300. However, larger Ns are required for smaller base rates. One rule of thumb is to anticipate having at least 30 taxon members in the sample. In other words,

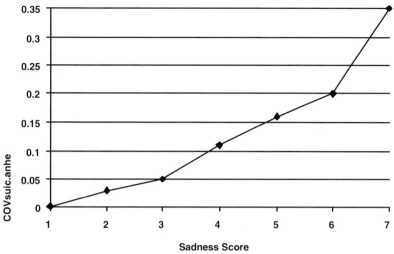

Figure 3.5. Cusping MAXCOV plot.

for a taxon with an expected base rate of three percent (e.g., obsessive–compulsive disorder in a community sample) an investigator should recruit at least 1,000 participants. A sample of such size can be difficult to get; one way around that is to sample from a different population, in which taxon members are expected to be more prevalent (e.g., a sample of anxiety patients) or screen the participants on a relevant factor. The 30 rule should allow for enough taxon members to obtain peaking graphs (rather than upward slopes) and should provide minimally reliable results (by having at least 15 people in the extreme right interval), that is, obtain reasonable support for taxonic conjecture. However, accurate *estimation of parameters* of the taxon requires many more taxon members than 30. We describe these parameters and explain why they are useful next.

A different way of approaching this issue is to manipulate the latent composition of the sample. The clearest taxometric findings are obtained when taxon members constitute 50% of the sample. This can be approximated by recruiting two groups of participants: one from a population where almost everyone is expected to be a taxon member (e.g., patients diagnosed with panic disorder for a study of a panic disorder taxon) and another from a population where almost no one is expected to be a taxon member (e.g., nonclinical, healthy individuals). Then these groups can be combined in equal proportion to produce a mixed sample with expected taxon base rate of 50%. There are few empirical studies that have used this approach in practice (Gleaves et al., 2000; Waller, Putnam, & Carlson, 1996).

The problem with this design is that it can produce spurious evidence of taxonicity. By combining two groups, the investigator in a sense drops the middle of the distribution and creates artificial discontinuity. This idea is best illustrated by the well-known "Tellegen's case" (Meehl, 1992). Suppose we mixed a sample of children with borderline intelligence and a sample of children with above average intelligence. If we administer an IQ test to this mixed group, we probably will get a clearly bimodal distribution and conclude that there is a taxon. Obviously, we will not obtain such evidence in any "natural" sample, where the range of intelligence scores is not restricted in such an unusual way.

One can argue that MAXCOV is not susceptible to this problem because it does not rely on bimodality of the overall score but evaluates correlations of the indicators. However, this question has not yet been evaluated. Other taxometric procedures, on the other hand, will definitely be affected. For instance, Mean Above Minus Below A Cut (MAMBAC)—one of the most popular CCK methods (described later in this chapter)—is undoubtedly susceptible to this problem. Gleaves and colleagues (2000) mixed a sample of 209 bulimics with a sample of 209 undergraduates who scored low on indicators of bulimia and found very strong support for a taxon with the base rate of 51%. Such a finding raises questions of whether it is an artifact of the sample mixture. Overall, we do not recommend using a mixed sample approach. If such an approach is used, the researcher should not use statistical methods that rely on means, variances, frequencies, or other statistics that can be affected by dropping middle cases (e.g., MAMBAC and Mixture Analysis).

As mentioned previously, the investigator can try to obtain adequate samples by screening participants. Screening can save resources when the assessment of putative taxon markers is labor intensive. However, the majority of current taxometric studies use self-report questionnaires, so it is often no more difficult to administer all of the indicators. For situations like this, Meehl (1999) suggested an internal screening procedure, which we refer to as *sample truncation*. First, the researcher standardizes the indicators to make sure that they are weighted equally and creates a composite by summing them. This composite is our best guess about taxon membership, with high scorers likely to be taxon members and low scorers likely to be nontaxon members. The researcher then selects a certain level on the composite and drops all cases that score below it. For taxa with an expected base rate of .25 or lower, the cutoff can be set at median; that is, the lower scoring half of the sample is "screened-out." For taxa with a very small base rate (less than .10), a higher cutoff can be used; for example, the bottom 70% of cases can be dropped.

Truncation does not increase number of taxon members in the sample, but it increases their base rate. Meehl suggested that having a base rate above .10 is important for the adequate performance of MAXCOV, even when the total number of taxon members is fixed. This claim has not been thoroughly evaluated, but results of a recent large-scale simulation study by Beauchaine and Beauchaine (2002) appear to be consistent with this assertion. Beauchaine and Beauchaine found that when the taxon base rate is low, MAXCOV has a tendency to underestimate the taxon base rate even further; if conditions are less than ideal, MAXCOV's ability to correctly identify a case as being taxonic or nontaxonic also suffers. However, it is unclear if sample truncation can enhance performance of other procedures. In fact, use of truncation with MAMBAC may yield uninterpretable outputs.

Another important advantage of sample truncation is that it can reduce nuisance correlations. The concept of nuisance correlation is explained later in this section, but we can also discuss this concept here in terms of taxonic and continuous variance. Consider that scores on real world indicators probably reflect both taxonic and continuous variance, and the presence of the latter can skew the results. Sample truncation essentially removes a big chunk of continuous variance, which can improve the accuracy of the results. It is, of course, important to ensure that taxonic variance stays intact. Almost any screener would screen out some taxon members, but our experiences with sample truncation suggest that it is usually possible to find a cutoff that removes a substantial number of nontaxon members without losing many taxon members.

The Hitmax and Base Rate

In addition to telling us whether a taxon exists, taxometric analyses have the potential to provide additional useful information about the nature of the taxon. The hitmax and base rate estimations are examples of this. The "hitmax" is that point on the graph's X-axis (input indicator) where the mixture of taxon and nontaxon members is at equal 50–50 proportions, which is also the point where the covariance peaks. On Figure 3.6, this point is marked with an arrow. The position of the hitmax is used in the computation of the taxon's base rate. In computing base rates, a value "K" is used, which is defined as $4 \times$ the covariance at the peak (i.e., hitmax).

For each interval on the X-axis (e.g., from 1 to 7 in the depression example), we solve for the base rate in that interval, which is:

$$p_{interval} = K \pm (K^2 - [4 \times K \times cov_{interval}])^{1/2} / 2K$$

The term "$cov_{interval}$" denotes the covariance for that particular interval. Note that the square root is taken of the elements within the parentheses. Note also that there is a "plus or minus" sign (i.e., $\pm$). For intervals to the right of the hitmax, use plus; for intervals to the left, use minus.

For each interval, we now have a value for $p_{interval}$ (the proportion of taxon members in that interval). We can then multiply $p_{interval}$ times n the number of participants in that interval, which will produce the number of taxon members in that interval (nontaxon members = total in interval – taxon members in interval). The sum of the taxon members across the intervals, divided by the total N, gives the taxon base rate (see Meehl & Yonce,

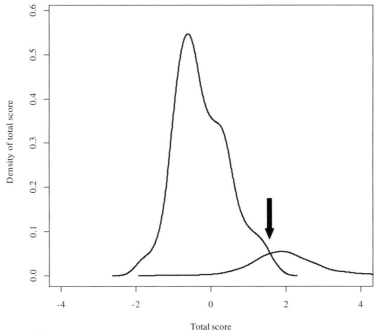

Latent Taxonomic Class Distributions

Figure 3.6. Hitmax.

1996). Each subanalysis will also produce estimates of the taxon base rate. An average of these estimates is called the *grand taxon base rate*.

Negative covariances may occur in some intervals and result in non-sense values, such as negative $p_{interval.}$ The convention in such cases is to assume $p_{interval} = 0$ in intervals to the left of the hitmax, and $p_{interval} = 1$ in intervals to the right of the hitmax. Also, covariance in an interval can be so high as to result in a negative number in the square root term. The convention in this case is to assume that the square root term = 0.

Let us review what we did with the depression example so far. First, we conjectured a taxon and three indicators. Next, we selected one of these indicators (anhedonia) as the input variable and two other indicators (sadness and suicidality) as the output variables. Input and output are labels that refer to a role of the indicator in a given subanalysis. We cut the input indicator into intervals, hence the word "Cut" in the name of the method (Coherent Cut Kinetics), and we looked at the relationship between the output indicators. Specifically, we calculated covariances of the output indicators in each interval, hence the word "Kinetics"—we moved calculations from interval to interval. Suppose that after all that was completed, we find a clear peak in the covariance of sadness and suicidality, which allows us to estimate the position of the hitmax and the taxon base rate. What next? Now we need to get multiple estimates of these parameters. To achieve this, we change the configuration and assign variables to different roles, e.g., use sadness as the input variable and anhedonia and suicidality as output variables. Our goal is to find out whether base rate estimates agree across these analyses, hence the word "Coherent." This, briefly, is Coherent Cut Kinetics; a method that looks consecutively at portions of the data and does so in various ways to get multiple estimates of latent parameters.

Consistency Testing

Use of consistency tests is one of the key principles of taxometric epistemology. A single taxonic finding, a single MAXCOV peak, can be a mistake for many reasons. Peculiarity of the sample, idiosyncrasy of the measures, an unforeseen influence of the specifics of the problem on the procedure, or a random fluctuation can result in a false taxonic finding. However, a constellation of consistent taxonic findings is much less likely to be a mistake. If an investigator finds an effect and it replicates across various analyses, he or she can conclude that there is strong evidence in support of the effect, although it is possible that these results are due to error. However, if the investigator also finds that the magnitude of the effect is essentially the same in all of these analyses, she or he has no other choice but to conclude that the effect is real. It is not possible for errors to produce consistent results across different methods and different samples; some real entity must exist that is responsible for consistent findings.

How exactly does one test for consistency? Our first impulse might be to devise some kind of statistical significance test. Interestingly, Paul Meehl, the author of MAXCOV, took a different route. In fact, none of the existing CCK procedures uses statistical significance testing. This is not an accident, for Paul Meehl is known for his position against statistical significance testing. His basic argument (Meehl, 1978) is that significance tests are weak and uninformative because any null hypothesis can be rejected given a sufficiently large sample size (an argument that the majority of statisticians accept). For a long while, Meehl encouraged researchers to abandon significance testing and use stronger tests; thus, he decided upon a very powerful test for taxometric research. Rather than trying to prove that a certain value is not zero, a taxometrician tries to prove that the set of values (parameters of the underlying distribution) can be consistently obtained multiple times using several dramatically different methods. A stringent test indeed! Utilization of stringent (or "risky") tests of theories is another epistemological tenet of the taxometric approach.

Of course, it would be unreasonable to expect that values of the parameters will be exactly the same in all analyses, even if a taxon really exists. We therefore set "tolerance intervals"—a predetermined limit on the degree to which estimates can deviate from one another—on each value being tested. If any estimate falls outside the interval, we should conclude that analyses showed evidence of inconsistency and the taxonic conjecture failed the test. Unfortunately, there are no established rules on what level of tolerance is optimal in a taxometric analysis. This is currently an important issue for taxometrics and hopefully will be resolved in the near future. At this point, investigators have to rely on their judgment about what is "close enough." There are two prototypic cases. One is that if all estimates of a particular value (e.g., taxon base rate) fall together in one tight cluster (e.g., all ten estimates are between 20% and 25%), then we conclude that there is consistency. The second case is that if the estimates are all over the place (e.g., range from 5% to 93%) without any evidence of clustering, then we conclude that the results are inconsistent. For intermediate cases (e.g., 7 of 10 estimates fall between 20% and 25%), the investigator needs to use some decision rules to help decide if the findings are consistent with the taxonic conjecture (e.g., if the standard deviation of the base rate estimates is greater than 0.10, the results are considered inconsistent).

To get some idea of reasonable sizes for tolerance intervals, we conducted a small simulation study specifically for this book. We applied MAXCOV to 20 simulated taxonic data sets created by Meehl and Yonce (1994, data set code D650v1). These data sets were generated to approximate data encountered in empirical work (e.g., indicators had limited validity and nuisance correlations were non-negligible). The only idealization of this simulation is that the taxon base rate was set at .50. One goal of the study was to provide guidelines for interval size (distance between the cuts) selection, discussed at the end of this section. As a result, each data set was analyzed 15 times using intervals ranging from .18 standard deviation (SD) to .32 SD (in .01 SD increments). We also performed MAXCOV analyses with 10 simulated dimensional data sets using the same approach. These data sets were created to match the distributional properties (e.g., interindicator correlations) of the taxonic data (Meehl & Yonce, 1994; data set code D600). There are four indicators in each data set. A total of 450 analyses were attempted and 409 of them produced usable data. MAXCOV yielded computational errors in the remaining 41 analyses. We used the taxonic status of the data sets as a criterion and performed stepwise multiple regression analyses to determine the combination of consistency tests that best distinguishes taxonic from nontaxonic data. In addition, we computed the discrepancy between the grand taxon base rate estimate and the true base rate (.50) for analyses of the taxonic data ($N = 287$). The absolute value of this discrepancy was used as an index of MAXCOV's accuracy and stepwise multiple regression was conducted to determine whether consistency tests can be used to evaluate the trustworthiness of the parameter estimates; that is, if they predict the magnitude of the discrepancy. We report results of this study below.

Due to paucity of simulation studies of taxometric procedures, there is a growing trend in substantive taxometric investigations to conduct one's own simulations. Full-blown simulation studies are labor intensive, so instead of generating hundreds of data sets, a researcher usually creates just one simulated taxonic data set and one simulated nontaxonic data set to serve as reference points. Comparisons between the research and the reference data can be vivid and compelling, but it is important to keep in mind that they represent only a comparison with an N of one, and should be interpreted with some skepticism. The main concern is that sampling error may cause a mistaken inference. For example, a single simulated continuous data set may appear similar to research data, but if analyses of 100 continuous data sets were averaged, it might become clear that the typical continuous data produces a pattern of results very distinct from that of the research data. Sampling error is a problem for all but the largest data sets (e.g., 10,000 cases) and is particularly troublesome for low base rate taxa—for example, even if the overall N is 1,000, a taxon with a .10 base rate would include just 100 cases.

We believe that only large scale simulation studies can truly advance the discipline by helping us establish acceptable tolerance intervals. However, individual (parallel) simulations such as those just described can also be useful. These simulations can serve as suitability tests; that is, they can tell the researcher whether a particular research data set can, in principle, answer the questions of interest. In other words, if taxonic and dimensional data are generated to simulate the research data and the researcher finds few differences between the simulated sets (e.g., they yielded the same number of taxonic plots), then there is little sense in analyzing the research data because it is unlikely to give a clear answer. With suitability testing, a modest simulation study (e.g., 20 taxonic and 20 continuous data sets) is preferred to individual simulations because it would yield clearer and more reliable results.

Let us put interpretational issues aside for now and describe the logic behind the various consistency tests. It is useful to distinguish between two types of consistency tests: internal consistency tests and external consistency tests. Internal consistency tests are conducted within a single analysis. The purpose of internal consistency tests is to evaluate whether subanalyses converged on the same values. In the depression example, MAXCOV is applied to a set of three continuous indicators, so we have three subanalyses and three estimates of taxon base rate. One way to test for internal consistency is to check whether all of these base rate estimates converge on the same number (e.g., taxon base rate of 13%). External consistency tests are conducted across different methods and studies. For example, if we apply a different analytic procedure (e.g., MAMBAC, described later in the chapter) to data from the depression example, we can perform an external consistency test by checking whether both procedures yield approximately the same estimate of taxon base rate. Ideally, we would require the conjectured taxon to pass multiple tests of both kinds (internal and external) before we consider it to be established. For example, with MAXCOV as the primary analytic procedure in the investigation, the following should be demonstrated in order to fully establish a taxon:

a. Graphs are clearly and consistently peaked across subanalyses.
b. The variance of base rates is low across subanalyses.
c. The Goodness of Fit Index (GFI) is above the threshold.
d. The distribution of individual subjects' taxon membership probabilities should cluster around 0 and 1 (more about this in the next section).
e. The same conclusions are reached using at least one separate taxometric procedure and one nontaxometric analytic procedure (some are described later in the chapter).
f. A through e is replicated on a separate sample.

This illustrates the general philosophy of taxometrics. For something to be deemed a taxon, it needs to clear several hurdles, which arguably makes taxometrics the most rigorous analytic approach to the study of taxonomy. The last two conditions (e and f) are external consistency tests and apply to all taxometric studies. On the other hand, a, b, c, and d are internal consistency tests. Some of them are specific to MAXCOV—other procedures have their own unique internal consistency tests—but a and b can be performed with any of the CCK methods. We will now consider the first three internal consistency tests (a, b, and c) in detail and postpone discussion of the distribution of taxon membership.

The first internal consistency test is a straightforward "nose count." The investigator uses visual inspection to identify the graphs that are peaking (consistent with the taxonic conjecture) and those that are not (inconsistent with the taxonic conjecture). This decision is usually made dichotomously, although some researchers use a three-point system: taxonic, nontaxonic, and ambiguous. Regardless of the rating scale, the "nose count" test is performed by comparing the number of taxonic and nontaxonic plots. What is the minimal ratio of taxonic to nontaxonic plots required for passing this consistency test? There is no definitive answer to this question, as once again this is an issue of tolerance intervals. The simplest approach is to require at least as many taxonic as nontaxonic graphs; that is, a ratio of 1:1. However, many researchers are concerned with false positive findings (mistakenly reporting discovery of a taxon) and use more stringent cutoffs, such as 2:1, meaning that there should be at least twice as many taxonic as nontaxonic plots. The most stringent cutoff we have encountered in the literature is 3:1. Our simulation study suggests that the 1:1 cutoff is perfectly adequate and may be superior to the alternatives. We found that less than one percent of the analyses of continuous data produced at least as many taxonic as nontaxonic plots. In fact, the 1:1 cutoff may be a bit too stringent, because in our study three percent of the analyses of taxonic data produced fewer taxonic than nontaxonic plots. We also found that the nose count is superior to all other consistency tests in detecting taxonicity. It alone accounted for 80% of the variance in taxonic status (taxonic or dimensional) of the data sets that were analyzed. On the other hand, when the taxonic data were examined separately, the nose count failed to predict how accurately MAXCOV estimated parameters of the underlying distributions.

It is important to note that if an indicator has little validity, its covariance with other indicators may not produce a clear peak. When there are reasons to believe that one of the indicators has poor validity—reasons that are more serious than not finding enough peaks in the output—it should not be automatically inferred from this failure of the nose count test that the taxon does not exist. The best way to solve this problem is to evaluate a different set of indicators or to drop the invalid indicator.

The second internal consistency test is called the base rate variability test. It compares base rate estimates across subanalyses. As mentioned before, MAXCOV allows for multiple assessments of the taxon base rate by evaluating different configurations of indicators. To do the test, all of these estimates are pooled together and the SD is calculated for this set of numbers. The magnitude of the standard deviation can be used as an index of consistency, with a large SD indicating a lack of consistency. Once again, there are no clear guidelines about the limits of tolerance on SD. In our research, we use SD of .10 or less as an absolute cutoff and consider SD of less than .05 to be strong evidence of taxonicity. This is just a plausible heuristic, but our simulation study allowed us to evaluate the performance of these cutoffs. First, we found that the base rate variability test is not the strongest index of taxonicity. It accounted only for 46% of the variance in the taxonic status of the data sets examined, and offered little incremental improvement beyond the nose count test, accounting for an additional 1% of the variance. Nevertheless, even a small incremental improvement should not be discounted outright. We also found that the nose count and the base rate variability tests interact to predict taxonic status of the data, and the interactive effect accounts for another 3% of variance. In other words, consistency between these two tests (i.e., both suggest taxonicity or both suggest dimensionality) strengthens the case for continuity or discontinuity beyond what an investigator could infer by evaluating these indexes separately. Furthermore, base rate variability was able to predict accuracy of the parameter estimation in analyses of the taxonic data sets. It accounted for 10% of the variance in the discrepancy between the estimated and the true base rate. Evaluation of various tolerance intervals revealed that the best cutoff for identification of taxonic data sets is actually an SD of .18 (sensitivity .90 and specificity .80). In fact, only 30% of the taxonic data sets had an SD of less than .10. However, consider that the taxon base rate was large and four indicators were analyzed in this study. Analyses of three indicators or a taxon with a lower base rate would generally produce a lower SD, so the .18 cutoff would be too liberal. More importantly, we found that the .10 cutoff is, in fact, the best cutoff for the identification of accurate results (defined as discrepancy of .05 or less, i.e., 10% estimation error). In sum, the base rate variability test is quite helpful in determining the taxonic status of a construct, and it is especially useful for evaluating the credibility of parameter estimates.

The third internal consistency test is the test of model fit. This type of testing is also employed in Structural Equation Modeling and many other statistical procedures. When we know all parameters of the model: taxon base rate and means and variances of latent groups (the method of calculating means and variances is described in the next section), we can use reduced Generalized Covariance Mixture Theorem (GCMT) to "predict" the observed variances and covariances of the indicators. This procedure is the reverse of a MAXCOV analysis. We compare the correlations "predicted" by the model to the observed correlations. If our model fits the data perfectly, the predicted correlations would equal the observed correlations. In all other situations, there will be some discrepancy. MAXCOV uses GFI to quantify the discrepancy. GFI ranges from 0 to 1.00, where 1.00 indicates perfect agreement (no discrepancy), and 0 indicates complete lack of agreement. One simulation study suggested that a cutoff of .90 should be set for the GFI (Waller & Meehl, 1998). The study found that the majority of GFIs in MAXCOV analyses of simulated taxonic data sets were higher than .90, while analyses of simulated nontaxonic data sets usually produced GFIs of .90 or less. However, more thorough investigations have raised some questions regarding optimal cutoff and even meaning of the GFI (e.g., Cleland, Rothschild, & Haslam, 2000).

The GFI should not be considered a true consistency test. To understand the role of the GFI, consider that it is based on *reduced* Generalized Covariance Mixture Theorem (Waller & Meehl, 1998). It tests a model that assumes nuisance correlations equal to zero. This assumption is rarely true, especially if similar measures are used as indicators (e.g., all of the measures are self-report questionnaires resulting in inflation of correlation due to method variance). Thus, a low GFI either means that the taxonic conjecture is wrong or that nuisance correlations are large. Findings from our simulation study support this notion. First, our findings were consistent with Waller & Meehl (1998) as we found that the GFI is associated with the taxonic status of a data set and the cutoff of .90 is appropriate for classifying taxonic and nontaxonic data (sensitivity .97, specificity .77). However, the GFI offered relatively little incremental improvement beyond the nose count test, accounting for an additional 4% of variance in the taxonic status. Second, we found that the GFI is the best test to predict the accuracy of parameter estimation in analyses of taxonic data sets. It accounted for 15% of the variance in deviations from the true base rate. The base rate variability test offered incremental validity over the GFI, so both indexes should be considered when evaluating the trustworthiness of parameter estimation.

Clearly, the GFI is a useful index. How should one interpret a low GFI? The only way to do so is by considering the results of the other consistency tests. If the nose count test failed, or cleared the threshold by a close margin, a low GFI can be taken as further evidence against the taxonic conjecture. However, if the analysis cleared the other hurdles with excellent results, a low GFI probably indicates high nuisance correlations. In this case, a low GFI signals substantial departure from ideal conditions in the data, and estimates of the latent parameters are probably somewhat degraded and should be interpreted with caution. We want to point out that the philosophy of taxometrics does not preclude model fit testing. However, taxometrics does not rely wholly on such tests, as some other procedures do.

The taxon membership test is described in the following section, so to conclude this section we would like to emphasize that the focus on consistency testing is a distinguishing mark of the taxometric approach. Taxometrics is explicitly concerned with coherence between various findings in the context of the nomological network. The term nomological network was first introduced to psychology by Cronbach and Meehl (1955) and refers to the entire body of knowledge about the construct of interest and its relations with other constructs. Ideally, this task goes beyond statistical evaluation of a single data set and into the realm of epistemological inquiry. This approach sets taxometrics apart from other approaches described later in the chapter (e.g., mixture analysis, cluster analysis) that are more concerned with maximizing fit with the data. The goal of these other techniques is to find a model that best describes a given data set with little regard to how meaningful the model is or how representative the data are of reality. *Fit-oriented* techniques are primarily concerned with statistical soundness, which does not always imply epistemological soundness. As a result, fit-oriented techniques are best utilized for data reduction. Taxometrics, however, is geared toward epistemological soundness and consistency with the nomological network; hence we classify it as a *net-oriented* (net for nomological network) approach. Taxometrics is often not the best approach to use for data reduction, but its utility for epistemological inquiry is unparalleled.

It is notable that the net-oriented versus fit-oriented distinction is not the same as the confirmatory versus exploratory division. Both confirmatory and exploratory procedures can be used either to maximize fit or to obtain the most meaningful results depending on investigators' goals. A net-oriented approach can be exploratory at earlier stages of the investigation and more confirmatory at the later stages. Thus, taxometrics can be used to generate new taxonic hypotheses, as well as to test existing theories.

Assigning Individuals to Groups (Diagnostics)

A MAXCOV analysis can yield additional, potentially useful information. MAXCOV can assign individuals to categories, which in the case of psychopathology would equal assignment of diagnosis. Suppose MAXCOV located hitmaxes on all indicators and produced a coherent result that passed

TABLE 3.1
Four Classification Parameters

	Below hitmax	Above hitmax
Nontaxon member	q_{nx}	p_{nx}
Taxon member	q_{tx}	p_{tx}

internal consistency tests. This means we can be reasonably sure that an actual taxon was identified, and we can use these results to classify people as belonging or not belonging to the taxon. The basic procedure for classification is as follows. Each indicator can now be viewed as a dichotomous variable: zero below the hitmax and one above the hitmax. Recall that the hitmax is the point at which the number of taxon members equals the number of nontaxon members; people who fall below the hitmax are more likely to be nontaxon members and people who fall above the hitmax are more likely to be taxon members. We can calculate this likelihood using four basic probabilities associated with each of our newly dichotomized indicators. These parameters (for a hypothetical variable, which we denote as X) can be depicted as a table (see Table 3.1).

These are well-known classification parameters: true positive rate (p_{tx}), false positive rate (p_{nx}), true negative rate (q_{nx}), and false negative rate (q_{tx}). They can be easily obtained from the previous computations where we calculated the number of taxon and nontaxon members in each interval. For example, to calculate the true positive rate, we sum the number of taxon members in intervals above the hitmax, plus half of taxon members in the hitmax interval and divide this by the total number of taxon members in the sample. To calculate the false negative rate, we sum number of taxon members in intervals below the hitmax, plus half of the taxon members in the hitmax interval and divide this by the total number of taxon members in the sample.

If we cross our newly dichotomized indicators, we obtain a cross tabulation with 2^k cells (k is the number of indicators). For instance, in the depression example, there will be $2^3 = 8$ cells, since there are three indicators. To give you a better idea, let's use three-digit notation to label these cells; for example (0,0,1), which means "below hitmax on anhedonia and sadness, above the hitmax on suicidality." Clearly there are 8 possible configurations that vary from (0,0,0)—below hitmax on all three indicators—to (1,1,1)—above hitmax on all indicators. Let's pick the (1,1,0) cell—above hitmax on anhedonia and sadness, below hitmax on suicidality—for further analyses. The probability that a randomly selected member of this cell belongs to the taxon can be estimated by calculating four classification parameters for each of the three indicators and combining them in one formula. Bayes' theorem provides the means for combining these parameters. Let us call anhedonia–x, sadness–y and suicidality–z; then probability of a (1,1,0) cell member belonging to the taxon is:

$$P(\text{taxon} \mid 1,1,0) = \frac{Pp_{tx}p_{ty}q_{tz}}{Pp_{tx}p_{ty}q_{tz} + Qp_{nx}p_{ny}q_{nz}}$$

Where P is grand taxon base rate (the average of taxon base rates across subanalyses), $Q = 1 - P$ is "base rate of nontaxon," and other variables are the classification parameters with subscripts x, y, and z denoting the indicator with which they are associated.

We provide this formula for illustrative purposes; the formula will change depending on which cell is being evaluated. For example, the formula for cell (1,1,1) is:

$$P(\text{taxon} \mid 1,1,1) = \frac{Pp_{tx}p_{ty}p_{tz}}{Pp_{tx}p_{ty}p_{tz} + Qp_{nx}p_{ny}p_{nz}}$$

For the general formula, see Waller and Meehl (1998, equation 3.16). For the purpose of this discussion, it is not important to understand Bayes's theorem, know how to derive these formulas, or memorize them; MAXCOV does all these computations automatically. The purpose of this description is to help readers understand that Bayes's theorem helps us link the position of a data point relative to hitmaxes with the probability that this data point is a taxon member. In other words, for a given individual we can compute the probability that he or she belongs to the taxon by comparing his or her scores to the hitmaxes. Moreover, we can calculate these probabilities for the entire data set and plot a histogram that shows how many individuals have each probability of belonging to a taxon. Figure 3.7 is an example of such a histogram.

These plots reflect the degree to which we can make an accurate "diagnosis" of taxon membership versus non-membership. Consider that we are able to diagnose individuals whose taxon membership probability is close to "1" or close to "0" fairly accurately, but we cannot be sure about diagnoses of individuals who fall in the middle range. Hence, an accurate "diagnostic scheme" will be represented as a U-shaped histogram (where the majority of cases fall close to "0" or "1"). This association can also be used for consistency testing. The basic idea is that if an actual taxon has been correctly identified, the histogram should be U-shaped. However, if a spurious taxon has been identified, many individuals would fall in the middle of the histogram, which would not produce a U-shaped distribution. There is a concern in the literature that correlated indicators can produce a U-shaped distribution even when the underlying data is continuous. However, our simulation study revealed that the shape of the histogram is strongly associated with the taxonic status of the data set. Specifically, 88% of analyses of taxonic data sets produced histograms that were more U-shaped than not, whereas the nontaxonic data produced such histograms in only 16% of the analyses. One

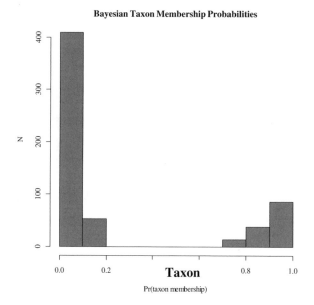

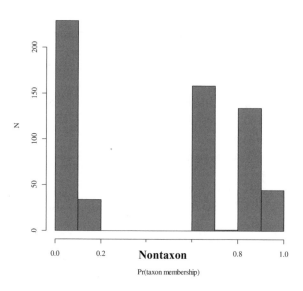

Figure 3.7. Histograms of Bayesian probabilities.

limitation of our simulation study is that we only examined indicators that correlated about .50. It is possible that more strongly related indicators would produce more spurious U-shaped distributions (false positives). One thing is certain, however; if the plot is not clearly U-shaped, group assignments will be plagued with error. It seems that this test is likely to be the best predictor of the accuracy of the group assignment. However, no simulation studies published to date (including ours) have examined this issue.

There is another useful application for taxon membership probabilities. We can use them to compute the average probability for the sample. This is done by summing the taxon membership probabilities for the entire sample and dividing the sum by the number of cases in the sample. Probability can be viewed as proportion, so this is another way to estimate taxon base rate. We will refer to this estimate as Bayesian taxon base rate, since we used Bayes's theorem in calculating it. Agreement between grand taxon base rate and Bayesian taxon base rate can be used as an index of accuracy of group assignment. If the Bayesian base rate is much smaller than the grand base rate (e.g., .05 versus .14), we can conclude that too many taxonic cases were not assigned to the taxon group. Conversely, if the Bayesian base rate is much larger than the grand base rate (e.g., .22 versus .14), too many nontaxonic cases were assigned to the taxon group. This reasoning is based on an assumption that the grand base rate is more trustworthy than the Bayesian base rate, which is plausible as the latter is based on the former (remember P in the equation), but involves more computational steps and hence provides more opportunities for error. However, no simulation studies have tested this notion.

Suppose we computed taxon membership probabilities for all individuals in the data set, plotted them in a histogram, and it came out U-shaped. Now we can go ahead with the group assignment. This is usually done by setting a cutoff for the taxon membership probability and placing cases that fall above the cutoff in the taxon group, while placing cases that fall below the cutoff in the nontaxon group. Two frequently used cutoffs are .50 and .90. The rationale for a .50 cutoff seems more straightforward as this cutoff will place those who are more likely to belong to the taxon group in that group and will place those that are less likely to belong to the taxon group in the nontaxon group. Also, by definition the .50 cutoff produces the lowest rate of misclassifications. Thus, any other value for the cutoff requires some special justification and should be spelled out. Use of higher cutoffs, such as .90, can be justifiable when it is critical to be certain about the taxonic status of the purported taxon members. One should be aware that this decrease in the number of false positive cases comes at the expense of increases in false negative cases. In fact, simulation studies of the MAXCOV procedure for group assignment suggest that the .50 cutoff tends to produce more false negatives than false positives (Beauchaine & Beauchaine, 2002). Therefore, utilizing a cutoff below .50 may be more justifiable than using a cutoff above .50, should the decision be made to deviate from the standard in the first place. Our general recommendation is to stick with the .50 cutoff, but we want to acknowledge that under certain conditions it may be better to use higher, more conservative cutoffs; for example, when the cost of a false positive is too high (e.g., stigmatization is likely), or when false negatives are not a concern.

Unfortunately, indicators of the taxon are fallible; thus, parameters that are used to calculate taxon membership probabilities will not be estimated perfectly. Hence, any group assignment will be only an approximation of the true membership. We can use this imperfect group assignment to improve the indicators and use them to do a more accurate group assignment.

BOOTSTRAPPING: STEPS TOWARD REFINING ASSESSMENT OF A DIAGNOSTIC CATEGORY

Bootstrapping is another important epistemological principle of the taxometric approach. The reality of research in psychopathology is that an investigation starts with a set of variables, which are only fallible indicators of the construct of interest. In most cases, these investigations do not contribute to improving the quality of the indicators. However, philosophers of science have shown that it is possible to start with fallible indicators and gradually improve on them, simultaneously refining assessment of the construct (Meehl, 1992, p. 141). This phenomenon is called bootstrapping. Let us walk through implementation of bootstrapping in taxometric research.

Suppose we conducted a taxometric analysis and obtained results that were consistent with the taxonic conjecture. Also suppose that these results (e.g., estimate of the taxon base rate) are not entirely accurate, which is expected in psychopathology research. Part of the problem is that the estimates are obscured by imperfections in the measures (e.g., nuisance correlations). This is not an easy problem to solve, as we lack gold standards for psychopathological constructs. A multistage approach is one way to tackle this issue. In the first iteration, we can review our approximated findings and use them to improve the indicators. In the second iteration, we take the improved set of indicators and do a taxometric analysis on it. If new findings still show evidence of unacceptably high error, we revise the indicators again and repeat this process. Ideally, researchers can continue with these iterations until the criterion of accuracy (whatever they chose) is satisfied. This is a general overview of the approach. We discuss some methods for improving indicators in chapter 4. However, we need first to establish procedures for assessing imperfection in taxon indicators. Specifically, there are two sources of imperfection: low indicator validity and high nuisance correlation.

Indicator Validity

After cases have been assigned to taxon and nontaxon groups, MAXCOV can begin the evaluation of indicators to determine whether they are good markers of the taxon, that is, measure their validity. A straightforward approach to evaluating indicator validity is to assess the simple differ-

ence between taxon members' average score on the indicator (e.g., anhedonia in the depression example) versus nontaxon members' average score
on the indicator; this idea is identical to calculating an effect size. To do this,
the indicator's mean among taxon members and the indicator's mean among
nontaxon members are needed. The equations for them are as follows:

Taxon Mean = Sum (midpoint$_{interval}$ × n (taxon) in interval)/ overall N in taxon

Nontaxon Mean = Sum (midpoint$_{interval}$ × n (nontaxon) in interval) /
overall N in nontaxon

In the depression example described earlier, the intervals have just one value
(i.e., 1 to 7); accordingly, that value would be used as the midpoint$_{interval}$ per
each interval. The various values for n and N are derived from the calcula-
tion of base rates, which was described above.

After the average difference is computed, it should be scaled to some
meaningful metric. In keeping with the convention for effect size computation, the difference is usually expressed in units of a latent group's standard
deviation. The taxon and nontaxon groups can have different standard deviations, and they often do, so the average of two SDs is usually used. If an
indicator has a validity of 1.50, it means that the separation between the
means of the two underlying distributions is one and a half times larger than
the average standard deviation of these distributions. To use this metric, it is
first necessary to compute the SD for taxon members and nontaxon members. Standard deviations of latent distributions cannot be measured directly,
but they can be estimated analogously to how latent means are computed.
There are a few other metrics that a researcher could use. For example, the
difference can be expressed in standard units of the overall, observed distribution (this metric is used for z-scores). However, the convention in
taxometric simulation studies is to use the average latent SD, and we dis-
courage the use of other metrics because this complicates the interpretation
of findings.

It is accepted that an indicator has good validity if it produces a taxon
versus nontaxon mean difference that exceeds two standard deviations (effect size of 2.00). Meehl (1995a) suggested that indicators with a validity of
less than 1.25 SD should not be used in taxometric analyses. There is some
evidence, however, that MAXCOV might work with indicators that have
validities below 1.25 SD (e.g., Meehl & Golden, 1982; Lenzenweger, 1993).
There are no data on the relation between indicator validities and the accurate detection of taxonicity, but simulation studies have examined the association between indicator validity and group assignment (Beauchaine &
Beauchaine, 2002). The accuracy of group assignment under ideal conditions (many indicators, no nuisance correlations) is very high with indicator
validities of 1.5 SD and above, but this level of accuracy drops off steadily as
the validities decrease. An average validity of 1.0 SD may be acceptable, but

classification becomes dangerously inaccurate below this level. Using measures with low validity may be acceptable for initial, exploratory study, but we recommend extreme caution in interpreting the results. In such a situation, it is likely that estimates of latent parameters have been degraded by low indicator validities, along with other potential problems. Moreover, we do not recommend retaining indicators that did not meet the 1.25 SD cutoff for future research, beyond the initial study.

An indicator validity of 1.25 SD may seem like an exceedingly high aspiration considering that an effect size of 0.80 is considered large in the social sciences (Cohen, 1988). Fortunately, taxometric empirical investigations conducted to date suggest that these high levels of indicator validity are not uncommon. Perhaps this discrepancy is due to the nature of group differences examined in these fields of research. In experimental research, group differences in the construct of interest are usually induced by external forces (e.g., experimental manipulation). On the other hand, group differences in taxometric research are part of the internal structure of the construct. Consider that if the taxon's mean falls at 90th percentile—a reasonable expectation for low base rate taxa—and the overall distribution is approximately normal, the taxon's mean z-score will be about 1.30 and nontaxon's z-score mean will be below zero. This suggests that the separation between taxon and nontaxon means will be at least 1.30 SD of the overall distribution. The standard deviations of latent distributions are likely to be smaller than the overall SD. Thus, when the separation is rescaled to the metric of effect sizes, it will be even greater than 1.30. This example shows that we can expect to find sufficiently large validities in taxometric research without having to look too hard.

We should also mention another approach to computing indicator validity. This approach is not based on Bayesian group assignment, but on the magnitude of covariance at the hitmax. For a given subanalysis, the covariance at the hitmax is one-fourth of the product of validities of the output indicators. Recall that the K parameter we used in earlier calculations is four times the covariance at the hitmax. Actually, K stands for the product of the indicator validities. Each subanalysis gives an equation with two unknown variables (validities of the output indicators), but these equations can be solved simultaneously and provide estimates of indicator validities. Let's consider the depression example one more time. Recall that we had three indicators, and hence three subanalyses, each providing an equation (see Table 3.2).

Here we have three equations and three unknowns ('V' stands for validity); by solving them, we find that the validity of anhedonia is fairly high (1.54 SD), but the validities of sadness and suicidality are marginal (1.01 SD and 1.04 SD, respectively). This method can be used when the group assignment is impossible for some reason, or as an additional consistency check. Also, a proposal was made in the literature (Blanchard, Gangestad, Brown,

TABLE 3.2
Computation of Validities From Covariances

Input variable	Covariance at hitmax (K)	Equation
Anhedonia	.399 =	$\frac{1}{4} * V_{sadness} * V_{suicidality}$
Sadness	.263 =	$\frac{1}{4} * V_{suicidality} * V_{anhedonia}$
Suicidality	.388 =	$\frac{1}{4} * V_{sadness} * V_{anhedonia}$

& Horan, 2000) that the average of two indicator validity estimations (obtained using group assignment and covariance at the hitmax) may be more accurate, but to the best of our knowledge this has not been tested empirically.

Nuisance Correlations

In the discussion of the mathematical basis for MAXCOV, we mentioned that ideal indicators of a taxon correlate only in mixed, but not in pure samples of taxon or nontaxon members. With real-world indicators and real-world data, this is rarely the case. Usually correlations between indicators in pure samples are not zero, although they tend to be much smaller than correlations in mixed samples. This departure from ideal conditions can cause significant problems for MAXCOV; thus, pure sample correlations are frequently referred to as "nuisance correlations." Specifically, simulation studies have demonstrated that high nuisance correlations (i.e., either taxon or nontaxon nuisance correlations > 0.50) can lead to an overestimation of taxon base rate estimates (Meehl, 1995a). These simulation studies have also suggested that MAXCOV results are not seriously degraded when there is a moderate departure from the assumption of zero nuisance correlations, which is usually considered to be .30 or less (see Waller & Meehl, 1998, Appendix A). Also, the magnitude of degradation depends on the difference between nuisance correlations in the taxon and nontaxon groups. The greatest degradation occurs when nuisance correlations are high in one group and low in the other. Base rate estimates will be relatively accurate even when nuisance correlations are substantial, if they are equally high in both groups. It is important to consider that high nuisance correlations tend to produce false nontaxonic findings and are not likely to make nontaxonic data appear taxonic (Meehl & Yonce, 1994, 1996). From the viewpoint of a researcher who is primarily concerned about false positives (false taxonic conclusions), the presence of nuisance correlations is not very problematic. Nuisance correlations cause the most trouble for investigators who are attempting to precisely estimate the parameters of latent distributions or who are trying to develop accurate classification schemes.

The reason nuisance correlations cause problems for MAXCOV is that the procedure relies on a reduced, rather than the full, version of GCMT. In addition to accounting for the main effect of mixing taxon and nontaxon members (effect that produces a hitmax), the full theorem also acknowledges correlations that exist within latent groups (i.e., nuisance correlations). The full GCMT is accurate but quite complex and difficult to solve. In order to make this problem tractable, MAXCOV assumes there is only the main effect and that correlations within latent classes are zero. Whenever this assumption is inconsistent with reality, we observe nuisance correlations that are within-group correlations, the existence of which we decided to ignore. Many CCK methods are based on reduced GCMT, and the level of nuisance correlation is an important concern with applying almost any CCK procedure. Meehl (1995b) proposed an algorithm for a generalized version of MAXCOV. This procedure is similar to regular MAXCOV but is based on full GCMT. However, application of this algorithm is not straightforward and there is no program that can perform generalized MAXCOV analyses.

Assessment and reduction of nuisance correlations is another goal of the taxometric approach. MAXCOV provides tools that can be useful for this purpose. When a taxon is identified, individuals can be tentatively sorted into taxon or nontaxon groups. Next, MAXCOV independently calculates correlations between indicators within each of these groups and provides a rough estimate of true nuisance correlations. These estimates tend to be inflated. As group assignment is imperfect, some cases from the other group are sure to end up among cases used in the estimation of nuisance correlations; their presence will drive nuisance correlations up for the same reason that indicators are correlated in a mixed sample even when nuisance correlations are zero. These misclassifications will make positive nuisance correlations appear more positive and negative nuisance correlations appear less negative. Unfortunately, this issue has not been examined in simulation studies, so we cannot make any specific recommendations.

Probably the only way to avoid misclassification is by estimating nuisance correlations in subgroups that are far from the hitmax and are fairly uncontaminated by members of the other group (e.g., nontaxon). However, it is difficult to define these groups in a way that will ensure their purity. John and Ayelet Ruscio (2000), for example, used the top and bottom quartiles for estimation, but this strategy works only when the taxon base rate is close to .50 and indicator validities are high. A bigger problem is that the selection of extreme subsamples (to ensure purity) can lead to restriction of range, thus deflating nuisance correlation estimates. The best solution seems to lie between these two approaches—not being overly inclusive or overly restrictive. However, procedures for selecting this middle point have not yet been worked out. We recommend sticking to the convention and using subgroups that are based on Bayesian group assignment (with .50 as a cutoff). Luckily, simulation evidence suggests that Bayesian group assignment has an accuracy of at least 75% under most circumstances and is sometimes much more accurate (Beauchaine & Beauchaine, 2002).

Taxometric Power Analysis

The conventional assessment of indicator validities and nuisance correlations requires some kind of taxon vs. nontaxon group assignment but this can only be accomplished after performing taxometric analyses. This is logical, because in order to ask questions about the validity of taxon markers, or about within-taxon correlations, the investigator has to have some evidence that the taxon actually exists. It is possible to get a rough idea about the parameters of putative latent groups even before conducting taxometric analyses. In the article mentioned above, Ruscio and Ruscio (2000) proposed a procedure that can be considered a taxometric power analysis.

This type of analysis begins with assuming that the taxonic conjecture is correct and making a guess about base rate of the taxon. This guess does not have to be based on direct evidence. One can then predict what portions of the distribution are fairly homogeneous and these can be used for the estimation of taxon and nontaxon nuisance correlations. Once nuisance correlations are known, it is possible to estimate indicator validities with formulas derived from full GCMT (Meehl & Yonce, 1996, p. 1146). These formulas require specification of the following parameters: indicator correlations in the overall sample (easily computed); taxon base rate (assumed); and nuisance correlations (estimated). Thus, the taxometric power analysis can be conducted before there is any evidence of taxonicity and can therefore be used to estimate the appropriateness of indicator selection before investing time and effort in extensive taxometric analyses. In fact, this procedure can guide indicator selection. The most important application of the method is for cases of null, nontaxonic findings. Failure to find a taxon may be due to poor indicator selection, and taxometric power analysis can be used to determine whether it was a problem. The standard procedure cannot do this as latent group assignment is impossible (or at least meaningless) in the absence of taxonic evidence.

There are some limitations to taxometric power analysis. First, it can be difficult to find homogeneous regions of the distribution for the estimation of nuisance correlations. If the base rate is low, a region for the estimation of within-taxon nuisance correlation may not be discernable by any means other than taxometric analyses. This happens when both taxon and nontaxon members have high scores on any given indicator and the knowledge of Bayesian probabilities is needed to make a clear differentiation. In fact, just knowing (or guessing) the taxon base rate is not enough for identifying pure regions. Their location also depends on indicator validities, with higher validities corresponding to broader regions. However, indicator validity is one of the parameters we are trying to estimate. An iterative procedure of going back and forth between estimating validities and safe regions could solve this problem but the development of taxometric power analysis has not progressed this far. Second, as mentioned, the pure regions approach underestimates the magnitude of nuisance correlations, which in turn leads to the overestimation of indicator validities. We have often observed this effect when applying taxometric power analysis to actual taxa. Thus, the pure regions approach can be misleading. Consider a case where the taxon actually exists, but the measures are not quite powerful enough to detect it (e.g., have validities around .80). Taxometric power analysis is likely to overestimate these validities and suggest that the study's failure to find a taxon is not due to measurement problems. Finally, taxometric power analysis hinges on a guess about the taxon base rate and an incorrect guess can throw off the estimation. For example, if a .25 base rate is assumed while the true base rate is .10, the indicator validities can be underestimated by 2.5 fold. Despite these limitations, taxometric power analysis is a necessary part of a taxometrician's arsenal and we look forward to the refinement of this procedure in the next few years.

Other Considerations

Thus far we have not considered differences in the objectives of the studies and in particular whether an investigation is confirmatory or exploratory. A confirmatory study is designed to test a particular theory (e.g., Meehl's theory of schizophrenia, 1962), while an exploratory study is conducted without the benefit of a clear theory. A general sentiment in psychology is that the confirmatory approach is preferred to the exploratory one. However, we do not share this view. Exploratory studies can be critically important by laying the foundation for theoretical development. It appears that there are relatively few well-articulated categorical models in the field of psychopathology (we do not consider the DSM a well-articulated model, since it is a pragmatic rather than a theoretical system), which perhaps stems from the historic lack of reliable methods for the identification of categories. Given the state of the discipline, taxometricians can either choose to be confined to areas where categorical models have been proposed, or they can push the boundaries of the field and let new theories grow from taxometric data.

In sum, we believe that both confirmatory and exploratory approaches to taxometrics are equally legitimate. However, the exploratory approach is undoubtedly more challenging. First, a categorical theory can prescribe a particular set of features–indicators that are supposed to define the category. An exploratory study does not have this kind of guide. Thus, indicator selection should follow a rigorous empirical procedure. Second, the nature of a category that is not grounded in theory is not immediately clear. Hence, it is necessary to establish the construct validity of the newly identified taxon. It is also important to justify the utility of this category, which can be done, for example, by examining its incremental validity. We think these considerations also apply to confirmatory studies and can enhance their value, but while any sound exploratory investigation has to incorporate these steps, they may not be necessary for all confirmatory studies. We also want to mention that it is critically important to demonstrate the construct validity and the appropriateness of measures for taxometric procedures, even if the investigation rejected the taxonic conjecture. Measurement problems can lead to a failure of taxometric methods to detect a valid taxon, so they have to be ruled out.

How does one select taxon indicators without the benefit of a theory? The first step, of course, is to define the construct under study as precisely as possible and to decide which measures assess it well. By assessing the phenomenon well, we mean at least two things: (a) the indicators define a coherent construct; that is, they are reasonably correlated, and (b) the indicators have adequate reliability. The next question is, What do we mean by "reasonably correlated"? There is no easy answer because interindicator correlations reflect a tradeoff between the validity and the level of nuisance correlations (redundancy). Weakly correlated indicators probably do not validly tap the construct, and highly correlated measures probably reflect the presence of large nontaxonic variance. Our rule of thumb is to strive for correlations in the .30–.50 range. The reliability of indicators is an important consideration, because low reliability can degrade interindicator correlations and make MAXCOV curves appear flat, thereby leading to false negative findings. Low reliability is unlikely to lead to false positive findings, but this in no way justifies utilization of unreliable markers.

In addition, it is important to consider the distributional properties of indicators. The measures should be sufficiently long (have enough levels) to allow for a large number of intervals, which is necessary for precise estimation. A general recommendation is that an indicator should have at least 20 levels (Waller & Meehl, 1998). Analyses with shorter measures are possible but produce less interpretable results. Indicator skew is another consideration. One critical feature of an indicator is its ability to separate taxonic and nontaxonic cases (indicator validity). Indicator validity is associated with indicator skew. If the taxon base rate is small (e.g., less than .30), then an indicator has to have substantial positive skew to be a valid measure of the taxon. Positive skew is necessary but *is not sufficient* for an indicator to be valid. This relationship does not hold for taxa with base rates around .50, and it is reversed (negative skew is necessary) for taxa with high base rates.

The final consideration in operationalizing a taxon is the number of indicators. Generally, greater numbers are preferred. MAXCOV requires at least three indicators and simulations suggest that three may work reasonably well, but this number is far from ideal. In a large simulation study, Beauchaine and Beauchaine (2002) found that an increase in indicator numbers from three to four and from four to five produced considerable incremental improvement. However, six appeared to be a point of diminishing returns; that is, five indicators performed almost as well as six. Moreover, MAXCOV outputs for six or more indicators are rather unwieldy. We believe it is better to have a few high quality indicators than to add low quality indicators to the set just to increase their number.

Up to this point, we've described indicator selection on the conceptual level, but a few quantitative procedures have been developed as well. The first method was proposed by Golden (1982). It is rather complicated, so we do not discuss this technique until chapter 5, when we illustrate it with concrete examples. The general idea of Golden's procedure is to select indicators that provide the most information at the level of the construct where the taxon and nontaxon groups are expected to overlap. This is accomplished by evaluating item difficulty and discrimination, which are parameters of Item Response Theory (IRT). The method only works with dichotomous variables and has not gained wide acceptance. The second method, termed TAXSCAN, was proposed by Meehl (1999). In TAXSCAN, correlations between candidate indicators are examined, and variables that do not correlate appreciably are removed. Next, the indicators are screened with a relatively simple CCK technique, such as MAMBAC (described later in this chapter), and variables that show taxonicity are subjected to more elaborate procedure, usually MAXCOV.

Indicator and sample selection are not the only choices a researcher has to make when using MAXCOV. A decision also has to be made about interval size, that is, how finely the input variable will be cut. Sometimes it is possible to use raw scores as intervals; that is, each interval corresponds to one unit of raw score (e.g., the first interval includes cases that score one on anhedonia, the second interval includes cases that score two). This is what we used in the depression example. This approach usually works when indicators are fairly short and the sample size is very large, since it would allow for a sufficient number of cases with each raw score. In our opinion, this is the most defensible method of interval selection and should be used whenever possible. However, research data usually do not fit the requirements of this approach (e.g., the sample size is too small). Instead, the investigator can standardize indicators and make cuts at a fixed distance from each other (e.g., .25 SD), thereby producing intervals that encompass a few raw scores.

How wide should the intervals be? Unfortunately, this issue has been completely ignored in the literature. The usual approach is to select an a priori interval size. However, this tactic ignores the fact that the selection of different interval sizes produces rather different results. For example, in our simulation study, different interval sizes produced base rate estimates that differed by up to .17. Thus, the choice of the interval size affected base rate estimates by as much as 34% of its true magnitude (.50). The average range of base rate estimates across different interval sizes was .10 (20% of the true magnitude). The same was true for the number of taxonic plots, with some counts differing by as much as six points (on a 13-point scale). In other words, the choice of interval size influenced the appearance (taxonic versus nontaxonic) of as many as half of the plots. The average range of plot counts across interval sizes was three. With variations in interval sizes producing such variability in results, it seems important to have a rigorous procedure for identifying the best interval size. We tried to develop such a method using this simulation study.

First, we correlated interval size with the absolute deviation from the true base rate and the number of taxonic plots. Both correlations were non-significant, suggesting that finer or thicker slicing does not systematically produce clearer or more accurate results for this type of data (N = 600, base rate = .50). Next, we thought that perhaps a post hoc procedure could be devised for selecting the best interval. The logic of such a procedure is to conduct analyses with various interval sizes, then look at consistency indices and decide which interval size worked best. Recall that the GFI and SD predict the accuracy of the analyses, so for each data set we selected one analysis (out of 15 possible) with the highest GFI and SD. We compared the average discrepancy between true and estimated base rate for analyses selected using this procedure and the standard approach (using the same interval size across analyses, .25 SD in this case). The difference between the two approaches was miniscule and not significant. Apparently the GFI and SD can predict the accuracy of analyses across samples, but within a given sample they cannot identify the interval size that produced the most accurate results.

We have to conclude that selecting an interval size a priori appears to be the best approach. However, things are more complicated in practice. When the data are far from ideal (e.g., the taxon has very low base rate, indicators are short, or sample size is small), an a priori approach may fail because it does not take these problems into account. For example, if indicators have only 12 levels (rather than the recommended 20), an interval size of .25 may produce "holes" in the taxonic plots because the indicators are sliced too finely and some of them fall in between raw values (e.g., an interval ranging from 1.05 to 1.90 on anhedonia does not contain any cases). On the other hand, a low base rate taxon may need very fine cutting for the full peaks to emerge. Under these conditions, an interval size of .25 may produce cusps because it allocates all of the taxon members to the final interval.

If one anticipates such problems in advance, the interval size can be set accordingly. However, there are no formulas for deriving the optimal interval size, and the investigator has to guess. Naturally, the guess is unlikely to be on the mark the first time and the investigator may have to try a few different slab sizes. MRIN may need to be adjusted a few times as well, as "15 cases per interval" is nothing more than a commonsense heuristic that may fail for certain data sets. To make this guessing process systematic, we recommend setting up a grid of values of procedural parameters (slab size and MRIN) that make sense for the given data and running MAXCOV analyses with each combination of slab sizes and MRINs that fall in the grid. For example, our experience suggests that with N = 1,000 and base rate of .25, the optimal interval size usually lies somewhere between .20 and .35—cutting finer than .20 produces too much noise and cutting broader than .35 may distort precise positions of hitmaxes too much—while the optimal MRIN is somewhere between 10 and 20—lower MRINs may produce pseudo-peaks on the extreme right due to sampling error and higher MRINs may turn some peaks into upward slopes. Multiplying these two ranges gives us $15 \times 10 = 150$ analyses. It may take a while to run these analyses, but they will provide the data necessary to choose optimal procedural parameters.

How does one identify the optimal parameters from this stack of outputs? We provided evidence that GFI and SD are not good guides for this. In fact, we believe that other numerical parameters are not very helpful either. The investigators should focus their attention on MAXCOV plots and study changes in their shapes across the grid. After reviewing a number of outputs, it will become apparent which curves are taxonic and which are not. Then the investigator should look for an output where all taxonic curves show complete peaks and all nontaxonic curves are reasonably flat. This will be the optimal analysis.

Currently, this grid procedure is based on common sense. Our simulation study did not really provide a test of this method, because the base rate in the simulation samples was .50 and the data were actually too good to require the grid procedure. Once again, the grid procedure is only needed when the circumstances are unfavorable for MAXCOV. If the data are reasonably close to the ideal requirements of MAXCOV, then nearly any a priori slab size and MRIN should do. We recommend using the a priori approach whenever possible, but when the researcher has to deviate from it, the rationale for the change should be stated and the parameter search procedure (e.g., the grid approach) should be explained in detail.

To finish the discussion of MAXCOV, we want to note that the assumption of zero nuisance correlation is not the only assumption of MAXCOV. Our interpretation of a hitmax as an interval with the 50/50 mix of taxon and nontaxon members is based on the presumption that two unimodal distributions underlie the data. There are two components in this assumption. The first component is presuming that latent distributions are unimodal. In other words, any kind of distribution will work as long as it has only one maximum, which encompasses the majority of distributions one finds in statistics textbooks (e.g., normal, chi-square, gamma and many others). This is an extremely lenient assumption, but it does pose some constraint on the flexibility of the procedure. However, we do not consider this restriction particularly important, especially in the context of our state of knowledge regarding psychopathology.

The second component is the assumption of *two* underlying distributions. This implies that if MAXCOV results are inconsistent with the taxonic conjecture, we can only conclude that there are *not two* underlying distributions (i.e., there can be one or three or four latent groups). In the presence of serious evidence against the taxonic conjecture we normally infer absence of a taxon, but there is also an alternative explanation that is frequently overlooked. It is possible that more than two latent groups reside in the distribution, and this overcrowding obscures the MAXCOV results. This alternative has not been thoroughly investigated, and we do not know what effect the presence of multiple latent groups has on CCK procedures. However, in the majority of cases this should not concern investigators. It is quite unlikely that all indicators in the set will discriminate appreciably between three groups (this is even less likely to happen when there are more groups). When a theory predicts a multi-group (meaning more than two) latent structure, the investigator has two options available. He or she can either try to find measures that uniquely discriminate the group (taxon) of interest, or try a non-CCK method (e.g., latent class analysis or mixture analysis; some are discussed later in the chapter).

SHORT-SCALE MAXCOV

To function, MAXCOV requires a minimum of three indicators of the construct and at least one of these indicators has to be continuous; only a limited number of consistency tests are possible when just the minimum requirements are met. Unfortunately, in many practical situations even the minimal requirements cannot be satisfied. Often only one or two measures that are relevant to the construct of interest are available to the investigator. In other situations, a sufficient number of indicators may be available, but none are long enough to be considered continuous (and employed as an input variable). It is not unusual for an investigator to have only a single inventory that consists of a dozen items rated dichotomously (true or false). Such data clearly do not fit the requirements of MAXCOV, but the problem can be solved by using each item as an indicator and then applying Short Scale MAXCOV (SSMAXCOV), which was specifically designed for this type of situation. SSMAXCOV was first proposed by Gangestad and Snyder (1985), and this article still gives the best description of the procedure available in the literature. Waller's package does not include SSMAXCOV. Also, several investigators wrote programs that perform SSMAXCOV analysis, but these programs were tailored to a specific research project. Two SSMAXCOV programs that can handle a variety of data sets can be obtained from Dr. Nader Amir (2001; http://nas.psy.uga.edu/TAX.html) and Dr. John Ruscio (2004; http://www.etown.edu/psychology/Faculty/Ruscio.htm).

SSMAXCOV Methodology

Let us look at the typical case in more detail. Suppose we have k dichotomous indicators. The basic strategy of SSMAXCOV is to take a pair (any pair) of indicators as output variables and combine the remaining $(k-2)$ indicators in one scale. In other words, the input variable is the sum of scores on all indicators, with the exception of the two that were taken as output variables. Then, covariances of the output indicators are computed and plotted for each level of the input variable ($k - 1$ levels in this case since the combined scale goes from zero to $k - 2$). At the next step, a new pair of indicators (it can include any one indicator from the previous pair) is taken as the output variables; all of the indicators except for the new pair are again combined to form the input variable. This process is repeated until all possible pairs are drawn (i.e., every indicator has been paired with all other indicators). Then all individual graphs are combined and the average graph is plotted.

For this average graph, no particular input variable is used as the X-axis; a hypothetical average input variable is presumed instead. Similarly, covariance of no particular indicator pair is used as the Y-axis; covariances are averaged across all pairs of indicators. The assumption of this technique is that indicators are interchangeable and nothing is unique about them, at least not for the purposes of these analyses. The average plot reflects the location of a hitmax on the latent continuum of the construct. Evidently, SSMAXCOV is best suited for analyzing items from a single homogenous scale.

It is instructive to consider a specific example. Suppose we have a hypothetical instrument that measures compulsive checking—an important aspect of obsessive–compulsive disorder symptomatology—and this measure consists of 8 true or false questions that ask about various checking behaviors. Furthermore, suppose we collected data on 1,000 college students with this inventory. Now we want to do a taxometric analysis to determine whether some of these students belong to a qualitatively distinct class of pathological checkers (possibly a subcategory of obsessive–compulsive disorder), or whether there are no qualitative differences in checking behavior in this sample. However, we have just this one measure available. How do we go about doing a taxometric analysis?

First, we conjecture that each item is a separate marker of the taxon. Now there is a pool of indicators to work with. Second, we choose a random pair of indicators, for example, item 1 ("When I go shopping, I check several times to be sure I have my wallet/ purse with me") and item 2 ("Before I leave my house, I check whether all windows are closed"), as the output indicators. Third, we sum scores on items 3 to 8, which makes a 7-point scale that ranges from 0 (*none of the 6 checking behaviors are endorsed*) to 6 (*all of the 6 checking behaviors are endorsed*); this is the input variable. Fourth, we calculate the covariance between items 1 and 2 in a subsample of individuals who scored 0 on the input variable, next we calculate the covariance for individuals who scored 1 on the input variable, and so forth. Fifth, we choose another pair of output indicators (e.g., items 1 and 3), and combine the other six items together to make a new input variable. This process is repeated 28 times until all possible pairs are drawn (1-2 and 2-1 are not considered different pairs). Next, we take 28 covariances from "0" subsamples and average them; we do the same for all seven sets of numbers and plot the average covariances. SSMAXCOV plots look similar to the plots from the MAXCOV section and are interpreted the same way.

This procedure can also be used with items that are not scored dichotomously; 4-point, 5-point, and so on, formats are perfectly acceptable. In fact, there is some concern in the literature that use of dichotomous indicators might lead to false taxonic results (Miller, 1996). This issue has not been fully resolved, although it appears that utilization of dichotomous indicators can cause problems only in extremely rare cases (Meehl & Yonce, 1996, p. 1111). Nevertheless, we recommend using longer scales if for no other reason than the higher reliability that these scales allow. One important source of unreliability of SSMAXCOV is the length of the input scale. Consider that if the hitmax erroneously shifts from 5 to 6 on a 7-point scale, this shift is likely to have a much greater impact on the taxon base rate estimate than a shift from 35 to 36 on a 40-point scale. In fact, the reliability of individual analyses is a notable concern. Most taxometricians deal with this issue by averaging the individual curves, as described above, and work with the single aggregate graph. We have two concerns about this approach. First, researchers often focus exclusively on the average plot. However, it is not possible to do consistency tests with one curve, so we recommend examining both the aggregate and the individual plots. Second, aggregation often ignores the fact that the metric of input variables differs across subanalyses. Mean, SD, and even range of the input variables vary as they are composed of overlapping, but not identical, sets of items. This can introduce considerable error and unreliability in the aggregate graph. A solution to this is to standardize the input variables, which would put the subanalyses on the same metric.

Another issue with SSMAXCOV is that the number of subanalyses grows rapidly with an increase in the scale length (number of items). For example, the application of SSMAXCOV to a 16-item scale will yield 120 subanalyses, and it may be difficult to compute and interpret so many outputs. The common practice is to reduce longer scales to eight items, which yields a more manageable number of subanalyses (28 in this case). There are a few ways to go about selecting these eight items. The most popular approach is to select items with the highest item-total correlations (e.g., Lenzenweger & Korfine, 1992), because they are believed to be most representative of the construct. However, some investigators have argued that this procedure can produce high nuisance correlations and limit the comprehensiveness of the analyses. Another approach is to select items with the least redundant content (Ruscio, Borkovec, & Ruscio, 2001). Unfortunately, no studies have evaluated and compared the merits of the two approaches so far. Probably the best tactic is to combine the two; first, select a set of indicators with highest item-total correlations and then drop or collapse variables that are highly correlated with each other.

Unfortunately, this strategy does not provide assurance that the selected items can discriminate taxon and nontaxon members adequately along the entire range of the construct. This can be achieved by using Golden's (1982) procedure or other applications of item response theory (IRT). These methods can be applied in conjunction with the strategies outlined above. It is also important to make sure that the construct's content is covered comprehensively and that the item selection procedure did not skew the representation of various components of the construct. This can be done rationally by comparing the content of the selected items with the content of the original scale. We also want to note that there is no reason (apart from saving time) for limiting SSMAXCOV analyses to eight items. Generally speaking, the more items included in the analysis, the more reliable the results will be. The main concern with using all of the available items is the potential for high nuisance correlations. However, if this issue has been addressed and more than eight indicators are available, we recommend using all of them.

In a situation when the scale in question is fairly long, we recommend performing a factor analysis before doing taxometric analyses. If a few interpretable factors emerge in the data, other possibilities are open to investigators. One option is to run SSMAXCOV within each of the factors separately. Alternatively, one overall analysis can be conducted using indicators that are selected to be representative of each factor. Yet another option is to drop a few of these factors completely, if they are theoretically uninteresting, and run analyses with the remaining factors.

Consistency Testing in SSMAXCOV

Current SSMAXCOV algorithms allow for two internal consistency tests: the nose count test and the base rate variability test. Both tests are performed in the same manner as described in the MAXCOV section. These tests are logical possibilities, since SSMAXCOV usually involves a considerable number of subanalyses. However, individual SSMAXCOV subanalyses tend to be fairly noisy and unclear (Meehl & Yonce, 1996, p. 1111). This is not surprising as SSMAXCOV usually employs short input variables, which is associated with a large sampling error, and single-item output variables, which tend to be unreliable. Hence, even truly taxonic data is likely to perform worse on SSMAXCOV than on MAXCOV consistency tests. Investigators should keep this in mind when setting tolerance intervals. The intervals should be wider, but how much wider is not yet established.

In addition to the two consistency tests, a unique test has been proposed specifically for SSMAXCOV (Ruscio, 2000). John Ruscio noticed that nontaxonic data rarely produce plots with elevations that are higher than .05. As a result, he recommends recording the height of the tallest elevation of the curve, and if it is under .05, this counts as a strike against taxonicity. This idea appears promising but needs further testing in simulation studies. It seems likely that various qualities of the analysis, such as the number of indicators, number of response options, and whether the input variable was standardized, will influence the optimal position of the cutoff.

Group Assignment and Bootstrapping in SSMAXCOV

The assignment of individuals to latent groups with SSMAXCOV is tricky. The usual MAXCOV procedure does not apply here, because it is not possible to calculate the position of a hitmax on any given indicator as a single indicator is never used as the input variable. One option is to classify cases as taxon members (falling at the hitmax or above hitmax) or nontaxon members (falling below the hitmax) in each subanalysis and then to count how frequently each case has been assigned to the taxon. The resulting frequency distribution can be treated as distribution of Bayesian probabilities, which assumes that the frequency of group assignment approximates the likelihood that a given case is a taxon member, and can be used for the final group assignment. This method seems quite reasonable, but it has not been tested. Another option is to simply assign the cases with the highest total scores to the taxon group. The proportion of cases assigned would equal the overall taxon base rate estimate. This approach seems to be fairly crude and it also has not been tested (for further detail see MAMBAC section, pages 79–81). Until the necessary testing has been conducted, we do not recommend performing membership assignment on the basis of SSMAXCOV. Membership assignment is the key to bootstrapping, so SSMAXCOV cannot estimate nuisance correlations and indicator validities.

MAXEIG-HITMAX

MAXEIG Methodology

MAXEIG-HITMAX is a multivariate generalization of MAXCOV (Waller & Meehl, 1998) that we will refer to simply as MAXEIG. The MAXEIG computer program can be obtained from the Taxometrics Home Page (Waller, 2004; http://peabody.vanderbilt.edu/depts/psych_and_hd/faculty/wallern/tx.html). Like MAXCOV, MAXEIG starts with a pool of indicators and selects one of them to be an input variable. Similar to MAXCOV, MAXEIG also cuts the input indicator in intervals. In MAXEIG, however, intervals are allowed to overlap. The magnitude of the overlap can vary, but the usual practice is to set it at 90%, meaning any two adjacent intervals will share 90% of their members. If a sample of 600 is cut in 180 intervals, cases 1–30 will be assigned to the first interval, cases 4–33 to the second interval, cases 7–36 to the third, and so on up to the 180th interval, which will be assigned cases 571–600. Thus, each individual, with the exception of the few laying at the extremes of the distribution, will be assigned to multiple intervals. For this reason, MAXEIG intervals have a special name; they are called "overlapping windows."

At this point, MAXCOV and MAXEIG procedures diverge. MAXCOV selects two indicators as output variables and evaluates their covariance. MAXEIG, in contrast, uses all of the remaining indicators as output variables and evaluates covariances among all of them simultaneously. In other words, MAXEIG can analyze more than three indicators at a time. In fact, it does not deal with individual covariances between indicators; it evaluates the matrix of covariances as a whole. MAXEIG applies multivariate statistical techniques to the covariance matrix and calculates parameters termed eigenvalues. For the purpose of this discussion, it is not important to know the precise definition of an eigenvalue. However, it is important to know that the first (and largest) of these eigenvalues reflects the overall level of covariance among a set of variables—in our case, the covariance between all available indicators other than the input indicator (for more details see Waller & Meehl, 1998). MAXEIG focuses on that first eigenvalue.

From this point on, MAXEIG again operates just like MAXCOV. It computes the first eigenvalue in each interval and plots their magnitudes. If the graph is clearly peaking, it is considered taxonic (consistent with the taxonic conjecture); if no peak is apparent in the graph, it is considered nontaxonic. The peak marks the location of a hitmax, and MAXEIG can calculate the taxon base rate from the position of the hitmax. However, the current version of MAXEIG does not use MAXCOV formulas for taxon base rate estimation. Instead, it just assigns cases above the hitmax to the taxon group and cases below the hitmax to the nontaxon group and uses this group assignment to compute the base rate. This method is only a rough approximation and relies on an assumption that the tails of underlying distributions are symmetrical relative to the hitmax; that is, that the number of taxon members falling below the hitmax equals the number of nontaxon members falling above the hitmax. This assumption fails under various conditions. For example, if the base rate of the taxon is small and indicator validity is relatively low, the tail of the nontaxon distribution will be longer than the tail of the taxon distribution, leading to an overestimation of the taxon base rate. In general, MAXEIG base rate estimates should be interpreted with caution. Examination of the latent distributions that MAXCOV generates can give clues regarding the accuracy of MAXEIG base rate estimates.

Clearly, MAXEIG is very similar to MAXCOV. In fact, when the methods are applied to a set of three indicators, they can be considered redundant. The results may differ somewhat between the procedures, because MAXEIG uses overlapping windows rather than (nonoverlapping) intervals, and it calculates eigenvalues, which do not exactly equal inter-indicator covariance. We want to note that a MAXEIG analysis is equivalent to a MAXCOV subanalysis—analysis of a single configuration of indicators. Waller's MAXEIG code does not analyze all of the possible configurations automatically, as it does not rotate the indicators; only one indicator is used as the input variable in an analysis. The investigator must rotate indicators by conducting a series of analyses: first do an analysis with indicator 1 as input variable, then change the setup and conduct a new analysis with indicator 2 as input variable, change the setup again, etc. Since this process is not automatic, Waller's MAXEIG program does not allow for the same kind of sophisticated calculations as MAXCOV; for example, it does not perform group assignment.

MAXEIG Group Assignment and Bootstrapping

MAXEIG cannot compute membership probabilities the way MAXCOV does, because MAXEIG locates only one hitmax in each analysis. To calculate taxon membership probabilities, one needs to locate a hitmax on each indicator. Because of this limitation, Waller's MAXEIG program does not evaluate the validity of indicators and does not estimate nuisance correlations. To overcome these limitations, Ruscio (2004; http://www.etown.edu/psychology/Faculty/Ruscio.htm) developed a new, expanded version of MAXEIG. His program runs all subanalyses automatically, and does group assignment and bootstrapping. With respect to parameter estimation (base rate, nuisance correlations, indicator validities), Ruscio's MAXEIG operates as MAXCOV does, except that in all calculations covariance is replaced by the first eigenvalue. This is an exciting development and we eagerly wait for this program to prove itself. However, this new MAXEIG program needs to be tested in simulation studies and applied to real psychopathology data before we can be sure there are no unforeseen problems with the algorithm and recommend it to readers. Hence, the focus of the section will remain on Waller's MAXEIG program.

MAXEIG Consistency Testing

The nose count and the base rate variability tests can be done with MAXEIG without too much difficulty. If the investigator runs all of the possible MAXEIG analyses (with each indicator taking its turn as the input variable), he or she will have multiple MAXEIG plots and multiple estimates of the taxon base rate, which will suffice for these two tests. The nose count test is conducted with MAXEIG exactly as described for MAXCOV. The only new consideration is that in most cases, MAXEIG would yield fewer graphs than MAXCOV. A small number of plots arguably makes the nose count test somewhat less reliable, but it can be informative nevertheless. For example, with a pool of four indicators MAXEIG will produce only four plots (MAXCOV will yield 12); however, if all four MAXEIG plots exhibit clear peaks, this should be considered strong evidence in support of the taxonic conjecture. The base rate variability test is also no different from the MAXCOV version, except that the investigator might want to report the range of base rate estimates rather than their standard deviation, because standard deviation is less meaningful for small numbers of estimates. As usual, it is up to the investigator to decide which statistic to use and what cutoff to set.

In addition to the usual two tests, MAXEIG has a unique internal consistency test called the "inchworm" test. This test is particularly useful for differentiating sampling fluctuations from true hitmax peaks (or upward slopes), a frequent concern in situations where low base rate taxa (base rate of 10% or lower) can be expected. The test is performed by increasing the number of windows (hence decreasing their sizes) on an input variable until a certain pattern emerges. If the data are taxonic, the graph will eventually assume the shape of an inchworm with its raised head on the right side of the plot. It will look something like Figure 3.8.

Frequently, this shape becomes more pronounced as the number of windows is increased, and can even turn into a peak. However, if the data are nontaxonic, the plot will remain a squiggly flat line with many elevations of comparable sizes, but without a major crest. It will look something like Figure 3.9.

Window sizes can vary greatly, which allows for substantial flexibility in the analyses. The only concern is maintaining a minimal number of cases per window. Recall that, for MAXCOV, we required at least 15 cases per interval. The same cutoff can be set for MAXEIG as well. This cutoff effectively sets the upper limit on the permissible number (size) of windows. In their book, Waller and Meehl (1998) give an example of MAXEIG analysis where up to 60 windows were used. However, the data set used in that example included only 40 cases. It is typical for taxometric studies to utilize samples at least ten times larger than that, and the window size can be set for hundreds. In fact, if the taxon has a low base rate, a complete peak may only emerge for a very large number of windows (e.g., 200 or 500).

MAXEIG Utility

In contrast to MAXCOV, MAXEIG has several important limitations. MAXEIG lacks many internal consistency tests. Tests applicable to MAXEIG are not as compelling as MAXCOV tests due to the smaller number of possible configurations. Moreover, MAXEIG does not provide the means for diagnostics and bootstrapping. Finally, MAXEIG may be negatively affected by high indicator skew. Specifically, right-end cusps may appear in positively skewed data and overshadow genuine peaks. These cusps are not likely to disappear or turn into peaks at any window size (number of windows). If this happens, MAXEIG estimates of the taxon base rate cannot be trusted.

The root of the problem is that positive skew makes windows at the extreme range of the scale much longer than average, as high scoring cases are spread out. This in turn produces high correlations–eigenvalues. This phenomenon can be thought of as the opposite of restriction of range.

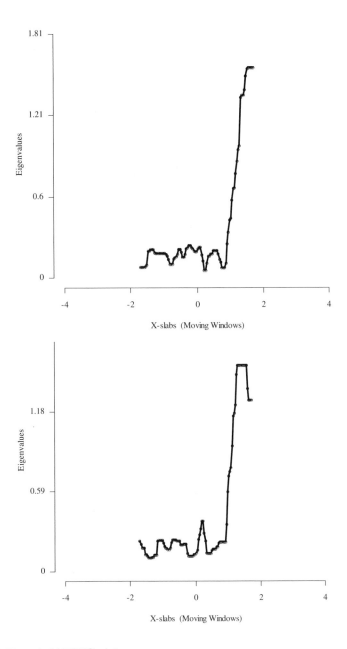

Figure 3.8. Taxonic MAXEIG plots.

MAXCOV does not suffer from this problem because the interval length is fixed in MAXCOV; it does not change along the scale. One possible solution to the problem is to drop the most extreme cases, as this may help the true peak to emerge from the shadow of the cusp. However, base rate estimates will need to be adjusted for the dropped cases (all of which can be considered to be taxon members). Another potential solution is to transform

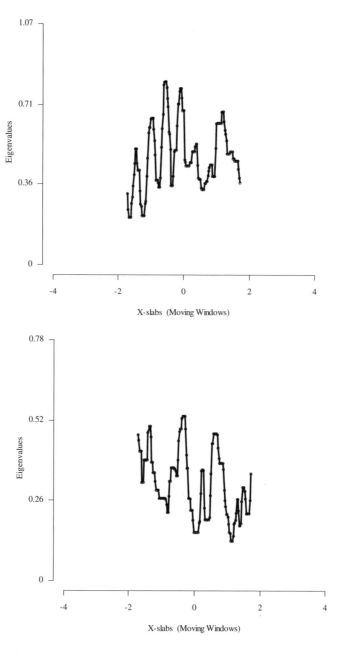

Figure 3.9. Nontaxonic MAXEIG plots.

the indicators to reduce the skew (e.g., take a natural log or a square root of scores). We do not recommend this approach. Reduction of indicator skew is likely to reduce indicator validity (recall our discussion of the relationship between validity and skew), which might reduce the accuracy of the analysis and make genuinely taxonic data appear nontaxonic.

On the other hand, MAXEIG has some advantages. It is a simple, straightforward procedure. It is much easier to evaluate MAXEIG outputs for evidence of taxonicity than the results of MAXCOV analyses. With MAXEIG, a taxonic judgment can be made on the basis of a few plots and a single parameter (taxon base rate), while MAXCOV outputs include multiple graphs and multiple parameters. Moreover, MAXEIG offers greater precision of estimation than MAXCOV. The principle of overlapping windows permits fine slicing of the input variable, which yields robust plots and reliable estimates of the taxon base rate. Also, MAXEIG can be used to investigate low base rate taxa, a condition where MAXCOV may fail.

Overall, MAXEIG is an excellent exploratory taxometric procedure, as it is flexible and does not require the monitoring of numerous parameters. MAXEIG can be used to get the feel for the data and estimate basic properties of the taxon. A more thorough assessment would require MAXCOV. MAXEIG can also be used for external consistency testing. MAXEIG is not the perfect choice for validating MAXCOV findings, as the two procedures are fairly similar. However, they are not identical so comparing results across these two procedures constitutes a legitimate (although not impressive) consistency test.

MAMBAC

MAMBAC (Mean Above Minus Below A Cut) is a simple but noteworthy technique. Unlike MAXCOV and MAXEIG, MAMBAC requires only two variables for an analysis. MAMBAC has a very different methodology and can serve as a stringent external consistency test for MAXCOV or MAXEIG findings. The MAMBAC program can be obtained from the Taxometrics Home Page (Waller, 2004; http://peabody.vanderbilt.edu/depts/psych_and_hd/faculty/wallern/tx.html).

MAMBAC Methodology

MAMBAC analysis starts with assigning one indicator to the role of an input variable and another one to the role of an output variable. Then a cut is made on the input indicator in the bottom portion of the distribution. This cut divides the data into two groups—we will refer to them as "above" and "below" groups. The average score on the output variable is calculated for each group; the score of the below group is subtracted from the score of the above group to yield the difference. Next, the cut is made farther up the input indicator and the difference between groups is calculated again. The cut continues moving progressively higher until it reaches the top end of the distribution. MAMBAC plots the resulting differences against the input variable. This graph reflects changes in the degree of difference between above and below groups that occurred as the cut moved along the input variable. Usually, the first and the final cuts are not made at the very extremes of the distribution. This is done to minimize the effects of sampling error, which can increase substantially when either the above or below group is small.

For illustrative purposes, consider a hypothetical example. Suppose we are interested in dissociation and collected data on a measure of depersonalization (the depersonalization scale, or DS) and a measure of amnesic experiences (the amnesia scale, or AS). A MAMBAC analysis with the DS as the input indicator and the AS as the output indicator is conducted. First we need to determine where to make the first cut. Suppose three individuals scored zero on the DS, eight individuals scored one, 23 individuals scored two, 37 individuals scored three, etc. To reduce sampling error, we need to have at least 25 people in the smallest group, so we make the first cut at the DS = 2.5. Then 34 people, who scored two or less on the DS, are in the below group and everyone else is in the above group. We then calculate the average AS score for each of the groups. Assume the average score for the below group is 0.8 and the average score for the above group is 2.6. We then record the difference of 1.8 and plot a point on the graph with coordinates (2, 1.8). Next, we move the cut to the DS = 3.5, and now 71 people, who scored three or less on the DS, are in the below group. Assume the new average scores are 1.1 for the below group and 3.0 for the above group. We record a difference of 1.9 and plot the second point with coordinates (3, 1.9). We continue in this manner until there are too few people (e.g., less than 25) in the above group, at which point we stop. If we stopped at the 10th cut, the graph will look like Figure 3.10.

To interpret this graph we need to go back to the theory. The basic premise of MAMBAC is that if there is no latent discontinuity, the difference between above and below groups should be small when the cut is close to the mean of the distribution and large when the cut is close to one of the extremes. In other words, if the construct is continuous, the MAMBAC plot will be concave, as seen in Figure 3.10. This makes intuitive sense. Assume we have a normal distribution that ranges from 0 to 30 with the mean of 15. If we compare the average score of the individuals who scored 29 or higher to the average score of individuals who scored 28 or lower, the difference will be large (probably around 13), since the bulk of people scored way below 29. However, if we compare the average of individuals scoring 15 or higher to the average of individuals scoring 14 or lower, the difference will be small (probably around 6), since the bulk of the people scored around 15. This example is not directly applicable to MAMBAC, since MAMBAC analyses involve two variables, but it illustrates the general idea.

Let's go back to the dissociation example. How would we interpret Figure 3.11? According to MAMBAC's rationale, when two groups underlie the observed distribution, the difference between the above and the below groups increases as the cut moves away from the extremes. This happens because

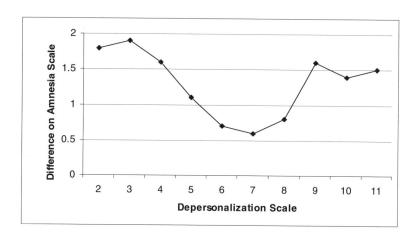

Figure 3.10. Nontaxonic MAMBAC plot.

greater numbers of cases are correctly classified as belonging in the above (taxon) or the below (nontaxon) groups. This idea can be illustrated with the following example. Assume we are comparing levels of testosterone between two groups drawn from a mixed sample of men and women. If we assign individuals to the above and below groups randomly, we will not find a significant difference. However, if we assign more men to the above group and more women to the below group, a difference will emerge. Assume we try several assignment procedures. The largest difference will be produced with a procedure that best separates males and females. A similar thing happens in MAMBAC. A cut placed close to either of the extremes will assign both taxon and nontaxon members to the same group, and the difference between the above and below group will not be large. If we have a sample of 1,000 participants, 300 of whom are taxon members, an extremely high cut—so only 30 people fall above it—would correctly classify 30 taxon members and misclassify 270. This would also be true for an extremely low cut. On the other hand, a cut placed closer to the middle would differentiate better between taxon and nontaxon members, resulting in a large difference. In other words, if the data are taxonic, the MAMBAC plot will take the shape of an inverted parabola, as seen in Figure 3.11, with the peak at the point of best classification.

We want to emphasize that the high point of the graph is *not* the hitmax. It is the point of best classification, which does not have the same properties as the hitmax (for details see Meehl and Yonce, 1994, p. 1066). For this reason, MAMBAC's method of calculating the taxon base rate is radically different from methods that other CCK procedures use. MAMBAC's approach starts with the assumption that only taxon members lie above the highest cut and only nontaxon members lie below the lowest cut. This is the only assumption of this method, and it should hold if the data set is fairly

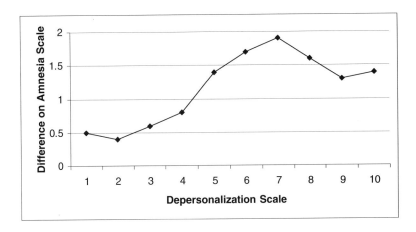

Figure 3.11. Taxonic MAMBAC plot.

large. Through a chain of equations that are not critical for this discussion (for details see Meehl & Yonce, 1994, p. 1117), the following formulas are derived:

$$P = 1/(R + 1), \text{ and } R = D_{hi}/D_{Lo},$$

where, D_{hi} is the difference (between above and below group) at the highest cut,

D_{Lo} is the difference at the lowest cut

and P is the taxon base rate

In other words, the taxon base rate is estimated from the positions of the left (low) and the right (high) ends of the MAMBAC plot. Low base rates cause the right end of the plot to rise relative to the left end, with the elevation being larger for smaller base rates. Moreover, the point of best classification shifts to the right as the base rates decrease. It is not uncommon to see an upward slope rather than a full parabola for taxa with base rates of .25 and smaller.

MAMBAC has several weaknesses. First, it produces taxon base rate estimates regardless of whether the graph is parabolic or concave. Fortunately, it is not difficult to detect nontaxonic results. If the data are not taxonic, there is no reason for one end of the plot to be significantly higher than the other end. Hence, nontaxonic data sets usually yield base rate estimates in the neighborhood of .50. If the taxon base rate is consistently estimated at .50, this should not be taken as evidence of taxonicity unless the estimates are accompanied by a series of clearly parabolic shapes. Second, we find that MAMBAC's method of estimating base rates is less reliable than the estimation procedure used by MAXCOV. This is especially true for low base rate taxa. If a MAMBAC plot does not produce a complete peak, the observed D_{hi} is likely to be lower than true D_{hi}, which would lead to an overestimation of the base rate. When nontaxon nuisance correlations are high, observed D_{lo} will be inflated—as sizable nuisance correlations tend to lift the left end of the plot (Meehl & Yonce, 1994)—which will also cause an overestimation of the taxon base rate. Hence, if unfavorable conditions are suspected, MAMBAC base rate estimates should be interpreted with caution. Indicator skew is also a problem for MAMBAC. MAMBAC analyses of dimensional data may produce cusping plots when the indicators are heavily skewed. Consider that if you have two 50-point scales with means of 10 (high positive skew), then the left end of the MAMBAC plot cannot be elevated by more than 10 points (10–0), while the right end can be elevated by as much as 40 points (50–10). However, there is no reason for skewed data to produce peaks, so indicator skew is not a concern if MAMBAC plots show complete peaks.

We should also note that there are other ways to plot MAMBAC results. The cut can be moved in increments (e.g., increments of .25 SD; Meehl and Yonce [1994]), or by a single point, which is the default setup in Waller's MAMBAC. These variations can alter the appearance of the graphs to some degree. Figure 3.12 depicts two graphs from the dissociation example with single point plotting (rather than single value plotting, which we used initially).

MAMBAC Consistency Testing

MAMBAC offers two standard internal consistency tests, the nose count test and the base rate variability test. MAMBAC allows for two analyses per pair of indicators, which means that two indicators produce two plots, three indicators produce six plots, four indicators produce 12 plots, five indicators produce 20 plots, etc. Waller's MAMBAC does not do this automatically, and the investigator has to run each analysis independently. Ruscio's software, on the other hand, is fully automatic.

MAMBAC Group Assignment and Bootstrapping

Waller's MAMBAC does not perform group assignments. The reason is that MAMBAC does not actually locate the position of a hitmax, thus there is no straightforward way of calculating taxon membership probabilities. Due to these limitations, Waller's MAMBAC is not able to estimate indicator validities and nuisance correlations.

Ruscio's software gets around these problems with *base rate based group assignment*. In this procedure, a certain portion of cases that score highest on the sum of indicators is assigned to the taxon group, and all other cases are assigned to the nontaxon group. The portion of cases assigned to the taxon equals the estimated taxon base rate, hence the name of the procedure. After cases are assigned in this fashion, Ruscio's MAMBAC can estimate all the parameters that MAXCOV estimates. However, we have two concerns with

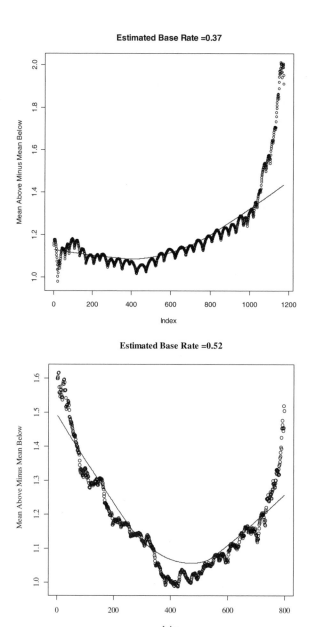

Figure 3.12. MAMBAC plots with case-by-case cut.

this method. First, as mentioned above, MAMBAC base rate estimation is often inaccurate, thus all parameter estimates may be off the mark. Second, even if the base rate is estimated accurately, group assignment based on the sum of raw scores is more likely to make missassignments than a procedure based on Bayesian probabilities. Unless indicator validities are very high, the latent distributions will be highly overlapping and missassignment rates may approach 50%; that is, almost 50% of those assigned to the taxon group would be nontaxon members and almost 50% of taxon members would be assigned to the nontaxon group. Poor group assignment would lead to problems with estimating latent parameters. Specifically, both nuisance correlations and indicator validities would be overestimated. These problems are precisely why the original MAMBAC does not perform group assignment. It is possible that the base rate based group assignment method may perform adequately under certain circumstances, but this issue needs to be thoroughly tested in simulation studies. To the best of our knowledge, such studies have not been conducted; therefore, we do not recommend using this approach.

MAMBAC Utility

MAMBAC is an excellent screening method for selecting potential taxon markers. MAMBAC only looks at indicator pairs, and such results are easy to interpret: Two measures either tap the same construct or they do not. On the other hand, several interpretations are possible with three indicators (e.g., MAXCOV analysis). Also, MAMBAC yields a manageable number of plots even for large numbers of indicators, unlike MAXCOV, which is impractical with more than five indicators. If the investigator starts with several potential taxon indicators, a quick series of MAMBAC analyses will provide some idea about properties of the taxon, if there is one. MAMBAC can also assist in the selection of indicators for a more detailed investigation with MAXCOV (Meehl, 1999; Waller, Putnam, & Carlson, 1996).

Unfortunately, MAMBAC tends to be less robust than MAXCOV under unfavorable circumstances, such as low taxon base rates, poor indicator validities, and high nuisance correlations. Specifically, taxonic plots often look flat and sometimes concave when the validity of indicators is less than 1.5 SD or when nuisance correlations are higher than .35 (Meehl & Yonce, 1994). A low taxon base rate can obscure the plots even more. For this reason, MAMBAC findings should be interpreted with special care and should be accompanied by MAXCOV analyses whenever possible. MAXCOV can assess the extent to which ideal conditions have been violated and can provide the investigator with information needed for making sound judgments about the trustworthiness of MAMBAC results.

MAXSLOPE

MAXSLOPE (Grove & Meehl, 1993) stands for MAXimum SLOPE and is another procedure that can be applied to two variables. MAXSLOPE was developed for a somewhat different purpose than other CCK methods. The primary goal of MAXSLOPE is to present data graphically in a manner that makes apparent whether a taxonic pattern is present or not, rather than providing precise estimates of latent parameters. In other words, MAXSLOPE does not involve fancy computations but provides the investigators with a graphical summary of the data that will be helpful in evaluating the taxonic conjecture and perhaps can serve as a starting point for calculating latent values with other programs. Waller's package does not include MAXSLOPE, but this program can be obtained directly from Dr. William Grove in the psychology department at the University of Minnesota in Minneapolis.

MAXSLOPE Methodology

To understand the rationale behind MAXSLOPE, consider the following. Assume we want to extend the applicability of MAXCOV to situations where only two indicators are available. We can approach this problem by assigning one indicator as the input variable and another indicator as the output variable. Our next step would be to calculate covariance, but we cannot do that because there is only one output indicator. The way out of this predicament is to compute covariance between the input and the output indicator. We can also do this by running a regression analysis, as regression analyses are not different in principle from covariance computations. From GCMT, we know that the covariance of two output variables peaks at the hitmax, if there is one. Analogously, the covariance of the output and the input indicators should also peak at the hitmax. In regression terms, higher covariance means a greater slope of the regression line; for example, the regression line describing two uncorrelated variables is flat. We can determine the location of the hitmax by finding an interval where the slope of the regression plot is the greatest. This is the basic idea of MAXSLOPE. We can now go through this procedure in more detail.

First, MAXSLOPE makes windows on an input indicator. The investigator sets window size by choosing the percentage of the sample that a window would cover. Recall that the investigator sets the number of windows in MAXEIG, rather than the number of people per window, but the general idea is the same. As with other procedures, the window should include enough cases to yield stable estimates. The first window starts at the lowest value of the input indicator, the next window is moved up one case (*not* one value); case by case the windows are moved up until they span the entire range of the input variable. This process yields a series of highly overlapping windows. In fact, two adjacent windows share all but two cases in common.

The regression slope is calculated in each window and a single continuous regression curve (not a straight line) is plotted on the basis of these values. It is often possible to see the hitmax area on this plot. This area manifests as an S-shaped curving in the graph—like the bend in the overall regression curve observed between X = 5 and 20 on Figure 3.1. To get a clearer picture, MAXSLOPE plots values of the regression slopes on a separate graph. The hitmax will manifest as a distinct elevation, but its exact position can be obscured by random fluctuations. Magnitudes of the slopes tend to vary substantially, especially in the neighborhood of the hitmax. To correct for that, MAXSLOPE locates the highest elevation in the plot and applies a smoother to the area around it. Next, MAXSLOPE locates the highest elevation in the smoothed curve and marks it on the graph. This is the final estimate of the hitmax's position. MAXSLOPE uses the position of the hitmax to estimate the taxon base rate.

MAXSLOPE automatically runs all possible combinations of indicators. Each pair of indicators yields two combinations. MAXSLOPE swaps the roles of the indicators; for example, in one analysis anhedonia is the input and sadness is the output, but in another analysis sadness is the output and anhedonia is the input. MAXSLOPE plots the graphs and reports averaged (across two analyses) taxon base rate estimates.

One critical limitation of MAXSLOPE is that the method locates the hitmax correctly only for certain types of latent distributions (e.g., normal distribution). For other kinds of distributions (e.g., chi-square distribution), the estimated location of the hitmax and the base rate may be substantially off the mark. In other words, when the underlying distributions are of the "difficult" kind, MAXSLOPE will detect taxonicity, but the estimated taxon base rate may be incorrect. Moreover, MAXSLOPE may fail to detect taxonicity under certain circumstances. Specifically, this will happen if:

$$(\Delta Y - b1 * \Delta X) < 0$$

where, ΔY – validity of a given output indicator
ΔX – validity of a given input indicator
b1 – average (between taxon and nontaxon) nuisance correlation

To understand this formula better, suppose that the average nuisance correlation is .33. Then MAXSLOPE will fail if the validity of the input indicator is three (or more) times greater than the validity of the output indicator. This limitation applies to both "easy" and "difficult" distributions.

MAXSLOPE Consistency Testing

Nose count and base rate variability consistency tests are possible with MAXSLOPE, although it is not yet clear how these tests behave when the underlying distributions are of the "difficult" kind. Luckily, MAXSLOPE puts less emphasis on internal consistency testing and stresses external consistency testing instead. MAXSLOPE is different from other taxometric algorithms and thus can provide a strong test of external consistency for other procedures.

MAXSLOPE Group Assignment

Although MAXSLOPE runs all of the subanalyses together (unlike MAXEIG and MAMBAC), it does not perform group assignment.

MAXSLOPE was conceived as a purely exploratory graphical procedure and was not intended for diagnostic purposes. Moreover, problems with locating a hitmax pose a significant obstacle to performing the computations necessary for group assignment.

MAXSLOPE Bootstrapping

MAXSLOPE does not estimate the latent parameters needed for bootstrapping, but statistically sophisticated investigators can use MAXSLOPE results as a starting point for calculating these latent parameters independently. Interestingly, these calculations do not involve group assignments, unlike approaches to bootstrapping that we have discussed so far. For instance, a nuisance correlation can be estimated by computing an average of regression slopes at an extreme of the observed distribution (e.g., taxon nuisance correlations will be calculated by averaging over the high end of the distribution). The appropriate size of the averaging area can be determined by examining MAXSLOPE graphs.

Several other useful values can be obtained with a complementary procedure, similar to MAXSLOPE except it calculates variances instead of regression slopes (see Grove & Meehl, 1993). An investigator can use these values to calculate parameters of latent distributions (e.g., mean and standard deviation of the taxon). These estimates are not biased by nuisance correlations, unlike MAXCOV estimates. Unfortunately, these calculations are fairly arduous, so we will not describe them here (for more details see Grove & Meehl, 1993).

In its current form, MAXSLOPE may be quite useful for statistically adept investigators who can do the additional calculations themselves and who want to have as much flexibility in the analysis as possible. Hopefully MAXSLOPE will be upgraded in the near future to be more automatic and accessible for less statistically inclined investigators. Another issue is that MAXSLOPE has not been sufficiently tested on simulated data. Consequently, we recommend using MAXSLOPE only for testing the external consistency of other taxometric procedures and would suggest caution when interpreting MAXSLOPE results. Due to the problems with locating the hitmax, external consistency testing can be done only in a general way by checking whether MAXSLOPE plots are S-shaped or not. Overall, MAXSLOPE is a very promising method, but it requires more development and testing.

OTHER TAXOMETRIC PROCEDURES

A few other taxometric procedures have been proposed in the literature, such as L-mode (L stands for latent: Latent mode; Waller & Meehl, 1998) and minimizing variance above the cut plus variance below the cut (SSa + SSb; SQUABAC; Meehl and Yonce, 1996, p. 1135), but they have not been studied as much as the five methods described above. L-mode and SQUABAC received limited attention in simulation studies and have been used in a handful of empirical studies. In our opinion, the available information is insufficient to develop guidelines for the application of these procedures; thus,we will only provide a brief summary of the methods. Interested readers can learn more about these techniques in Waller and Meehl (1998) and Meehl and Yonce (1996).

L-mode infers taxonicity from the bimodal distribution of scores. This is an intuitively appealing approach; however, taxometricians have long recognized that bimodality in raw scores is not necessary for taxonicity and that this pattern can be observed only with powerful indicators. Consider the example of Figure 3.13. The observable distribution is hardly skewed and certainly does not show evidence of bimodality, but the underlying structure is clearly taxonic. In fact, the separation between the latent groups is almost two SD. On the other hand, factor scores are considered to have less measurement error than raw scores and therefore possess greater ability to reveal latent bimodality. This idea is the central rationale behind L-mode. Specifically, L-mode performs a factor analysis with all available indicators and plots the distribution of scores on the first unrotated factor. Then the investigator examines the graph for evidence of bimodality and determines the taxonic status of the data. Figure 3.14 shows examples of two clearly interpretable L-mode plots and one ambiguous plot. If the investigator finds the second mode, it can be indicated to the program. The software can find the first (highest) mode automatically, but it needs help finding the second mode. L-mode uses the locations of two modes to compute independent estimates of taxon base rate. It also can compute the Bayesian base rate estimate. Variability of these three estimates is the only consistency test available with L-mode. The nose count test is not possible because the procedure yields only one graph.

In short, the logic of L-mode is to combine the taxon indicators and optimally weight them to produce the single most powerful indicator possible. However, keep in mind that only very powerful indicators can expose bimodality (indicator validity of at least 2.0 SD is necessary even under the best circumstance; Meehl, 1995a). The first unrotated factor is probably the most valid single indicator that can be constructed with given data, but is it valid enough? Unfortunately, virtually nothing is known about how much L-mode enhances the validity of the indicators and how well it performs relative to other taxometric procedures. Moreover, opinions differ regarding the interpretation of ambiguous plots. Some researchers interpret the presence of a plateau rather than a clear second peak as absence of a taxon (e.g., Tylka & Subich, 2003), while others consider it suggestive of taxonicity. In fact, the ambiguous plot shown in Figure 3.14 was produced with simulated taxonic data that was created to resemble actual psychopathology data. The vertical right line, one that goes through a plateau, roughly corresponds to position of the mode of the taxonic distribution.

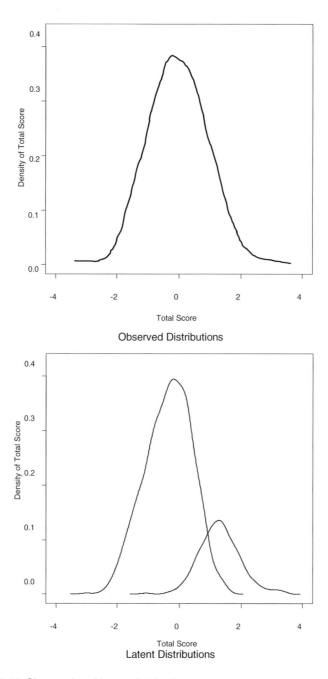

Figure 3.13. Observed and latent distributions.

In sum, it seems plausible that L-mode may be prone to false negative results; that is, it may overlook taxonicity. Consequently, we recommend applying this technique with caution and weighting the results of L-mode less heavily than the findings of more established procedures. It is important

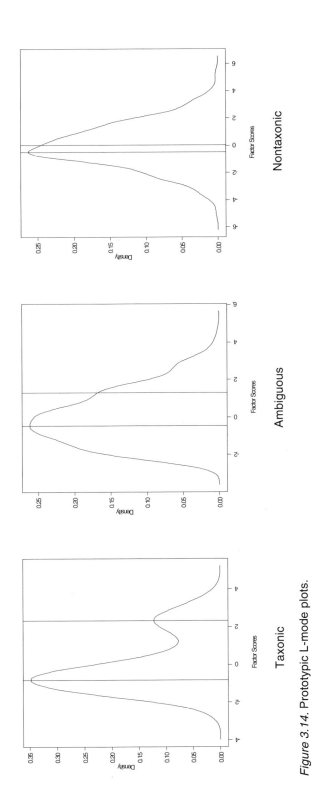

Figure 3.14. Prototypic L-mode plots.

to note that the performance of L-mode appears to improve proportionally to the number of indicators; hence, results of analyses that use eight markers may be more trustworthy than results of analyses with four variables. On the other hand, we believe that the usual rules apply here, and continuous distinct indicators with established validity are preferable to individual items or measures with poor psychometric characteristics.

SQUABAC or "minimizing SSa + SSb" has received even less attention than L-mode. This procedure is conceptually similar to MAMBAC, but it evaluates the behavior of variances rather than means. The only computational difference between the two methods is that the SQUABAC plot reflects the sum of variances of two groups (above and below the cutoff) instead of the difference between means of these two groups. Interpretation of SQUABAC graphs is the direct opposite of how one evaluates MAMBAC. Consider that if a taxon in present, a cut that produces optimal assignment to the groups should minimize variances within these groups. As the cut moves to the right from the optimal position, more and more taxon members get assigned to the nontaxon (below) group, thus introducing more and more between-group variance, which results in an upward slope on the plot. A similar thing happens when the cut moves to the left from the optimal position. Consequently, the presence of a taxon is indicated by a convex or parabolic shape; a concave or peaking shape suggests the absence of a taxon. Little is known about performance of this procedure, and we are unable to offer any further comments.

SUMMARY OF CCK-BASED TAXOMETRIC PROCEDURES

In this chapter we described statistical procedures that are usually classified as taxometric methods. They all rely on the CCK principle but differ in a number of other respects, such as the type of statistic being evaluated and the number of indicators required. Moreover, some procedures differ in relatively small details while others are more distinct. To help readers organize this information, we graphed these relations on a "genealogical tree" of taxometric methods (see Figure 3.15). Now that we have discussed taxometric procedures, let us briefly consider other statistical methods that can be used in taxometric investigations.

Nontaxometric Approaches to Identifying Taxa

Taxometrics was developed by clinical psychologists to study the taxonomy of psychological disorders. Many other disciplines, including medicine, biology, and economics, have been concerned with taxonomic questions. Research in different disciplines takes place under different conditions: The context of taxonomic questions varies, as well as the questions them-

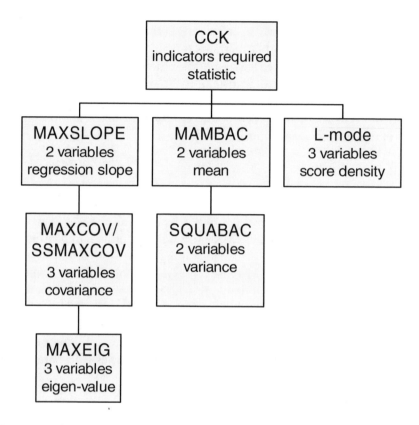

Figure 3.15. Genealogical tree of CCK procedures.

selves. A physicist might be reasonably sure that two well-established enti-ties (e.g., protons and neutrons) are responsible for the observed distribu-tion. The physicist's objective is to identify known entities in the given data set, which is a signal detection problem. Conversely, a psychologist might hypothesize the existence of a latent entity without any direct empirical evi-dence in support of this conjecture. The psychologist's objective is to obtain convincing evidence that will support (or refute) this ontological hypoth-esis. To give another example of variability in research contexts, a biologist might be interested in identifying several taxa in a single analysis, while an oncologist might be interested only in distinguishing pathological from nonpathological cases.

Different taxonomic questions call for different methods. Taxometrics is one of many systematic approaches designed to investigate taxonomic puzzles. In fact, some other techniques offer computational advantages over CCK procedures. However, no other method provides the level of epistemo-logical rigor that taxometrics offers. The task of establishing an empirically sound classification of mental disorders is a complex and difficult one, and we would argue that it is best addressed using a rigorous, epistemologically grounded approach. We have argued at length that taxometrics is best suited for the task; why discuss other methods in this book? Taxometrics is more than a statistical procedure; it is a philosophical approach, and it can be complemented by a variety of statistical techniques. In this section, we will briefly describe three popular non-CCK methods and make recommendations about how they can be incorporated in the taxometric approach to the study of psychopathological taxa.

Latent Class Analysis

Latent Class Analysis (LCA) is a family of methods designed to identify latent groups in categorical data; that is, LCA allows one to study the taxonic structure of constructs defined by nominal or ordinal indicators. LCA can also be applied to quasi-continuous indicators, such as total scores on self-report measures, by treating these scores as ordinal variables. Sometimes LCA is defined more broadly, but we chose this narrow definition for reasons of clarity. LCA was originally developed as a qualitative analog of factor analysis; earlier versions of LCA approached the search for latent groups in much the same way that factor analytic procedures search for latent dimensions (Green, 1951, 1952). In fact, these two approaches still share a lot in common.

LCA and CCK, on the other hand, appear to be strikingly dissimilar. All CCK procedures require at least one quasi-continuous indicator, and if there are none, the investigator has to create such an indicator (e.g., SSMAXCOV procedure). In contrast, LCA does not require continuous indicators and only deals with categorical data. In the case of categorical data, the patterns of interest are usually apparent, so there is no need to summarize the data with correlations. Therefore, LCA evaluates cross-tabulations and compares the number of cases across cells. This shift in representation of the data necessitates other basic changes. For example, LCA operates with proportions instead of covariances and yields tables rather than plots. These differences aside, the two approaches share a lot in common. LCA, like CCK, starts with a set of correlated indicators. It also makes the assumption of zero nuisance covariance—in the LCA literature this is called the assumption of local independence, and it means that the indicators are presumed to be independent (i.e., uncorrelated) within latent classes. Moreover, LCA and CCK (MAXCOV in particular) use similar procedures for group assignment and both of them involve Bayes's theorem.

One distinctive feature of LCA is that it allows the investigator to examine more than two latent groups in one analysis. Hence, the investigator has to make a guess about how many latent classes are in the data before starting the analysis. This can be just a guess, in the purely exploratory sense, or a theory-driven hypothesis. In fact, depending on the context, the investigator has a choice between exploratory and confirmatory LCA, which relate to each other in much the same way exploratory factor analysis relates to confirmatory factor analysis. Details of LCA are beyond the scope of this book, so we refer interested readers to McCutcheon (1987); we found his exposition of the method to be fairly accessible. Two other possible reading sources are Clogg (1995) and Lazarfeld & Henry (1968).

To make the discussion of LCA more concrete, consider an example. Assume we are investigating depression and conjecture three classes: individuals with major depression, individuals with dysthymia, and individuals with no depression. After the number of classes has been posited, we can define a mathematical model that links parameters of the latent classes (e.g., base rates) to proportions of cases in each cell of the cross-tabulation. LCA imposes this model on the data set and estimates parameters of the latent classes. This estimation is an iterative process. In the beginning, the investigator provides initial values for each parameter, to get the computation started somewhere. Initial values can be based on a completely unsubstantiated guess. Inaccurate guesses should not prevent LCA from eventually recovering the correct values. An accurate guess, however, would shorten the computation time.

LCA uses the initial values and the data to calculate maximum likelihood estimates for parameters of the model; that is, find a set of numbers that are most likely to be the correct values of the parameters. Assume we initially guessed that in this particular sample the prevalence of major depression is 20%, the prevalence of dysthymia is also 20%, and the rest of the individuals (60%) are not clinically depressed, but LCA arrived at a substantially different set of numbers—for example, 5%, 25%, and 70%, respectively. These estimates are likely to be "contaminated" by the initial values, which apparently were off the mark. To "purify" these estimates, we repeat the procedure again, but now the starting values are not provided by the investigator; values from the previous iteration are used. These starting values are still somewhat contaminated by the initial guess, but to a lesser degree. The process is repeated until the estimates stop changing appreciably from one iteration to the next, which means the procedure arrived at a set of reasonable numbers. Are these estimates accurate? There is no way of knowing with certainty, but we can test this by redoing the analysis with a different set of initial values. If all reanalyses converge at the same set of estimates, we can be confident that the estimates are accurate, at least for the given data set.

Among other parameters, LCA calculates conditional probabilities. A conditional probability is the proportion of members of a given class that scored a certain value on the indicator. Assume that in the depression example we have an indicator of severity of depression that reads: "How much does your depressed mood interfere with your life?" Assume further that three latent classes have the following conditional probabilities (see Table 3.3). Notice that the numbers in the columns add up to one, but the rows do not.

TABLE 3.3
Conditional Probabilities

	Major depression	Dysthymia	No depression
Not at all	0.08	0.12	0.45
Somewhat	0.14	0.19	0.49
Quite a bit	0.35	0.41	0.05
A lot	0.43	0.28	0.01

The rows do not need to equal one, since people in different classes can have similar preferences for the same option, although this probably would mean that the indicator is not valid. We can use Bayes's theorem to combine the conditional probabilities of all indicators used in the analyses and calculate the probability that members of a certain cell of the cross-tabulation belong to a certain latent class. If members of a cell are more likely to belong to the Dysthymia class than either the Major Depression or the No Depression classes, then all of them will be assigned to Dysthymia. Moreover, conditional probabilities can be used to calculate indicator validities. However, validity is not expressed as a standardized separation between two classes in LCA. LCA uses discrimination (a parameter from Item Response Theory) instead. Finally, we want to note that most LCA methods do not evaluate the original assumption of local independence (i.e., zero nuisance covariance), but investigators can do it themselves after individuals have been assigned to classes. They just need to compute correlations between indicators in each group.

Everything looks great so far, but we still have not answered the question of whether our tri-class model is an accurate reflection of the true state of affairs. LCA does not really pose this question. Instead, it investigates whether the model approximates the data well. LCA does that by comparing the number of cases in each cell, as predicted by the model, with the actual number of people in the cell. Then any index of fit (e.g., chi-square) can be used to evaluate the discrepancy between the data and the model. A variety of models can be evaluated and compared on the index of fit, and the best fitting model should be selected as most appropriate. Unfortunately, such comparisons generally provide fairly weak epistemological tests. A taxon that survived the full rigor of taxometric testing is a meaningful category indeed; whereas, a "taxon" derived with LCA alone is really only a taxon candidate. In our view, this is the major disadvantage of the LCA approach because it is oriented towards maximal fit rather than maximal coherence with the nomological network.

On the other hand, LCA has a number of important advantages. One of them is the ability to estimate a full set of latent parameters from categorical data. SSMAXCOV can analyze categorical data, but it cannot estimate any latent parameters other than the taxon base rate. A second advantage of LCA is its ability to simultaneously evaluate the existence of multiple taxa. This feature of LCA can be invaluable in situations when more than one taxon is expected to be present in the data. There is a danger of testing in-creasing numbers of latent classes until a near perfect fit is achieved without considering the meaning of these taxa and their places in the big picture. This is the reason taxometrics has focused on the simple two-class latent structure. Instead of pitting various statistical models with different numbers of latent classes against each other, taxometrics tests a single model against the gold standard of skepticism.

As we have described, LCA is in many ways superior to SSMAXCOV; however, there are situations in which the latter is preferable. SSMAXCOV is best suited for analyzing items from a single homogeneous scale. Items from homogeneous scales tend to correlate highly, due in part to some redun-dancy in the content of the items, which can produce significant nuisance correlations. Both SSMAXCOV and LCA make an assumption of zero-nui-sance correlation, but it appears that LCA is more vulnerable to a violation of this assumption. This question has not been rigorously investigated, but we tentatively recommend using SSMAXCOV rather than LCA for within-scale analyses.

Golden (1982) attempted infusing some features of the taxometric ap-proach in the methodology of traditional latent class analysis. His goal was to alleviate the epistemological weakness of LCA while preserving its strength in analyzing dichotomous data. Golden, however, had to sacrifice the flex-ibility of LCA. He restricted the application of his procedure to the two latent class (taxon vs. nontaxon) problem, which was primarily done to avoid epistemologically unsound guessing about the number of classes. The main limitation of the traditional LCA is that it does not allow for multiple inde-pendent ways of evaluating the taxonic conjecture and estimating param-eters of latent distributions, which severely restricts opportunities for consis-tency testing. Golden was unable to resolve this issue, so he worked around it. Golden's procedure did not use standard consistency checks, such as the nose count and base rate variability test. Instead, he employed indirect con-sistency tests; that is, tests that evaluate the indicators rather than the result itself. Specifically, Golden added another iterative procedure on top of the one used by traditional LCA. Following are the steps of the procedure (Golden, 1982, pp. 407–408):

1. Select indicators with clinical or face validity that are positively cor-related in a mixed sample.
2. Run traditional LCA analysis, then:
   - Exclude or combine indicators that have high nuisance correla-tions.
   - Delete indicators that do not discriminate sufficiently between la-tent groups; that is, are not valid.
3. Do consistency tests:
   - Compare the taxon base rate to previous research and clinical ex-perience.

- Check that the Bayesian taxon membership probabilities of the sample cluster around 1 and 0.
- Check that errors of parameter estimation are within tolerance limits. Golden proposed an index that can be used to evaluate these errors. This index specifically focuses on errors that arise from the degrading effects of nuisance correlation and ignores sampling errors, as they cannot be minimized.

4. Repeat Step 2 until all criteria of Step 3 are met.

This procedure has been used in several empirical studies (Golden & Meehl, 1979; Macfarlane, 1997). However, it has not been subjected to adequate simulation testing. Moreover, the procedure does not allow for some of the powerful consistency tests that are possible with MAXCOV. We find Golden's approach interesting, but its validity and utility require further investigation.

Overall we recommend using LCA in conjunction with taxometric analyses. In most cases, LCA provides an excellent test of external consistency for CCK procedures. In order to apply both approaches to the same data, an investigator could do taxometric analyses with continuous indicators and then break them down to form a pool of ordinal or dichotomous taxon markers.

Mixture Analysis

Mixture Analysis (MA) is similar in many respects to LCA (for a detailed treatment see McLachlan, 1988). MA also shares common features with CCK. For example, MA was developed to work with quasi-continuous rather than categorical indicators. However, two critical features distinguish MA from both LCA and CCK. First, MA does not make the assumption of local independence (zero nuisance covariance). Second, MA can be conducted with a single indicator.

MA can evaluate the existence of any finite number of latent distributions (groups, classes). The investigator starts by making a guess about the number of latent distributions. Usually these latent distributions are expected to be significantly overlapping or mixed (if they were not mixed, the investigator should have been able to classify cases by inspection without using fancy statistical techniques); hence, the name of the approach. In addition, the investigator specifies what kind of latent distributions he or she is looking for: normal, chi-square, gamma, and so on. In the case of both CCK and LCA, there is no need to stipulate the type of distributions beyond the supposition that they are unimodal. This new stipulation is the tradeoff for not making the assumption of zero nuisance covariance. How can the investigator determine what kinds of distributions underlie the data? Unfortunately, there are no sound rules for that, and the investigator must simply use common sense and guess. Usually there is little information that can help these

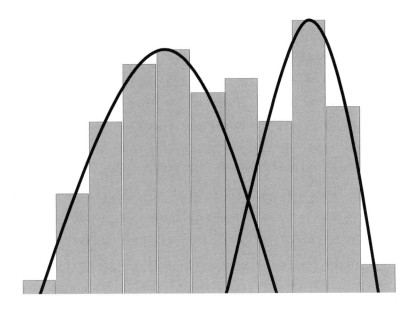

Figure 3.16. Fitting two normal distributions.

guesses; thus, MA investigators frequently presuppose normal distributions because of their convenience.

After the investigator specifies the number and the type of distributions, straightforward mathematics is used to define relations between the model and the data. Similar to LCA, an iterative maximum likelihood procedure is used for estimating parameters of the model (e.g., base rates, latent means, latent standard deviations, etc.). MA also starts with initial values provided by the investigator and continues until the estimates stop changing appreciably. In essence, it is a curve-fitting procedure; that is, MA varies parameters of latent distributions until it can best reproduce the observed curve. For example, Figure 3.16 is a histogram fitted with two normal distributions. However, even the best fitting latent distributions almost never fit the data perfectly. This discrepancy can be captured by a number of fit indexes (e.g., chi-square) and used to compare various models with different numbers or types of distributions.

Clearly, MA is a fit-oriented approach, and it is exposed to the same danger as LCA—the investigator can completely lose sight of interpretability while searching for the best fit and trying out various models. On the bright side, MA is more flexible than either CCK or LCA, it can work even with one indicator, and it does not assume zero nuisance covariance. We recommend using MA as a consistency test for the other two approaches, but the number of distributions and their type should be decided upon ahead of time. In fact, the decision-making process is pretty straightforward: the number of distributions should be the same as in the other analyses, and the distribution type should usually be set as normal, unless there is very substantial skewness in the data. If the taxon is expected to have a low base rate in the given sample, more skewed distributions, like chi-square distributions, may be preferable.

Cluster Analysis

Cluster analysis (CA) is probably the most common approach used to evaluate latent groups. It was proposed for use in the social sciences in the 1930s and gained considerable popularity after the development of powerful computers. Since the 1930s, a variety of CA methods have been designed. In fact, there are now over 100 different CA procedures (Blashfield, 1976). CA is often used to group related variables, but it can also be used to generate groupings of individuals. The latter purpose is the primary interest here. Unfortunately, the majority of CA procedures are nothing more than plausible heuristics as they are not supported by rigorous statistical reasoning. Certain CA algorithms are more statistically sound than others, but all of them are based on induction rather than risky tests of a conjecture.

Three statistical approaches described so far (CCK, LCA, and MA) rely on statistical models. They make certain assumptions about the latent structure, which allows them to define models and then evaluate these models with the data. CA is radically different; it goes "bottom-up" from the data and does not make any structural assumptions whatsoever. CA is inductive and exploratory in nature. Is this advantageous? We will come back to this question, but first let us get better acquainted with the methodology.

Describing CA is tricky, because the 100 plus CA algorithms vary dramatically from each other. A comprehensive description of all these procedures is certainly beyond the scope of this book, so we have to narrow this discussion to one method as an illustration of the general approach (for a more detailed treatment see Aldenderfer & Blashfield, 1984). One thing that unites all CA algorithms is their reliance on the concept of similarity. This should not be surprising, as the notion of similarity (between members of a taxon) and dissimilarity (between members of different taxa) is fundamental to the process of classification. The similarity of two individuals on a set of indicators can be expressed in multiple ways; for example, Euclidean distance. To calculate the Euclidean distance between two cases, we determine their coordinates in the indicator-space by using indicators as coordinate axes, analogously to the width, length, and height in spatial problems. The rest is a simple geometrical problem of calculating the distance between two points in space. After an index of similarity has been selected (e.g., Euclidean distance), CA applies an algorithm to the similarity data and assigns individuals to clusters by putting similar cases in the same clusters and dissimilar cases in different clusters. This is usually done in an iterative fashion.

There are several types of CA algorithms for the investigator to choose from, including hierarchical agglomerative, hierarchical partitioning, density search, and a few others. Hierarchical agglomerative algorithms are much more popular than other types of algorithms. Hierarchical agglomerative methods start by regarding each case as a cluster in itself. Then they fuse these micro-clusters one by one following a simple heuristic until all are joined in a few big clusters. Sometimes all the data points end up being fused in one large cluster, which suggests that there is no evidence for multiple latent groups. Fusion heuristics vary among the procedures. To get a better understanding of how they work, consider in detail one of these algorithms—the single linkage method. The basic idea of the algorithm is that a case is added to a cluster if there is at least one data point in the cluster that is more similar to the case than any of the points that do not belong to the cluster. In other words, to be added to a cluster, a point has to be very similar to at least one point already in the cluster, and it can be rather dissimilar from other points of the cluster.

This is how a single linkage procedure is done in practice. It starts with N micro-clusters, each containing one case. In the first iteration, the two most similar clusters are fused together to form a two-case cluster. In the second iteration, two clusters that have the shortest single link are fused, and so on for $N-1$ iteration, until all cases are joined in one super-cluster. Figure 3.17 demonstrates how the process might look for six individuals. Evidently this process will continue until all clusters are fused unless the investigator specifies a termination point. In this example, two clusters are clearly apparent in the data, so an investigator can specify that the process should be terminated when only two clusters remain independent; that is, at the $N-2$ iteration.

How can we determine the termination point more rigorously? In fact, this is a restatement of the key question of taxometrics—"are there two latent groups underlying the data"—so we should answer this question as rigorously as possible. CA employs a number of indexes that can be used to formalize the decision. Most are based on a straightforward approach. The idea of the approach is to measure the dissimilarity of clusters that are being fused at each of the $N-1$ iterations. In our selected single linkage algorithm, length of the link at a given iteration can be employed as the index of dissimilarity. It can be plotted against the number of clusters remaining at the given iteration, which produces a plot that is analogous to the "scree plot" in factor analysis. The idea of the test is to go backward through iterations and decide at what point splitting a cluster does not substantially improve the homogeneity of the resulting clusters. Similarly to the scree plot, there will be a rapid decrease in the index of dissimilarity in the beginning, then the plot will flatten out, which means that further splitting offers diminishing returns. It is assumed that the point of diminishing returns marks the true number of latent clusters. In the example we are considering, the drop stops

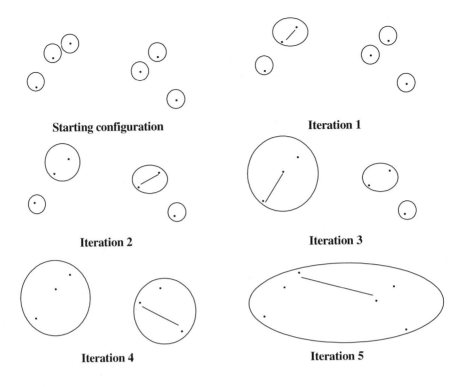

Starting configuration

Iteration 1

Iteration 2

Iteration 3

Iteration 4

Iteration 5

Figure 3.17. Cluster analysis.

at two clusters—splitting them in three did not substantially increase the homogeneity of the clusters—so we can conclude that there are two latent groups in the data.

Other CA tests are similar in that they are single-number indexes of fit and do not require confirmation of risky predictions or any kind of cross-analyses corroboration. Clearly, CA is a fit-oriented approach and it may be useful for describing the given data set, but it is often inadequate for uncovering true latent structures. A number of simulation studies compared the ability of CA and taxometric approaches to determining whether the data are taxonic (two clusters) or not (one cluster; Beauchaine & Beauchaine, 2002; Cleland et al., 2000, Grove & Meehl, 1993). The unanimous conclusion is that the taxometric approach is superior to CA. In line with this, Meehl (1979) made a general observation that despite the considerable popularity of CA, not a single entity in medicine or psychology has been discovered with CA.

Another problem with CA is associated with diagnostics. Even if CA correctly determined the number of latent groups, this is not a guarantee that it also accurately determined group membership. Unfortunately, there are no adequate ways to assess the validity of CA group assignment. Empirical evaluation of a variety of CA methods suggests that CA procedures are actually very poor at correctly detecting group membership (Meehl & Golden, 1982). A large-scale simulation study comparing a leading CA algorithm and MAXCOV supported the diagnostic superiority of MAXCOV, especially for low base rate taxa (Beauchaine & Beauchaine, 2002). Another problem with the CA approach is that different algorithms often do not agree with each other and sometimes they do not detect established taxa. Unfortunately, there is no accepted criterion to determine which CA classification to trust, and there are no theoretical grounds for preferring one method over the other (Meehl & Golden, 1982). Thus, there are considerable costs associated with abandoning a deductive, assumption-limited approach to classification employed by CCK, LCA, and MA. CA does not force us to make assumptions, which may or may not apply to the data set at hand, but the price we pay for this freedom appears to be too high. Overall, we do not recommend use of cluster analysis for identifying taxa or for consistency testing, with a possible exception of data that are not suitable for taxometric procedures.

SUMMARY OF NON-CCK TAXOMETRIC PROCEDURES

In the second part of this chapter we described the basic principles of three other families of categorical methods. To help the reader integrate this information with discussions of the taxometric procedures, we plotted another genealogical tree that includes classes of procedures rather than individual methods (see Figure 3.18).

The procedures are grouped in two general classes: "inferential" and "descriptive." These labels are not an established convention, but rather, are used to highlight the fundamental difference between the completely "atheoretical" approach of CA and the model-guided approach of the other methods. Among the inferential methods, CCK is based on the strictest model, LCA makes fewer assumptions, and MA uses a bottom-up, fit-oriented approach.

The methods discussed in this chapter vary in terms of their sophistication and epistemological rigor; all of them are just statistical procedures and cautions that have been noted regarding other statistical analyses apply to them as well. The procedures do not determine whether a taxon exists; they just provide outputs for a researcher to interpret. In the end it is the scientist, not the procedure, that decides the epistemological status of a putative taxon. In other words, the taxometric enterprise involves a certain degree of subjectivity and even experts may disagree regarding the taxonicity of certain data. Also, the taxometric approach is not infallible, despite its thoroughness. Taxometrics can be expected to sometimes miss actual taxa and sometimes mistake genuine continua for taxa. Moreover, it may detect taxa that are trivial and uninteresting (Widiger & Frances, 2002). Unfortunately, little is known about the limitations of taxometrics at this time. We believe science can learn about the utility of this methodology only by applying it and by

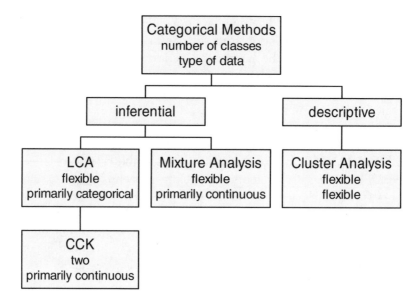

Figure 3.18. Genealogical tree of families of categorical methods.

examining the construct validity and practical significance of the identified taxa. We also believe that taxa or taxometrics as an approach will not become truly established until their practical utility is shown. Thus, despite these uncertainties, we encourage researchers to use taxometrics and to study the meaning and utility of the identified taxa. Some of the initial conclusions may turn out to be incorrect, but ultimately we are likely to find taxometrics to be more helpful than confusing.

4

DIAGNOSING A TAXON: SPECIFIC APPLICATIONS FOR THE *DSM*

There is one thing even more vital to science than intelligent methods;
and that is, the sincere desire to find out the truth, whatever it may be.
—Charles Sanders Pierce

Having outlined the conceptual and analytic basics of taxometrics in previous chapters, we now focus specifically on the application of taxometrics—Coherent Cut Kinetics (CCK) methodology in particular—to the *Diagnostic and Statistical Manual of Mental Disorders (DSM)*. Until this point we have used broad psychological or psychopathological constructs such as anxiety or depression to illustrate taxometric procedures. While these constructs are likely to be related to the *DSM*, they are certainly not isomorphic with *DSM* diagnostic entities. As the central theme of this book is the utilization of taxometric procedures as a guide for future iterations of the *DSM*, this chapter specifically describes taxometric approaches to testing the viability of existing diagnostic entities.

In chapter 5 we review taxometric research in psychopathology. This body of research has largely tested the latent discontinuity hypothesis on general psychopathological constructs such as psychopathy, dissociation, or worry (Harris, Rice, & Quinsey, 1994; Ruscio, Borkovec, & Ruscio, 2001; Waller, Putnam, & Carlson, 1996). Waller et al., for example, were interested in determining whether dissociation rests on a continuum. In their report, CCK analyses identified a pathological dissociation taxon. This dissociation taxon should be related to *DSM* dissociative disorders such as dissociative identity disorder. However, specific diagnostic entities were not directly assessed, so it is difficult to make specific recommendations regarding the *DSM*.

Other taxometrics research has evaluated the validity of theoretical psychopathological subtypes. For example, Haslam and Beck (1994) used CCK procedures to test whether five proposed subtypes of major depression (e.g., endogenous, sociotropic, autonomous) reflect underlying categories. Again, because these theoretical subtypes of depression are not necessarily represented in the *DSM*, they do not speak directly to psychiatric nosology.

To date, CCK studies have rarely attempted to test the taxonic status of diagnostic entities specified in the *DSM*. In other words, there are few examples of taxometric analyses that utilize *DSM* criteria or focus on a *DSM* diagnosis. In one study that did use this strategy, Trull, Widiger, and Guthrie (1990) applied SSMAXCOV to diagnoses of borderline personality disorder and dysthymic disorder. Trull et al. conducted analyses using *DSM–III–R* symptom criteria as indicators of the corresponding disorders (American Psychiatric Association, 1987). They concluded that there is no support for the categorical view of borderline personality disorder and dysthymic disorder. In our view, this conclusion is questionable. Evaluation of the Trull et al. findings suggests that the cusp on the SSMAXCOV plot is suggestive of a low base rate borderline personality disorder taxon, rather than the absence of a taxon. We suggest that this study indicates that borderline personality disorder might be an actual entity, while dysthymic disorder seems to be an artificial category that designates the extreme portion of a continuum.

If corroborated, these findings can have important implications for the definition of these two disorders in the *DSM*. For example, the set of borderline personality disorder diagnostic criteria can be revised using CCK analyses to include only the most valid criteria and to identify a cutoff that best distinguishes between individuals with and without borderline personality disorder (e.g., by requiring six out of nine criteria for the diagnosis, rather than five out of nine as is done currently). If Trull et al. (1990) are correct that dysthymic disorder is continuous, this condition should be represented in a different manner in the *DSM* (see Beutler & Malik, 2002 for a review of continuous approaches to representing psychopathology).

While we believe there are compelling reasons to think that taxometric research is needed for advancing psychiatric nosology, few studies have exposed specific *DSM* criteria to CCK procedures. Direct tests of the viability of the diagnoses defined in the *DSM* are likely to provide an impetus to change our understanding of diagnostic entities and, therefore, guide future revisions of the *DSM*.

EXAMPLES OF TESTING TAXONICITY OF *DSM* DIAGNOSES

In this section, we selected several representative diagnoses from the *DSM* and outlined approaches to analyzing them with CCK procedures.

Example 1: Is Narcissistic Personality Disorder (301.81) a Taxon?

Nearly all the personality disorders are defined in a manner that should facilitate taxometric evaluation. This is noteworthy because there is a general lack of empirical support for the validity of personality disorder diagnoses, along with considerable controversy about the dimensional nature of personality and personality disorders (Clark, Livesley, & Morey, 1997; Clark & Watson, 1999; Widiger & Frances, 2002). As a result, we expect taxometric investigations to be particularly fruitful in this area.

Narcissistic personality disorder, which is organized similar to other personality disorder diagnoses, is described as a pervasive and enduring pattern of behavior indicated by at least five of nine criteria, including

1. grandiose sense of self-importance;
2. fantasies of power, brilliance, and so forth;
3. belief that one is "special" and unique;
4. requires excessive admiration;
5. sense of entitlement;
6. interpersonally exploitative;
7. lacks empathy;
8. envious of others; and
9. arrogant.

Unlike many other *DSM* conditions, there are no explicit exclusionary criteria for narcissistic personality disorder. Thus, CCK analyses can be done without special considerations for the sample composition. The sample can be drawn from almost any population and no exclusion rules are necessary. However, sampling from a population with a higher prevalence of the putative taxon (e.g., psychiatric patients) is likely to aid the analyses. The general scheme for this analysis will not differ from the procedures outlined in the previous chapter. The only additional challenge in analyzing simple *DSM* diagnoses, such as narcissistic personality disorder, is the choice of taxon indicators. Operationalization of general psychopathological entities, such as depression, is usually a straightforward task because one can rely on existing measures with established subscales. Operationalization of *DSM* definitions, on the other hand, can be done in several ways. Following are three main options from which investigators can choose.

Option one is to consider each criterion an indicator, score it either dichotomously or using a short scale—for example, the Structured Interview for DSM–IV Personality (SIDP-IV; Pfohl, Blum, & Zimmerman, 1997) has a four-point system for scoring diagnostic criteria, where zero is not present, one is subthreshold, two is present, and three is strongly present—and then apply SSMAXCOV. This is exactly what Trull et al. (1990) did in their study. Other CCK methods might be appropriate, especially if indicators have several levels; that is, if indicators are not dichotomous.

Option two is to group criteria in a smaller set of indicators. This grouping can permit the application of MAXCOV when the resulting indicators are sufficiently long. As noted in chapter 3, MAXCOV offers several advantages over SSMAXCOV. More importantly, this grouping approach might be necessary in certain cases because sets could include similar criteria. For example, narcissistic personality disorder criterion three (belief that one is "special" and unique) is similar to criterion five (sense of entitlement), and criterion one (grandiose sense of self-importance) is similar to criterion two (fantasies of power, brilliance, etc.). Such similar criteria tend to be highly correlated and produce high nuisance correlations, which can be a problem for CCK methods. Hence, the best way to approach certain diagnoses is by grouping criteria. The grouping can be done rationally or with the aid of factor analysis. It is important to realize that these clusters of criteria might reflect redundancies in the definition of the diagnosis rather than different facets of the construct. Principal components analysis (one of the several factor analytic methods) could be the most appropriate technique, as it aims to reduce data rather than to uncover the underlying structures, which is the goal of other factor analytic methods.

Option three is to develop a separate continuous measure for each of the criteria—as mentioned previously, it is desirable for these measures to have at least 20 levels—and use them as indicators. MAXCOV can definitely be used with such indicators. An indicator can be a single-item measure (e.g., a rating of arrogance made by a clinician on the scale from 0 = *none* to 20 = *extremely*), but it is much better to have several items rated on a short scale and then sum these items to form an indicator with a sufficient range. The latter approach is preferable because single-item measures are not very reliable. Moreover, long scales force raters to make fine distinctions (e.g., choosing between 13 and 14 on a 20-point scale), which often are not done consistently and can decrease the reliability of the measure further (Clark & Watson, 1995). Option three is difficult to carry out in practice, but it provides the most informative and methodologically sound test of the taxonic conjecture; serious taxometric studies should consider taking this approach.

After choosing among these three options, an investigator should also decide on the measurement method. A structured diagnostic interview is considered the gold standard of diagnostic assessment, but self-report and peer-report methods are also acceptable and sometimes desirable. For example, patients with narcissistic personality disorder often lack insight into their behavior, which shifts the burden of obtaining diagnostic information to the clinician; however, the clinician might fail to notice qualities such as lack of empathy or need for excessive admiration in the course of a single interview. Peer-report, on the other hand, is more likely to reveal these traits. The best approach is to combine different methods on the criterion level; that is, include information from different methods in each indicator. We caution against using different methods as different indicators—the latter approach will not clarify the definition of a disorder but can only be used to compare the relative merits of various sources of information. The methods can be combined either by a clinician (best-estimate diagnosis) or statistically as a composite of the ratings (e.g., a sum of standardized scores).

Once these basic decisions have been made, the investigator can proceed in the manner outlined in chapter 3.

Example 2: Is Panic Disorder (300.01) a Taxon?

Most of the Axis I conditions are organized in a more complex fashion than personality disorders. Panic disorder is used as an example. Panic disorder is defined by the *DSM–IV–TR* (American Psychiatric Association, 2000, p. 402) as follows:

A. Both (1) and (2) are required for a diagnosis:
    (1)   recurrent unexpected panic attacks (PA)
    (2)   at least one PA followed by one month or more of:
        (a)   persistent concern about additional PA
        (b)   worry about the consequences of PA
        (c)   significant change in behavior associated with PA
B. PA not due to physiological effects from a substance or from a general medical condition
C. PA are not better accounted for by some other mental disorder

Panic attacks are further described as intense fear or discomfort with the confluence of at least 4 of 13 symptoms within a 10-minute period of time.

Essentially this is a four-component definition. First, the person has to have panic attacks. Second, these attacks should not be caused by a substance or general medical condition, or be accounted for by another mental disorder. Third, at least two of these panic attacks have to be unexpected. Fourth, they should lead to a clinical syndrome that includes concern about additional attacks, worry about the consequences of panic, or significant behavioral change as a result of fear of panicking. This syndrome is the heart of panic disorder, and taxometric analyses would focus on it. However, an investigator should deal with the other components first.

The first task is to select some operationalization of a panic attack. The investigator can rely on the *DSM* definition or she or he can perform a CCK analysis of the phenomenon. Specifically, panic attack symptoms can be analyzed following one of the approaches described in the narcissistic personality disorder example. Given that panic attack criteria are narrow, concrete symptoms that are somewhat independent from each other, option one seems most appropriate. Although SSMAXCOV provides limited information, it can answer central questions such as whether there is a panic attack taxon and how many panic symptoms are sufficient to diagnose it. The DSM assumes there is a qualitative change associated with having more than three symptoms. It seems important to test this arbitrary threshold empirically. If no detectable discontinuity underlies panic attack symptoms, then a different definition of panic attacks can be developed; perhaps a definition that does not focus on the number of symptoms but on the severity or clinical significance of a loosely defined surge of fear. Now that we have a certain appreciation for the complexity of this decision, we assume that some definition of a panic attack was selected and proceed further.

The investigator then needs to decide how to handle the exclusion criteria. To appreciate the meaning of exclusion criteria, consider the distinction between syndromes, disorders, and diseases (Lilienfeld, Waldman, & Israel, 1994). Syndromes are simply constellations of signs and symptoms. Disorders are syndromes that are not produced by other conditions (e.g., refusal to fly on airplanes due to fear or distress is a syndrome, and it is usually considered a disorder-specific phobia. However, if the person is distressed only because he or she has to sit in close proximity of others, specific phobia will not be diagnosed. The syndrome is present, but it is not an independent disorder. Diseases are disorders with known pathology and etiology. Although the etiology and pathology of mental disorders is unknown (Lilienfeld et al.), which means they cannot be considered diseases, creators of the DSM have tried to elevate psychiatric diagnoses to disorder status by specifying exclusion criteria in addition to syndromal descriptions in definitions of mental disorders. DSM exclusion criteria do not help define a syndrome; they rule out individuals who exhibit the syndrome for reasons other than the target disorder. That is not to say there are no classification systems that use exclusion criteria to define clinical syndromes. For example, the Flexible System for diagnosing schizophrenia (Carpenter, Strauss, & Bartko, 1973) includes the absence of affective features (e.g., no elation, no early morning awakening) in its description of the syndrome. In contrast, significant affective disturbance is an exclusion criterion for a DSM schizophrenia diagnosis. Taxometric procedures are designed to work with indicators that play an equal role in the definition; that is, no indicator is privileged or has primacy over the others. As the DSM holds exclusion criteria and syndrome descriptions on different levels, we recommend using exclusion criteria as a screen in sample selection, rather than including it in taxometric analyses per se.

In the case of panic disorder, the exclusion criteria specify that only certain types of panic attacks are relevant to this diagnosis (i.e., panic attacks resulting from drugs, other anxiety disorders do not count). One could simply exclude all patients with irrelevant panic attacks. Another option is to retain these cases in the sample, but not count panic attacks that fall under exclusion criteria in the analyses. For simplicity, suppose that the first option is chosen. Thus, the second step after defining a panic attack is to apply a filter based on the exclusion criteria to subject selection. Then the investigator will have a sample that includes only subjects who experienced at least one panic attack of the target type. This is a rather restricted sample, and the researcher should keep in mind a potential base rate problem. As mentioned previously, for CCK analyses the optimal range of taxon base rates is 10% to 90%. If the taxon base rate is expected to be over 90%, it might be useful to "dilute" the sample with some nontaxon cases. This, however, is not likely to be a problem when analyzing panic disorder, because 20% of the population experiences a panic attack at least once in their life (Barlow, 2002) while the lifetime prevalence of panic disorder is only 3%. We want to note that exclusion criteria for panic disorder are similar to exclusion criteria for most other DSM entities; hence, the same consideration will apply when evaluating other diagnoses.

It is less clear how one should handle the requirement of unexpected and recurrent panic attacks. This is an inclusion criterion in form, while it is an exclusion criterion in function. This requirement can be operationalized either as a selection filter or as a component of the syndrome. We think it useful to break up "unexpected and recurrent" into two components and consider them separately. The unexpectedness of the panic attack is such a fundamental requirement in the DSM definition that it makes sense to operationalize it as a selection criterion. According to the DSM, individuals who have only experienced situationally bound panic attacks cannot have a panic disorder diagnosis, which can happen if this criterion is used as an indicator in CCK analyses. An individual can become a taxon member by being elevated on some, but not necessarily all, indicators. Moreover, unexpectedness of a panic attack cannot be easily coded as a continuous variable, which can present computational difficulties, especially for MAXCOV.

The recurrent nature of panic attacks can be viewed as an exclusion criterion, but it can as easily be considered an integral part of the syndrome, especially if one adopts a position that a person who had one panic attack but is severely impaired and a person who is mildly impaired but has frequent panic attacks should both qualify for the diagnosis. Since the DSM requirement of "at least two unexpected panic attacks" seems arbitrary, we would analyze recurrence as one of the criteria. Specifically, we propose to operationalize recurrence as a simple frequency measure, the history of unexpected panic attacks (i.e., 1, 2, 3).

In terms of the other criteria, each of the three components of worry— worry about panic likelihood, worry about panic-related consequences, and behavior change associated with panic-related worry—can be operationalized as separate indicators. However, this operationalization might be a bit tricky.

One can either measure the highest severity of the worry symptoms or measure how long they were present. We think that level of severity is more central to the definition and the measures should focus on it. The *DSM* requires worry to be present at least for one month; we recommend obtaining severity ratings for the month when the patient's worry was at its worst. However, the one month requirement is arbitrary; one can test it using CCK methodology by assessing how long each symptom was present and then deriving temporal cutoffs empirically. A different question is whether worry length has any diagnostic validity to begin with. This question can be examined with CCK if worry length is operationalized as a separate indicator; that is, three indicators are severity of worry symptoms during the worst month and the fourth indicator is the length of time while at least one worry symptom was present. Another option is to combine length and severity in one measure, for example, by calculating the burden of worry; for example, the amount of time the person has been extremely disabled by panic-related worry.

More can be said about considerations involved in the operationalization of worry symptoms, but further discussion goes beyond the scope of this chapter. In the end, the investigator will have four indicators of the panic disorder syndrome (number of unexpected panic attacks and severity ratings for the three worry component), which is more than enough for CCK analyses. If panic disorder is in fact taxonic, the analyses will tell us what combinations of criteria are sufficient for the diagnosis. Perhaps the *DSM*'s demarcation of two unexpected panic attacks plus one worry symptom will be supported by the data, but the investigator might find that a larger number of panic attacks or presence of two worry symptoms define taxon membership better.

It is important to mention that a researcher might want to relax certain exclusion criteria to test various structural hypotheses, such as the one that panic disorder is only associated with unexpected panic attacks. Specifically, the investigator can test this hypothesis by creating two samples, one that requires unexpectedness of panic attacks and one that does not, and then performing separate CCK analyses in each sample. These tests can inform us about etiology of the disorder. However, other well-known methods, such as construct validation—for example, contrasting profiles of various groups on theoretically important variables to determine whether and how these groups are different—can also do the job.

Example 3: Is Bipolar I Disorder, Single Manic Episode (296.0x) a Taxon?

Bipolar I Disorder, Single Episode (296.0x) is one of many *DSM–IV* diagnoses for which the taxonic status cannot be directly tested (American Psychiatric Association, 1994). The problem lies with the structure of the 296.0x diagnosis. Unlike the definition of panic disorder, 296.0x lacks a unique syndromal component. This diagnosis has one inclusion criterion, history of a manic episode, and several exclusion criteria. As explained in the previous section, exclusion criteria should not be included in taxometric analyses. Moreover, the only inclusion criterion for 296.0x is shared by several *DSM* entities—various Bipolar I diagnoses. Thus, taxometrics cannot be applied to the 296.0x diagnosis itself, but taxometric procedures can be used to validate the categorical status of the disorder indirectly. One can follow a procedure alluded to in the previous section. First, the investigator needs to select a sample of patients using exclusion criteria for 296.0x as filters. Then the researcher can apply CCK methods to the manic episode criteria in this restricted sample. This is really a test of the taxonicity of a manic episode, but because of the particular sample selection procedure, it can also validate 296.0x. Thus, evaluation of this particular diagnosis boils down to the question regarding the taxonicity of manic criteria for the particular subgroup of individuals filtered through the exclusion criteria.

The exclusion criteria for Bipolar I Disorder, single Manic Episode (ME; 296.0x) are (a) history of a major depressive episode and (b) a single manic episode that is not better accounted for by another disorder, such as schizoaffective disorder or delusional disorder. The first criterion is straightforward; the investigator can simply exclude patients with a history of a major depressive episode (defined by *DSM* or *DSM*-based taxometric studies). The second criterion is trickier because in order to identify subjects whose mania is due to other conditions, we need to know what mania is, and we don't have a satisfactory definition of a manic episode at this point. There are a few ways to handle this issue (listed from most to least stringent). The researcher can simply exclude all patients who have potentially confounding disorders (e.g., schizoaffective disorder). Another option is to focus on patients with clinically significant manic symptoms, which might or might not meet criteria for a ME, and exclude patients whose symptoms are accounted for by other disorders. The last option is to do the same for patients with full ME, either defined by the *DSM* or derived with CCK procedures in an unrestricted, general patient sample.

How would one test the taxonicity of ME (in a general or restricted sample)? According to the *DSM*, a manic episode is defined as:

A. Distinct period of abnormally and persistently elevated, expansive, or irritable mood lasting at least one week (or any duration if the person is hospitalized).

B. Three or more of the following symptoms must be significant during the episode:
 (1) grandiosity
 (2) decreased sleep
 (3) pressured speech
 (4) racing thoughts
 (5) distractibility

(6) increased goal-directed behavior

(7) excess in pleasurable activities with probable adverse consequences

C. The episode must cause marked impairment.

D. In addition, the mood disturbance is not due to a substance or general medical condition.

The standard exclusion criteria, not due to a substance or general medical condition, can be handled using sample selection filters as were described in the Panic Disorder section. The disability criterion can be considered either inclusionary (i.e., a part of the syndrome) or exclusionary. As there is no established objective cutoff for what constitutes marked impairment, it might be beneficial to consider the disability criterion as a part of the syndrome and let the CCK analyses identify the best cutoff. The drawback of this approach is that it might allow a person to be a taxon member without being significantly impaired. It is important to remember that elevation on all indicators is often unnecessary for taxon membership. On the other hand, the problem with treating the disability criterion as exclusionary is that there is no objective impairment cutoff that can be used in sample selection. Until such a cutoff is derived, investigators will have to choose between two evils: assigning some well-functioning cases to the taxon group, or tolerating a certain level of arbitrariness in the definition of the taxon. We leave this choice to the readers. It is worth noting that in either case one needs to use a psychometrically sound measure of impairment. For example, the Sheehan Disability Scale (Sheehan, 1983) is a commonly used scale for assessing the level of impairment created by psychiatric symptoms. Disability scales like this one are more reliable than dichotomous clinician ratings (significantly impaired versus not) and hence they should be incorporated in taxometric investigations.

Criterion A (distinct period of abnormal mood) is an inclusion criterion, but it has primacy over other components of the syndrome—symptoms listed in Criterion B—and as explained in the previous section, it should not be thrown in the analyses with other symptoms. An additional complicating factor is that there is an arbitrary length requirement (episode duration of at least one week) built into this criterion. We propose dealing with Criterion A in the following manner. Criterion A is not used explicitly in the analyses; instead, subjects are asked to recall the most severe episode of elevated or expansive mood they experienced, and the presence of Criterion B symptoms during that episode is assessed. The episode length requirement seems to be ignored here, but consider that the purpose of this requirement is to ensure the episode's severity, and severity is represented with the impairment criterion. Moreover, if the manic episode taxon is identified, it is easy to determine, using standard psychometric techniques or CCK, whether the episode length requirement is diagnostically useful and how it can best be operationalized. Another option is to accept the DSM definition of Criterion A and treat it as an exclusion criterion; that is, include only subjects who report at least a week of elated mood or who were hospitalized because of it.

Finally, each Criterion B symptom (e.g., grandiosity, decreased sleep, etc.) can be assessed and analyzed using CCK procedures. Considerations regarding this stage of investigation were described in detail in the section on narcissistic personality disorder. Several outcomes are possible in this investigation. If CCK fails to identify a taxon in both general and restricted samples, the current conceptualization of manic episode would be considered questionable. We would have to start conceptualizing mania as a continuum, or design a new definition of manic episode and test it for taxonicity. If the taxon is detected in the general sample but not in the restricted sample, the validity of the 296.0x diagnosis is undermined. This pattern of findings suggests that manic episode is a categorical syndrome, but 296.0x is not an actual disorder. In other words, the exclusion criteria of 296.0x "threw the baby out with the bathwater" and excluded etiological components responsible for the taxonicity of mania. This is a rather strong and potentially highly informative conclusion, but before asserting it, the investigator needs to consider methodological artifacts as alternative explanations. For example, perhaps the base rate of the taxon was too high in the restricted sample. Finally, if the taxon is identified in the restricted sample, the categorical view of 296.0x diagnosis is validated. It is important to note that this finding increases our confidence in conceptualizing 296.0x as a disorder, but only studies of the underlying etiology and pathology of mania can resolve this issue definitively.

It is important to note that many diagnoses, especially mood disorder diagnoses, also include specifiers. For example, clinical status and features of the recent episode (296.0x) can be further described in the *DSM* with specifiers such as mild, moderate, severe without psychotic features, severe with psychotic features, with catatonic features, and with postpartum onset. Taxometrics can test the validity of this system by examining whether the disorder can be further divided into small taxa that correspond to the specifiers. As the goal of these analyses is to distinguish various forms of one disorder, it is best to restrict the sample to patients with 296.0x diagnosis or members of 296.0x taxon (assuming it has been identified). However, depending on the taxometric method used, non-manic individuals can be included as well. A critical question is whether we have enough cases in each subtaxon for good parameter estimates. If there is enough power to detect the subtaxa (see chap. 3 for recommended N), CCK methods are appropriate for these analyses when the definition of the specifier can be broken down into enough components to operationalize the subtaxon with the number of indicators required for the planned CCK analysis (three or more, but two are acceptable). CCK techniques will validate specifiers by performing separate analyses for each of them. Mixture Modeling may be an appropriate method as well. However, Latent Class Analysis seems to be the best choice. In fact, LCA has been used in a number of subtype analyses already (e.g., Fossati et al., 2001; Kessler, Stein, & Berglund, 1998; Sullivan, Prescott, & Kendler, 2002). This is due in part to the fact that LCA works well with dichotomous indicators, and most specifiers are scored dichotomously. It is important to note that CCK procedures have a disadvantage in subtype analyses. They cannot model the presence of more than two groups, and thus it is safer to use CCK methods in samples that do not include non-manic individuals—otherwise the procedures might pick up on the manic versus non-manic distinction rather than distinguish a specific type of manic individuals from other forms of mania. Another way to approach these analyses is to use the procedure that we described for 296.0x diagnosis: select a restricted sample of cases using a specifier as an exclusion criterion, perform CCK analyses, and use the previously outlined logic to interpret the results.

We want to make a final point regarding the use of historic (lifetime) and current data. Earlier, we outlined procedures that rely on historic data, for example, by asking about the worst month of panic-related worry, or worst manic episode, or history of panic attacks. We recommend this approach mostly for pragmatic reasons; taxometric analyses require large samples, and it is easier to obtain them under a lifetime framework. However, there are certain problems with retrospective reports. Memory for details of past events deteriorates rapidly (Robinson & Clore, 2002); recall can become untrustworthy within one week after the event. There is evidence that specific ratings required for diagnostic assessment are not reliable when based on retrospective reports. For example, the stability of lifetime obsessive–compulsive disorder diagnosis in the Epidemiological Catchment Area study was very poor (kappa of .18) at the one year retest, presumably due to the unreliability of retrospective reports (Nelson & Rice, 1997). For this reason, we recommend focusing taxometric assessments on current symptoms, that is, if a sufficient number of taxon members can be expected in the data—the number of subjects qualifying for the current diagnosis can serve as a rough guide.

We hope these examples make another important idea apparent. The DSM should be evaluated from the bottom up, starting with basic syndromes such as panic attacks or manic episodes and working up toward complicated disorders. Syndromes are building blocks of the DSM diagnoses, and there are considerably fewer syndromes than there are disorders. Evaluation of syndromes seems to be a logical place to start.

IMPEDIMENTS TO CONDUCTING TAXOMETRICS ANALYSES ON DSM-DEFINED ENTITIES

In this section, we briefly reiterate some impediments to conducting taxometric analyses specifically directed at DSM entities, as well as propose solutions for dealing with these difficulties.

Data Derived From Structured Diagnostic Interviews

There are a number of problems associated with these data. First, most existing data from these interviews are not dimensional—diagnostic criteria are assessed categorically (present, absent)—structured diagnostic interviews are the most typical means of assessing disorder criteria. Moreover, structured diagnostic interviews often contain instructions to skip sections that are deemed irrelevant. For example, in the Structured Clinical Interview for the DSM (First, Spitzer, Gibbon, & Williams, 1994), patients not meeting certain "necessary" criteria do not receive the remainder of the interview for that particular diagnosis.

Possible solutions: modify existing diagnostic assessment instruments so criteria are assessed more dimensionally (no sxs, mild sxs, mod sxs, clinically signif sxs, severe sxs), plus assess for every diagnostic criterion; use those taxometric procedures that can adequately deal with categorical data.

Large Patient Samples Are Needed for Taxometric Analyses

It is not easy to obtain measures on hundreds of patients. This is particularly an issue when investigating more specific subgroups, such as those we discussed for the mood disorders. Conceivably, the taxonicity of 296.40 with seasonal pattern can be tested separately from 296.40 with rapid cycling, but of course, these analyses would require access to extremely large samples.

Possible solution: "enrichment" strategies in which 50 or so likely candidates are collected and paired with 250 unlikely candidates. Another option would be to establish multi-site trials.

Some Diagnoses Do Not Lend Themselves to Taxometric Analyses

There are some diagnoses that are too diverse and are likely to include multiple taxa. Consider some of the exclusionary criteria we have discussed. In many cases, these criteria are also used to specify diagnoses such as anxiety disorder, mood disorder, and psychotic disorder due to a general medical condition or due to a substance. In the case of a disorder due to a general medical condition, the disturbance is the direct physiological consequence of a medical condition. In the case of anxiety disturbances that are included in this diagnosis, examples include pheochromocytoma, hyperthyroidism, hyperadrenocorticism and a number of other diseases, each of which could be considered a taxon. One can argue that these conditions are etiologically different, but on the descriptive level, they share the same syndrome. There are other diagnoses with which it would be difficult to come up with the kinds of indicators needed for taxometrics. For example, shared psychotic disorder (297.3) specifies that a delusion is developed in the context of a close relationship with another person who already has a similar delusion. Thus, we need to appreciate that taxometric procedures may be limited or inappropriate for certain diagnostic entities.

5

TAXOMETRIC STUDIES OF PSYCHOPATHOLOGY: WHERE ARE THE TAXA?

Once the toothpaste is out of the tube, it's hard to get it back in!
—H. R. Haldeman

The primary purpose of the final two chapters is to give the reader a sense of how well taxonicity of various forms of psychopathology has been explored, what conclusions can be drawn from this literature, and whether the evidence supports the taxonic conjecture or not. In chapter 5, we review areas of psychopathology that are sufficiently studied to draw conclusions about their taxonic status. In chapter 6, we discuss taxometric research in areas that are not sufficiently understood to allow firm conclusions.

Our review will focus on studies applying Coherent Cut Kinetics (CCK) methodology to psychopathological constructs that were published between 1990 and mid-2003. A few substantive taxometric studies were published before 1990, but these were excluded from the review because they tended to use older methodologies and discussing them may prove to be more confusing than helpful. Moreover, almost all of the earlier findings have been replicated with newer CCK procedures. A number of methodological papers have been written about taxometrics over the years, and we reference many of them in chapter 3, but a detailed review of the methodological literature is beyond the scope of this book. We refer readers interested in a more comprehensive overview of taxometric literature to a recent, excellent review by Haslam and Kim (2002).

ESTABLISHED AREAS OF TAXOMETRIC RESEARCH

Three psychopathology domains have been the focus of numerous taxometric investigations: schizotypy, dissociation, and psychopathy. In the following sections, studies in these areas are critiqued.

Schizotypy

Schizotypy is a relatively narrow area of psychopathology, but it has received more attention from taxometricians than any other domain in the field. This is not surprising, as Meehl started developing CCK procedures with the explicit goal of testing his theory of schizophrenia (Meehl, 1962, 1990). According to this theory, a single gene, termed *schizogene*, is responsible for the development of schizophrenia. It is further postulated that the schizogene does not have complete penetrance; that is, having the gene is necessary but not sufficient for the development of schizophrenia, and a large proportion of gene carriers (90%, according to the theory) will never suffer from psychosis. However, almost all of the gene carriers have a certain personality type: schizotypy. The idea behind taxometric investigations of schizotypy is that the identification of a schizotypy taxon will allow us to identify gene carriers, which should aid genetic and preventive research. Originally, Meehl (1962) conceptualized schizotypy as having four primary features, the most important of which are cognitive slippage (mild form of positive schizophrenic symptoms, such as unusual perceptions and magical beliefs) and anhedonia (mild form of negative schizophrenic symptoms, such as not enjoying social interactions). Two decades later, the concept of schizotypy was also recognized by the *DSM* (starting with *DSM–III*; American Psychiatric Association, 1994), which operationalized it as schizotypal personality disorder. The definition of schizotypal personality disorder includes cognitive slippage and social anhedonia, as well as other features such as odd speech and odd behavior. It is important to recognize that schizotypy and schizotypal personality disorder are overlapping but distinct constructs. Unfortunately, some researchers use these broader constructs while they actually measure only a subset of their defining features (e.g., only cognitive slippage), and this led to some confusion in this literature.

The best-known measures of schizotypy are the product of long-standing research by Jean and Loren Chapman on psychosis-proneness. Inspired by Meehl's theory, they developed two measures of cognitive slippage: a 34-item Perceptual Aberration Scale (PAS; Chapman, Chapman, & Raulin, 1978) and a 30-item Magical Ideation Scale (MIS; Eckblad & Chapman,

1983). They also developed two measures of anhedonia: a 61-item Physical Anhedonia Scale (PhA; Chapman, Chapman, & Raulin, 1976) and a 40-item Revised Social Anhedonia Scale (RSAS; Eckblad, Chapman, Chapman, & Mishlove, 1982). All four measures utilize a true or false format. The PAS, the MIS, and the RSAS assess features of schizotypy that are also included in the definition of schizotypal personality disorder, while physical anhedonia is not an explicit part of the DSM criteria. With this in mind, let us review schizotypy literature.

Tyrka et al. (1995) performed perhaps the most rigorous investigation of the schizotypy taxon. They analyzed data obtained from 207 offspring of schizophrenic mothers (high risk group) and 104 matched offspring of normal controls (low risk group). The children were assessed in 1962 when they were about 15 years old. The data were collected in the form of teacher reports or psychiatric interviews. The participants were rated on a variety of items. Items that did not discriminate high and low risk groups were dropped and the remainder were aggregated in ten dichotomous composite variables. This set of variables taps all facets of schizotypal personality disorder, although it is noticeably different from the DSM criteria. The authors also had data on the diagnostic status of the participants when they were approximately 39 years of age and nearly out of the risk period for developing schizophrenia.

The study primarily relied on Golden's procedure (a variant of latent class analysis described in chap. 3; Golden, 1982) to evaluate the taxonicity of the construct. This method was somewhat popular in the 1980s but has not been used much since that time, so relatively little is known about the accuracy and robustness of the technique. However, Golden's procedure has several attractive features, such as the ability to analyze dichotomous indicators. This procedure also has a variety of consistency tests—many more than what is available with SSMAXCOV, which is the other option for analyzing dichotomous data. Tyrka et al. (1995) tested their set of variables against three consistency hurdles and selected only the indicators that passed all of them.

First, all but one indicator were summed to create an overall composite scale, with the remaining variable used as the target. Next, some level of the scale was selected (e.g., three on this 10-point composite) and the average difference on the *target indicator* was calculated between cases that fell below the selected level (scores zero, one, and two) and the remaining cases (scores three through ten). The magnitude of this difference gives a rough approximation of item discrimination, which is a parameter commonly used in item response theory (IRT). The difference between the above and below groups was calculated for each level of the scale. An indicator was deemed acceptable if it produced a difference of at least .10 at each level of the composite; in other words, if it had good discrimination (was informative) at each level of the construct.

The authors reviewed the results of this procedure and selected items that showed the highest discrimination in approximately the same region of

the composite scale (in IRT terms, this means that they have similar difficulty values—difficulty is another IRT parameter). Items that did not meet
this criterion were dropped. After this, the indicator validities were estimated.
Golden and Meehl (1979) derived formulas that allow for estimation of indicator validity from false-positive and true-positive rates, and these rates were
estimated for each indicator. The false-positive rate was defined as the percentage of individuals in the lower quartile of the composite scale who scored
positively on the indicator, and the true-positive rate was the percentage of
individuals in the upper quartile scoring positively. Indicators with low estimated validity were dropped. Due to lack of research, it is difficult to com-
ment on the soundness of this indicator selection procedure, but we can at
least conclude that the last test should probably be modified when a low base
rate taxon is expected.

As a result of this protocol, four indicators were dropped because in
each case, they did not pass the first consistency test, that is, failed to discriminate adequately at all levels of the scale. Next, Tyrka et al. (1995) calculated the taxon base rate for each indicator using a hybrid of MAXCOV
and Latent Class Analysis estimation procedures (for details see Golden, 1982)
and adjusted the estimate for the true- and false-positive rates computed earlier. The average taxon base rate was .49. The authors did not report a variability statistic, but a simple computation shows that SD of base rate estimates was .04.

Knowing the base rate estimate, true-positive rate, and false-positive
rate for each indicator is sufficient to calculate Bayesian taxon membership
probabilities. This is what Tyrka et al. (1995) did and found a clearly U-
shaped distribution. The authors defined taxon members as cases with a Bayesian probability of .90 or above and found that 39% of the sample could be
classified as taxon members according to this rule. The authors defined
nontaxon members as cases with a Bayesian probability of .10 or below and
used these two groups (taxon and nontaxon members) to estimate the level
of misclassification in their diagnostic scheme. This parameter is often referred to as *implied misclassification*. Tyrka et al. took all nontaxon cases, calculated their average probability of taxon membership and multiplied this
probability by the number of nontaxon cases. The resulting value is the implied number of taxon members misclassified as nontaxon cases. Next, the
authors took all of the taxon cases, calculated their average probability of
taxon membership, subtracted it from one, and multiplied this value by the
number of taxon cases. This value is the implied number of nontaxon members misclassified as taxon cases. This procedure is a straightforward quality
check on group assignment. It is logically appealing, but to our knowledge, it
has not been tested against an external criterion (e.g., known taxon membership in Monte Carlo simulations). Although the implied misclassification
test has been used for many years (e.g., Golden, 1982), its utility is still
unknown. Tyrka et al. found that the total implied misclassification rate of

their diagnostic procedure was 20%. However, the actual rate is definitely higher, since the most troublesome probability regions (.10 – .90) were excluded.

The authors also estimated indicator validities, which they defined as the proportion of cases classified as taxon members scoring positively on an indicator. This time, however, taxon membership was defined as a Bayesian probability of .50 or higher. The average validity was .83, but it is difficult to evaluate this value as the authors used a nonstandard approach to estimating indicator validity. We note that the inconsistent use of cutoffs for classification of taxon members employed in this investigation is confusing and hardly justifiable. We recommend using a single cutoff (e.g., .50) for all analyses.

Finally, Tyrka et al. (1995) performed an SSMAXCOV analysis and plotted the overall SSMAXCOV curve derived from the average of 15 subanalyses with various parings of the six indicators. Averaging was done without standardizing the input variable. The plot had a clear central peak but the highest covariance was only .035 (below the .05 cutoff), which somewhat undermined the strength of this finding. SSMAXCOV allows for estimation of taxon base rates for each subanalysis, which can serve as an internal consistency test (variability of individual base rate estimates) and as an external consistency test (as comparison to Golden's base rate), but unfortunately SSMAXCOV base rates were not reported.

The authors examined the validity of their taxon by relating it to external measures of genetic liability. Compared to low-risk participants, they found that a much higher percentage of high-risk participants were taxon members (58% vs. 28%). Also, of the 48 individuals who developed schizophrenia or schizophrenia spectrum disorder by the end of the follow-up period, 73% were taxon members, which is significantly higher than the 48% expected by chance. Importantly, taxon members were not found to be at increased risk for other mental disorders. Combining predefined groups in one analysis (e.g., high and low risk group) is potentially problematic because this method can lead to spurious evidence of taxonicity, with taxonic results simply reflecting a selection factor. However, this is not likely to be the case in this study, since the taxon did not clearly map onto one of the groups.

These results suggest that the taxon is overinclusive: It includes 28% of low-risk participants—instead of the 10% predicted by Meehl's theory—and misses some cases that later become symptomatic. This might mean that the identified taxon is not isomorphic with specific genetic liability for schizophrenia and reflects a construct that is overlapping, but not identical to, the genetic risk factor. Another explanation is that the *DSM* criteria for schizophrenia and spectrum conditions may be too broad. Tyrka et al. (1995) proposed this hypothesis and estimated that at least two-thirds of the misses (symptomatic cases not assigned to the taxon) can be accounted for by errors in the taxon classification scheme, but the remaining misses are due to overinclusiveness of the *DSM*. Overall, this is an ambitious and methodologically sophisticated study. A particular strength of this study is external validation of the taxon, which produced interesting results. On the other hand, the reliance on nonstandard techniques is a significant limitation.

While Tyrka et al. (1995) examined carefully selected samples assessed on a range of behavioral indicators, most taxometric studies of schizotypy use student samples and self-report measures. In the first of this series of studies, Lenzenweger and Korfine (1992) evaluated a sample of 1,093 college freshmen. All participants were administered the PAS, which taps the core feature of cognitive slippage, and an infrequency scale, which measures deviant or careless responding. Participants who scored high on the infrequency scale were dropped from the sample. The authors selected the eight PAS items that correlated most highly with the rest of the scale and that were not highly intercorrelated or redundant. This is a reasonable strategy, but it is inferior to Golden's item selection procedure because the approach used by Lenzenweger and Korfine does not necessarily select items that are informative (have high discrimination) at the level of the construct. In other words, items with high item-total correlations could be useful at the middle range of the construct, but these same items could be uninformative at the extreme end, and hence may fail to identify a taxon if it has a low base rate.

Lenzenweger and Korfine used SSMAXCOV, which produced 28 individual plots and an average plot (calculated without standardizing the input). A smoothed curve was then created by applying Tukey's procedure (1977) to the average plot. The authors used both average smoothed and unsmoothed curves to obtain taxon base rate estimates, which were .088 and .096, respectively. The average plots are generally consistent with the taxonic conjecture, although the unsmoothed curve is so variable that it is hard to be sure whether it is really taxonic. Unfortunately, the graphs exhibit right-end cusps rather than complete peaks. The problem with cusps is that the true hitmax may be much further to the right than the observed crest, which means that the true base rate of the identified taxon can be anywhere between .097 and zero. Moreover, Lenzenweger and Korfine did not report their MRIN; therefore, it is possible that there were too few cases in the hitmax interval for reliable cusp detection and reliable estimation of hitmax covariance, and the base rate estimate depends on these.

Unfortunately, no consistency tests were reported in this study. Furthermore, instead of reporting the 28 individual base rate estimates, the authors reported an overall base rate estimate for each item, averaging over analyses in which the item was an output variable. This can be somewhat confusing because MAXCOV base rate estimates are associated with the input variable, not the output variable. The reason for this is MAXCOV base rate estimation is tied with locating the hitmax on the input indicator so that each base rate estimate is attached to a certain input indicator. This, however, does not work for SSMAXCOV, because the input variable is not an indicator but a composite of many indicators.

To get an idea of the internal consistency of the analysis, we computed the variability of these eight averaged base rate estimates and found them to be somewhat inconsistent (SD = .10). It is difficult to interpret the meaning of this value, as it does not reflect the consistency of individual estimates. However, we expect the variability of individual estimates to be greater than the variability of the averages. Bayesian probabilities, indicator validities, and nuisance correlations were not estimated, which is a limitation of relying on SSMAXCOV. The taxon's construct validity was not examined either, and it would have been very difficult to do so without computing Bayesian probabilities.

In a replication study, Korfine and Lenzenweger (1995) analyzed the same eight PAS items in a representative sample of 1,646 freshmen. The methodology of the replication study was identical to the initial report. The unsmoothed SSMAXCOV plot was again highly variable. The MRIN was not reported, but the authors reported that covariance could not be calculated in the hitmax interval for 13 of 28 subanalyses (making them unusable), either because there was only one case in the interval or because there was no variation in output variables, which also suggests a very low interval n. The taxon base rate was much lower in this sample (.034 for the unsmoothed and .032 for the smoothed curves). The discrepancy between the two studies is surprising given the similarities in the populations and selection procedures. In the second sample, we find that endorsement frequencies for the eight items were substantially lower, suggesting that there were fewer schizotypes in that sample. The level of variability across the Korfine and Lenzenweger studies adds to the uncertainty about the true prevalence of the schizotypy taxon in the undergraduate population.

Korfine and Lenzenweger also conducted a taxometric analysis of feminity to compare with the schizotypy analysis, because feminity was hypothesized to be nontaxonic. The authors selected eight items from the Bem Sex Role Inventory (Bem, 1974), scored on a seven-point scale, dichotomized them, and used SSMAXCOV. The resulting average curve was clearly flat even without smoothing. This failure to find a taxon in the feminity data suggests that the taxonicity evidenced when using the PAS is not simply an artifact of SSMAXCOV.

Of course, even this comparison cannot fully alleviate concerns associated with dichotomous data, so Lenzenweger (1999) decided to replicate the taxonic findings using MAXCOV. A new sample of 430 undergraduates was administered three measures of cognitive slippage: the PAS, the MIS, and a 34-item Referential Thinking Scale (REF; Lenzenweger, Bennett, & Lilenfeld, 1997), which taps cognitive slippage in conjunction with paranoid thinking, as well as an infrequence scale—to ensure valid responding.

Lenzenweger (1999) performed MAXCOV using the three scales as taxon indicators. He used an interval size of .50 SD and MRIN of 15. Two of the plots showed clear peaks, and one produced a cusp. The one incomplete peak was probably a consequence of the interval size being set too high, which allowed for only seven intervals on the input variable. A lower interval size would have produced a finer gradation and probably allowed the cusp to turn into a full peak. However, this may not have been possible due to the modest size of the sample. The base rates estimates were .11, .22, and .13. The author did not report a base rate consistency test, but one can easily calculate the SD of the three estimates to be .06, which is somewhat high but probably acceptable.

Bayesian probabilities were calculated and exhibited a U-shaped pattern. Cases with a probability of .90 or higher (eight percent of the sample) were assigned to the taxon group and the remaining cases were assigned to the nontaxon group. This dichotomous taxon membership was then related to a self-report measure of paranoid schizophrenia (Pz) and was found to correlate .43 with it (Cohen's $d = 1.62$). On the other hand, the median correlation between the three continuous taxon indicators and Pz was .63. Although this finding provides some convergent validity for taxon membership, it is unclear what we should make of this pattern of correlations. The author claimed that the correlation between taxon membership and Pz was not entirely due to the association between taxon indicators and Pz. However, this claim was not supported statistically. One could evaluate this proposition by testing whether the relation between taxon membership and Pz remains significant after the three taxon indicators are controlled for. No further validation or consistency tests were performed, and indicator validities and nuisance correlations were not reported.

These findings were also replicated by Meyer and Keller (2001) in a large sample of young German adults ($N = 809$) from vocational schools and industrial organizations. This sample is probably more representative of the general population than are college undergraduates, although the response rate in the Meyer and Keller study was lower than the response rate in the Lenzenweger and Korfine (1992) studies (65% vs. 84%). The participants were administered three measures of schizotypy, the PAS, the MIS, and a brief version of the PhA. Each scale was analyzed independently using SSMAXCOV. Following common practice, the authors selected eight items with the highest corrected item-total correlation for each measure. They did not screen the indicators for overlapping content or high inter-item correlations, and some of the selected items were rather redundant (e.g., "I have often found walks to be relaxing and enjoyable" and "After a busy day, a slow walk has often felt relaxing" were both included).

The average SSMAXCOV curve for the PhA had a clear complete peak with the highest covariance of .04; the MIS curve was flat with the highest covariance under .03; and the PAS curve had two equal peaks with the highest covariances of about .06. The latter shape can be interpreted as lacking a clear reliable peak and thus is consistent with nontaxonic conjecture. However, the authors thought that the pattern was ambiguous rather than nontaxonic and applied Golden's consistency tests to the eight PAS indicators to clarify the situation. Two indicators failed the consistency tests and were dropped. The average covariance curve of the resulting six items had a single complete peak. This post hoc approach has limited appeal; a sounder approach is to apply Golden's consistency tests to each of the three sets of items. The base rates of PhA and PAS taxa were .13 and .11, respectively. No further analyses were reported.

In summary, a cognitive slippage taxon has been identified in a number of studies and it appears to be a fairly reliable phenomenon. The fact that the taxon has been studied and identified across different populations and cultures is a significant accomplishment attesting to the robustness of this taxon. This line of research is still developing and it is too early to draw firm conclusions. Researchers have started addressing limitations of the initial studies in recent, more sophisticated investigations (e.g., Lenzenweger, 1999), but a definitive study has not been conducted. Two important issues need to be addressed. First, it remains to be seen whether the taxon can pass all of the epistemological hurdles of taxometrics. Second, no one has conducted a comprehensive assessment of the taxon's construct validity.

Unlike cognitive slippage, anhedonia has received relatively little attention from taxometricians. The only taxometric study in this area, with the exception of the Meyer and Keller (2001) analysis of the PhA, is an evaluation of social anhedonia conducted by Blanchard, Gangestad, Brown, and Horan (2000). The authors administered the RSAS to 1,526 undergraduates recruited from various psychology courses. Blanchard et al. wanted to use MAXCOV rather than SSMAXCOV. To obtain sufficiently long indicators, they conducted a principal component analysis of the RSAS, which identified four factors. The resulting four scales were fairly short (ranging from six to nine levels) and not very reliable (alphas ranging from .57 to .70). Factor or principal component analysis is probably the best way to prepare this type of data for taxometric analyses, but in this particular case, the procedure had limited utility because the pool of items was relatively small and the items were dichotomous.

The authors used an MRIN of 25 and generally set the interval length to be equivalent to each raw score. To ensure that there were enough cases in the most extreme interval, they had to combine a few extreme intervals into one. For example, on a six-point indicator there could have been 500 cases at level 0, 400 cases at level 1, 350 cases at level 2, 250 cases at level 3, 20 cases at level 4, and six cases at level 5. Then the authors assigned cases from levels 0, 1, 2, and 3 to the corresponding four intervals, but assigned cases from levels 4 and 5 to the same interval, thus placing 26 cases in the fifth interval. This combining of extreme intervals might seem questionable, because it distorts the original scoring scheme. The RSAS, as well as the majority of self-report measures, is best conceptualized as an ordinal scale and the combining procedure does not distort the essential properties of ordinal data. The procedure, however, does lead to some loss of information (e.g., the distinction between individuals who scored 4 and 5), but this is necessary to ensure the reliability of MAXCOV in this instance. In general, this sort of procedure appears to be reasonable, but given the lack of data, we recommend caution in using it.

Despite increasing the usable range of the indicators, the MAXCOV plots yielded cusps rather than complete peaks. The estimated base rates were .085 for unsmoothed and .083 for smoothed plots. The range of estimates was small (.02). However, this is likely to be an underestimate because it is based on four estimates derived from four aggregated plots averaged over three subanalyses with the same input indicator. This atypical presentation makes the findings difficult to interpret.

Blanchard et al. (2000) also corrected the base rate estimate for nuisance correlations using General Covariance Mixture Theorem, which lowered the taxon base rate to .054 for unsmoothed and .043 for smoothed curves. However, as the plots did not peak completely, even corrected estimates only provide an upper boundary estimate of the true base rate. We note that this is one of the few studies that adjusted base rate estimates for nuisance correlations. Base rate adjustment appears to be a sound practice, although it has not been tested in simulation studies. To approximate nuisance correlations, the authors used correlations in the lowest and highest intervals of an indicator, as estimates of nontaxon and taxon nuisance correlations respectively. We note that the adjustment for nuisance correlation was thoroughly discussed by Meehl (1995b), but he did not completely delineate one step of the procedure—estimation of nuisance correlations. As discussed in chapter 3, there is no adequate method for an a priori estimation of nuisance correlations, although estimation based on groups derived from Bayesian probabilities seems to be most accepted. In this study, nuisance correlations were probably overestimated in the taxon and underestimated in the nontaxon groups.

The authors estimated indicator validities using both methods described in chapter 3 (separation of the groups and covariance at the hitmax) and used their average as the final estimate. Validities corrected for the presence of nuisance correlations ranged from 1.07 to 2.02 SD (mean = 1.4 SD). Interestingly, the two methods varied considerably. Blanchard et al. also computed Bayesian probabilities and found them to be clearly U-shaped. Finally, the authors conducted a MAXEIG analysis to serve as a consistency test of MAXCOV. The number of windows was varied from 5 to 450. MAXEIG produced taxonic plots, although only one of them showed a complete peak. The other three curves had peaks, but these peaks were obscured by highly elevated cusps. The authors did not report base rates estimated by MAXEIG, but the shapes of the graphs suggested that the estimates were very low. It seems likely that in each of the three cusping MAXEIG plots, a genuine peak was overshadowed by an extremely high right end, which was probably driven by indicator skew.

Blanchard et al. did not investigate the validity of the taxon, but they examined the factor structure of the data and found that removing taxon members from the sample did not change the factor structure, although the interfactor correlations dropped from about .37 to .17. This dramatic decrease in the correlations seems to be consistent with the taxonic conjecture, but to our knowledge this issue has not been previously discussed in the literature, so it is difficult to adequately evaluate this finding.

Overall, the Blanchard et al. study provided fairly strong evidence in support of the RSAS taxon. However, it does not tell us whether the RSAS taxon is a schizotypy taxon or a distinct entity, perhaps a form of extreme introversion (e.g., schizoid personality disorder). The second possibility seems likely given that RSAS and PAB correlate only modestly in the general population (Chapman, Chapman, & Kwapil, 1995). This possibility can be examined by assessing both social anhedonia and cognitive slippage taxa in the same sample. If the two taxa reflect the same phenomenon—schizotypy—almost all members of one taxon should also be members of another taxon. We are more likely to find, however, that the two taxa overlap more than expected by chance, but not completely. Such a pattern may suggest that two independent but related entities were identified. On the other hand, this pattern is also consistent with Meehl's most recent model of schizotypy (2001) wherein cognitive slippage is the central feature of schizotypy and social anhedonia is a secondary feature that is continuously distributed. According to this model, social anhedonia shows taxonicity because it is "dragged along" by the primary feature—it correlates with cognitive slippage. This model can be evaluated by dropping members of the cognitive slippage taxon from the sample before conducting a taxometric analysis of social anhedonia. If Meehl is right, CCK analyses should fail to find a social anhedonia taxon after the cases are dropped.

Taxometric investigations of various personality traits associated with schizotypy (cognitive slippage, anhedonia, and a subset of schizotypal personality disorder criteria) show evidence of taxonicity, but they do not definitively answer the key question as to whether a single dominant gene is responsible for schizophrenia. Detection of a schizotypy taxon is consistent with both the polygenic multifactorial threshold model (Gottesman, 1991), as well as Meehl's single dominant gene model. In other words, the observed qualitative break might reflect a threshold effect or presence of a single gene. This issue cannot be answered by taxometric analyses of self-report questionnaires. Now that the taxon has been identified, other types of research (e.g., behavior genetics) are required to help determine its nature. Also, additional taxometric studies are needed to refine the assessment of the schizotypy taxon, but researchers should keep in mind that the examination of descriptive features (symptoms and personality traits) is not likely to advance this area much further. Taxometric studies of schizotypy should include measures of pathology and determine what types of pathology are responsible for taxonicity.

Dissociation

Dissociation is the core feature of the dissociative disorders; it is defined by the *DSM–IV* as "a disruption in the usually integrated functions of consciousness, memory, identity, or perception of the environment" (American Psychiatric Association, 1994, p. 477). Dissociation is usually assessed as a continuum, most often using the Dissociative Experiences Scale (DES; Bernstein-Carlson & Putnam, 1986), a 28-item self-report measure. The DES items are rated on a scale reflecting the frequency of dissociative experiences (0-to-100% in 10% intervals). Factor analyses of DES items have led to the development of three subscales (Carlson et al., 1993; Frischholz, Braun, Sachs, & Schwartz, 1991; Ross, Joshi, & Currie, 1991). They are (a) Absorption, which reflects dissociation from surroundings (e.g., daydreaming); (b) Amnesia, which reflects dissociation from past experiences; and (c) Depersonalization–Derealization, which reflects dissociation from the body or senses.

Waller, Putnam, and Carlson (1996) conducted the first taxometric study of dissociation using DES items in a combined sample of 228 individuals diagnosed with multiple personality disorder and 228 normal controls. The authors used a mixed sample because CCK analyses work best when the taxon base rate is close to .50, and as the majority of individuals with multiple personality disorder are expected to be members of the putative taxon, this mixed sample should have a taxon base rate of about .50. Waller et al. screened the DES items with MAMBAC to select items that showed evidence of taxonicity. MAMBAC analysis of all possible pairs of 28 items is unwieldy since it would generate 756 plots. To ease computations, only items that loaded on one of the three subscales were selected (18 out of the 28) and these items were only paired with items from other subscales. This procedure reduced the number of plots to 216. The authors did not pair items that came from the same subscale to avoid high nuisance correlations, as these items share subscale-specific variance. Apparently, Waller et al. assumed that subscale-specific variance is continuous in nature and can only obstruct the taxonicity of the general dissociation construct. An alternative view is that some forms of dissociation are taxonic (e.g., depersonalization) while other forms are not (e.g., absorption). Within-subscale analyses allow for a direct test of this hypothesis, but the authors chose to evaluate it indirectly. They scored MAMBAC plots on a three-point scale (−1 = *clearly nontaxonic*, 0 = *ambiguous*, 1 = *clearly taxonic*) and selected items that had a score of seven or above (that is, an item had to receive at least 75% of the highest possible score for it to be selected). Seven items passed this criterion: three were Amnesia items and four were Depersonalization items.

On this basis, Waller et al. (1996) concluded that Absorption is a non-pathological form of dissociation, while Amnesia and Depersonalization tap into pathological dissociation. This inference is perhaps too strong given the available data and should be investigated further using within-subscale analyses. Also, consider that the Absorption items are less skewed in the general population relative to the Amnesia and Depersonalization items. For low base rate taxa, such as pathological dissociation in the general population, indicator validity is associated with skew. A skewed indicator is not necessarily valid, but a valid indicator is likely to be highly skewed. Following this logic, perhaps absorption is actually taxonic but the DES does not have valid markers of pathological absorption because it includes normal-range, rather than extreme, items. This possibility casts additional doubt on the statement that Absorption is generally nonpathological.

The authors combined the seven selected items into a new scale that they called the DES-T (T for taxon). Since 10 DES items were not yet examined for taxonicity, further MAMBAC analyses were performed so each of the remaining 10 items was paired with the DES-T. One item, concerning alterations in identity, had a sufficiently high rating and was added to the DES-T. Hence, the final version of the DES-T included eight items and only these items were used in further taxometric analyses.

MAMBAC analyses of the DES-T items yielded 57 base rate estimates. The average of these estimates was .33, but no variability indexes were reported. Waller et al. also performed MAXSLOPE, but instead of using individual items, they created two mini-scales, each with four randomly selected nonoverlapping items. Two hundred nonredundant pairs of mini-scales were generated, and all were subjected to MAXSLOPE, thus producing 200 semi-independent taxon base rate estimates. The average of MAXSLOPE estimates was .37, and half the estimates fell in the .28–.40 interval, which corresponds to an SD of about .09, suggesting that variability was fairly high but probably acceptable. An SSMAXCOV was performed as well. The input was standardized before averaging covariances. The average smoothed curve had a clear peak (highest covariance of .11). Instead of computing the taxon base rate by solving General Covariance Mixture Theorem (GCMT) equations in each interval, the authors approximated the base rate by assigning all participants who fell in the hitmax interval or above to the taxon, which yielded a taxon base rate of .37. In sum, the three CCK procedures produced similar base rate estimates, and the dissociation taxon cleared the most stringent taxometric hurdle.

The Waller et al. taxonic results do not appear to reflect a sample selection factor. If the findings resulted from combining predefined groups (individuals with multiple personality disorder and nonclinical controls), base rate estimates should have been about .50. The .37 taxon base rate suggests that not all individuals diagnosed with multiple personality disorder experience the pathological form of dissociation and are probably misdiagnosed. Waller et al. also conducted MAXCOV analyses of individual DES-T items, which yielded 168 subanalyses. The resulting Bayesian probabilities were clearly U-shaped, and the authors assigned cases with the probability of .50 or above to the taxon. Unfortunately, no other MAXCOV findings were reported, although it would have been useful to examine the consistency between MAXCOV and the other three procedures. Apparently, MAXCOV was done only to supplement SSMAXCOV in calculating Bayesian probabilities, as they cannot be obtained with SSMAXCOV.

The authors also examined the validity of the taxon by comparing scores of different diagnostic groups. However, they did not use Bayesian probabilities and examined the validity of the DES-T instead. This choice may be puzzling at first, but this method is more likely to be robust across various samples due to the fact that Bayesian probabilities and DES-T scores offer two ways of scoring the same responses. The DES-T score is a simple sum of an equally weighted response, whereas Bayesian probabilities are scored by dichotomizing and weighting responses. Item cutoffs and item weights are likely to vary considerably between populations, thus the Bayesian scoring scheme derived in one sample may be inappropriate for a different sample. Simple scoring rules such as the one used in computing DES-T scores, on the other hand, are likely to be appropriate across samples. This issue has not been examined in the taxometric literature, but investigations of other scoring techniques suggest that simple summation is generally preferable to complicated weighting schemes (e.g., Fabrigar, Wegener, MacCallum, & Strahan, 1999).

The sample used to derive the taxon was a part of a much larger data set ($N = 1,574$) that included 11 diagnostic groups. The groups were sufficiently large for reliable comparisons (smallest $n = 61$). Waller et al. examined the average score for each group on the DES-T and compared it to the DES. Seven groups had low scores on the DES-T: nonclinical adults, nonclinical college-aged people, patients with neurological disorders, anxiety disorders, mood disorders, less common psychiatric disorders, and eating disorders (in the order of elevation from lowest to the highest). Patients with schizophrenia had moderate scores, patients with PTSD and patients with dissociative disorder NOS (not otherwise specified) had high scores, and patients diagnosed with multiple personality disorder had very high scores. This pattern of elevations is almost identical to the one produced by the DES. There were a few differences between the two measures, however. Scores on the DES-T were much lower relative to the DES for all groups other than multiple personality disorder, and the DES-T variance increased for dissociative disorder NOS and MPD and decreased for the other groups. These findings suggest that the DES-T is a purer and more informative measure of pathological dissociation than the DES. If researchers inspired by Waller et al. want to study the dissociation taxon without conducting their own independent analyses, their best bet is to use the DES-T; this is the reason it is important to examine the construct validity of this measure.

In many respects, the Waller et al. study is an exemplary taxometric report. The authors used multiple taxometric techniques and examined the construct validity of the taxon. However, three issues were not clarified in the report. First, only base rate estimates were reported and there was no discussion about shapes of the plots, so it is unclear how many of them were taxonic. Also, only one type of consistency test—cross-method consistency—was reported in the study; although the different procedures were consistent with each other, it is difficult to determine the strength of each individual piece of evidence. Second, mini-scales were used for MAXSLOPE but not for the other analyses. The authors indicated that they created mini-scales because individual items are not very reliable. However, it is unclear why this would not also have been beneficial to the MAMBAC and MAXCOV analyses. Third, nuisance correlations and indicator validities were not computed. It is thus unclear how well the data conforms to CCK requirements, and how much we can trust the estimates. Moreover, this information could have been useful in assembling the DES-T.

Waller and Ross (1997) followed up the initial study with a taxometric examination of dissociation in an epidemiological sample of community-dwelling adults. The sample was recruited from the greater metropolitan area of Winnipeg, Manitoba, in Canada. The response rate was 69%, which is a bit low, but the sample appears to be representative of the Winnipeg population. In this study, the DES items were scored on a 21-point scale (in 5% increments).

MAXCOV analysis of the eight DES-T items yielded 168 base rate estimates with the median value of .055. The variance of base rate estimates was not reported quantitatively, but a histogram revealed that most estimates clustered between 0 and .10 with a few outliers, some of which are as high as .40. The authors noted that some of the items had similar content, so they rationally grouped three amnesia items and two depersonalization items in two parcels. Waller and Ross did a MAXCOV analysis using the two parcels and the three remaining items as indicators. This analysis yielded 30 base rate estimates with a median of .045 and only a few outliers. Unfortunately, interval size and MRIN were not reported for either analysis, and nothing was mentioned about the shapes of the curves. It is worth noting that parceling is a sound practice. It can reduce nuisance correlations and increase reliability of indicators, though, if possible, it is best to parcel all items, rather than use a mix of parcels and individual items.

Waller and Ross also conducted MAXEIG analyses in this study. MAXEIG plots were consistent with the taxonic conjecture and showed clear peaks. However, only one of eight sets of plots was reported. Moreover, no MAXEIG base rate estimates or variabilities were reported. The overall result, unfortunately, was a less informative set of MAXEIG analyses.

Next, Bayesian probabilities were computed and these produced a clear U-shaped pattern. The authors assigned cases with the probability of .90 or above to the taxon, and found that 35 individuals were identified as taxon members by these rules, that is, the prevalence of this taxon was 3.3%. Note that the .50 cutoff is generally associated with the lowest overall rate of misclassification, but the .90 cutoff may be preferable under certain conditions. In epidemiological studies, however, accuracy—a low rate of misclassification—is the primary consideration. In fact, the actual prevalence of the taxon in the Waller and Ross study appears to be about 5% based on the non-Bayesian base rate estimates. Thus, it appears that the use of a conservative cutoff in this study may produce somewhat misleading findings.

The authors now had a reasonable program for scoring Bayesian taxon membership, so they decided to revisit the full data set reported by Waller et al. (1996) and examined the construct validity of the taxon by applying the program to those data. The program classified 8% of patients with schizophrenia and 18% of patients with posttraumatic stress disorder as taxon members, which is much greater than 3.3% expected by chance. The overlap probably would have been much larger if the .50 cutoff was used. These findings suggest that some schizophrenia and posttraumatic stress disorder diagnoses may have been misdiagnosed. Alternatively, the findings indicate a link between these disorders and pathological dissociation.

The authors also evaluated the performance of various DES-T and DES cutoffs for detecting taxon members defined by Bayesian probabilities. Waller and Ross found that DES-T cutoffs work much better than the cutoffs on the DES because they have higher sensitivity, specificity, and positive and negative predictive values. One could say that the authors stacked the deck in favor of the DES-T, as the Bayesian probabilities and DES-T scores are based on the same data. However, this redundancy is unavoidable, since there is no other method of assessing taxon membership. It is important to evaluate the qualities of DES-T cutoffs for studies that will use the DES-T, rather than the Bayesian scoring scheme.

Deriving a scheme for scoring Bayesian probabilities in the general population opens many new opportunities. A general population scheme can be used in various samples without having to derive new scoring every time. Consider that each individual is a member of the general population, and thus can be classified according to the rule developed for this population. Deriving a Bayesian scoring scheme is analogous to norming a measure, and following this analogy, general population "norms" are produced for assessing the probability of taxon membership.

These norms, of course, are not ideal. First, the Winnipeg sample may not be representative of the general population of the United States. Second, the sample size is too small to provide adequate general population norms. The reliability of estimates that the scoring scheme is derived from (e.g., taxon base rate, indicator validities) depends on the number of taxon members in the sample. With only 35 taxon members, we cannot consider these estimates to be accurate, and consequently the scoring scheme itself cannot be considered very trustworthy. Finally, there is an issue of norm relevance. Although all Americans are members of the general U.S. population, and national norms apply to every resident to some extent, each American is also a member of smaller, more specific population(s)—based on factors such as ethnicity, age, and religion—and norms of these subpopulations may be more relevant than the general norms. This is the reason the Minnesota Multiphasic Personality Inventory (MMPI; Tellegen, Ben-Porath, McNulty, Arbisi, & Graham, 2003) has separate norms for men and women, and the Wechsler Adult Intelligence Scale (WAIS; Wechsler, 1997) has separate norms for different ages. In fact, Waller and Ross do not recommend using a fixed cut-off on the DES-T or the DES for the identification of pathological dissociation, because the position of the best cutoff depends on a variety of factors, such as prevalence of taxon members in a given subpopulation. Bayesian scoring programs rely on cutoffs, and the same reasoning applies to them. Perhaps over time schemes for scoring pathological dissociation will be derived for various subpopulations, but this is not yet the case. Despite its limitations, development of this scoring scheme is an advancement, and we encourage researchers to use it with the cautions indicated here (the scoring scheme is given in the appendix of Waller & Ross, 1997). Another reasonable option is to use the DES-T and define taxon members as cases that fall above a certain threshold (presumably derived in a taxometric study of the target population). This approach may be particularly appealing given the limitations of the current scoring program.

Waller and Ross further advanced our knowledge of the construct validity of the dissociation taxon by examining its biometric structure. They administered the DES to a sample of 280 MZ twins and 148 DZ twins. The participants were adolescents (mean age just above 15 years). The authors estimated genetic, shared environmental and unique environmental variances for the DES-T and Bayesian probabilities. The two sets of results were similar; shared environment contributed substantially (about 0.40) to the scores, in contrast to the complete absence of genetic contribution. This pattern is consistent with the view that pathological dissociation is primarily due to processes occurring in the family environment, such as abusive parenting (Putnam, 1989). The findings are particularly striking given that few personality and psychopathology variables have considerable shared environmental variance (Plomin, DeFries, McClearn, & Rutter, 1997).

These are exciting findings, but there are some concerns about their validity. In the biometric analysis, taxon membership was operationalized with continuous measures, which are arguably inferior to dichotomous taxon membership (dichotomized Bayesian probabilities). This is because continuous measures are probably somewhat contaminated by the dimensional variance associated with the construct, whereas dichotomous taxon membership is the purest measure of the taxonic variance available. Also, in practice, taxonic status is most likely to be operationalized as a simple member–nonmember dichotomy rather than a continuous measure. Apparently, the authors could not use dichotomous taxon membership because there were too few taxon members in the twin sample. Another concern is that the current Bayesian scoring scheme may be inappropriate for adolescents. There are notable differences in the reported levels of dissociation between adolescent samples and the general population (Ross, 1996). Moreover, the Winnipeg sample did not include any individuals under 18 years of age as they were not a part of the target population. In summary, the existing Bayesian scoring scheme cannot be considered appropriate for adolescents. This means that the Bayesian probabilities used in computing the biometric structure may have been biased, perhaps to a substantial degree.

Another challenge of the biometric findings comes from examining the taxon's stability (Watson, 2003). Watson examined the stability of the taxon over a three month interval in a sample of undergraduates ($N = 465$) and found that the DES-T was significantly less stable than measures of personality. For example, the stability of Neuroticism in this study was $r = .83$, while the stability of the DES-T was only $r = .62$. Bayesian membership had even lower stability ($r = .32$), and the dichotomously scored taxon was unstable ($r = .29$). The lack of stability raises a question about whether the dissociation taxon is really a product of early traumatic events. In fact, these data imply that the taxon reflects a qualitatively distinct but transient dissociative reaction, rather than a stable pathological experience.

Let us examine how this interpretation fits with the biometric data. If the taxon simply reflects a transient reaction, it does not necessarily have to show strong associations with stable predispositions, such as inherited characteristics. However, it should covary with the presence of dissociation-provoking stressors, and adverse family environment is perhaps one of them. This account may or may not be able to explain the seeming inconsistency between the stability and biometric data. The issue needs to be explored in future studies, but it certainly highlights the importance of a thorough construct validation for newly discovered taxa.

Only two taxometric analyses of dissociation have been published to date and both came from the same research group. These studies are among the most rigorous taxometric investigations conducted. In fact, the identification of the dissociation taxon has had more impact on nontaxometricians than the detection of any other taxon. To date, the DES-T and the Bayesian scoring program have been used in a number of nontaxometric studies (e.g., Allen, Fultz, Huntoon, & Brethour, 2002; Leavitt, 1999; Seedat, Stein, & Forde, 2003; Waldo & Merritt, 2000). The success of this work can likely be attributed to the use of diverse taxometric techniques, which left little question regarding the existence of the taxon, and to the development and validation of a classification procedure.

However, two important issues remain in this literature. First, there is a question about the reliability of estimated taxon parameters. Both taxometric studies relied on individual items as taxon indicators, and single items tend to have low reliability. Moreover, in Waller and Ross (1997), items were rated on a 21-point scale, which may have further decreased reliability by taxing the respondents' capacity to make meaningful distinctions (see Clark & Watson, 1995). In addition, the number of taxon members in the Waller and Ross (1997) sample was low, leaving considerable room for sampling error. Second, construct validation of the taxon is far from complete as evidenced by questions raised by recent findings regarding taxon instability (Watson, 2003).

Psychopathy

Psychopathy is a personality type associated with persistent criminality. It includes a number of features first systematically described by Cleckley (1941). Although terms such as *psychopath* or *psychopathic personality type* are frequently used in the literature, the underlying assumption is that psychopathy is a continuous construct (Harris, Rice, & Quinsey, 1994). The Psychopathy Checklist–Revised (PCL-R; Hare, 1991) is the most widely used measure of psychopathy. The PCL-R is continuous and reflects the extent to which an individual matches the prototypic psychopath as described by Cleckley. The measure is composed of 20 items scored on a three-point scale (0 = *absent*, 1 = *some indication that the feature is present*, 2 = *present*) with a range of scores from 0 through 40. The PCL-R is usually administered in the form of an interview, but it can also be scored from detailed clinical files. A score of 30 is considered a cutoff for a psychopathic personality, but it was not derived from quantitative analyses and reflects pragmatic convenience, rather than the categorical conceptualization of the construct.

Factor analyses of the PCL-R (e.g., Hare, 1991) identified two underlying factors: interpersonal–affective (Factor 1, including such traits as "callous") and antisocial behavior (Factor 2, e.g., "juvenile delinquency"). The interpersonal–affective features are generally considered to be central to the construct (e.g., Harpur, Hart, & Hare, 1994). It is important to note that a similar construct is included in the *DSM*—antisocial personality disorder— but it is defined primarily in behavioral terms and does not match many of the nonbehavioral aspects of Cleckley's description. Moreover, both constructs overlap substantially with the concept of criminality, but they are not isomorphic with it. An individual can be a psychopath and can still be successful and without a criminal record.

Harris, Rice, and Quinsey (1994) were the first researchers to examine the taxonic structure of psychopathy. The motivation for this study was not based on a theoretical model. Instead, the study had a pragmatic basis and was focused on investigating the common practice of dichotomizing psychopathy (e.g., using 30 cutoff on the PCL-R). In other words, this was an exploratory study, conducted primarily to inform the existing assessment practice. Participants in the study included 653 male offenders; 365 of them were treated at the research site and 288 were assessed at the site but were not treated there. A variety of variables including the PCL-R were coded from each participant's file. One additional variable—criminal recidivism—was scored from data obtained from other institutions. Some variables were categorical while others were continuous, but the authors dichotomized all of them for the taxometric analyses (for the PCL-R, only the clear presence of a feature counted). This was not altogether necessary, as taxometric analyses such as SSMAXCOV can be performed with trichotomous and polichotomous data, and in fact these types of data are preferred to dichotomous data (A. M. Ruscio & Ruscio, 2002).

First, the authors examined the distribution of total PCL-R scores using special probability graph paper (Harding, 1949). This method is a predecessor to mixture modeling; it allows for estimation of taxon base rate, means, and standard deviations of latent distributions. The procedure suggested the presence of two latent distributions, with the hitmax at the PCL-R total score of 18. Harding's method is appropriate conceptually and simple computationally, but it became obsolete with the advent of powerful computers. On the other hand, there is no reason to believe that it was grossly inaccurate in this study.

To perform SSMAXCOV, Harris et al. selected the eight PCL-R items that correlated most highly with the total score. No efforts were made to reduce nuisance correlations or ensure adequate coverage of the construct. SSMAXCOV analyses were apparently done without specifying MRIN or standardizing inputs. The SSMAXCOV curve was clearly taxonic, with the highest covariance of over .12. The plot was not smoothed, since the "raw" average plot was already clear. SSMAXCOV analyses were also performed with Factor 1 items and then with Factor 2 items. The SSMAXCOV curve for Factor 1 was flat (although the highest covariance was .08) and the plot for Factor 2 had a distinct peak. This is somewhat surprising especially given that the initial set of eight items included two Factor 1 items. The nontaxonic finding may mean that the affective–interpersonal features of psychopathy do not define a taxon. An alternative explanation is that an affective–interpersonal taxon exists, but Factor 1 items are not sufficiently valid and fail to identify it. The authors did not evaluate these two accounts. SSMAXCOV was also applied to eight adult antisocial history variables (e.g., violent offense history, escape from an institution) and eight childhood history variables (e.g., childhood aggression, parental alcoholism). Unfortunately, the authors did not report how they selected these items. The adult history curve was clearly flat and the childhood history graph was clearly taxonic, although the highest covariance was only .04, which is slightly below the cutoff. The childhood variables were labeled Childhood and Adolescent

Taxon Scale (CATS) and were later used in other studies. This finding suggests that the nature of criminal behavior changes across the life span: in childhood it is reflective of latent taxonicity, but it primarily taps continuous variance in adults. This conclusion is somewhat at odds with the finding that Factor 2 of the PCL-R (antisocial behavior) is taxonic. Perhaps the inconsistency reflects a disconnection between criminality and behavioral manifestations of psychopathy.

The authors also applied two consistency test variants of Golden's procedure to the 20 PCL-R items. The first procedure eliminated one item, and the second eliminated an additional 11 items—eight items passed all of the consistency tests. Bayesian probabilities were computed for both analyses and were clearly U-shaped. Cases with a probability of .10 or below were assigned to the nontaxon group and cases with a probability of .90 or above were assigned to the taxon group. On the PCL-R, the taxon had a mean of 24.2 with SD = 6.1, and the nontaxon had a mean of 10.1 with SD = 6.3. Validities and nuisance correlations were not estimated for individual items, but the study statistics suggest that the validity of the PCL-R as a whole was about 2.3 SD in this sample, which is very good. This value, however, is an overestimate because some cases (with Bayesian probability between .10 and .90) were dropped from the analyses, which artificially increased the separation between groups and decreased the variability within groups.

The two variants of Golden's procedures essentially identified the same individuals, yielding a classification accuracy—agreement between two dichotomized Bayesian probabilities—of 90%. In one sense this is not surprising, as the two methods are very similar. On the other hand, the classifications were based on overlapping but distinct sets of data. Thus, the high level of agreement between them is notable. This result, however, was weakened by the findings that the application of Golden's procedure (without consistency tests due to small number of items) to Factor 1 items, and to the adult criminal history variables, also yielded U-shaped distributions. This inconsistency between SSMAXCOV and the U-shaped test may be attributable to the weakness of the latter method, which was discussed in chapter 3. There was also substantial agreement between the two classifications described above and classification based on CATS (65% agreement). The level of agreement is fairly high, and it is unclear whether this overlap should be interpreted as indicating that CATS and the PCL-R tap the same latent category or whether we have two semi-independent taxa.

Harris et al. also tested the taxonic conjecture by examining one of the logical consequences of taxonicity, a prediction that taxon membership should emerge as the first unrotated component in principal component analysis (Meehl, 1992). The idea behind this corollary is that in the absence of nuisance correlations, all observed correlations between indicators are due to latent taxon membership. Furthermore, the purpose of a principal component analysis is to reduce the observed correlations to a smaller set of factors and reveal the latent origins of the correlations. If the data are taxonic, taxon membership should emerge as the main factor (first unrotated component). This logic is sound, but it only works when nuisance correlations are low. If the influence of nuisance correlations rivals the impact of taxon membership, the first component may be reflective of continuous variance associated with the measures (e.g., shared content, a response bias), while taxon membership would emerge as a subsequent component (second, or third, and so on). However, if the conditions are right, indicator loadings on the first unrotated component should be approximately equal to correlations between indicators and group membership. This is exactly what the authors found for both variants of Golden's procedure. The mean difference between loadings and correlations were very small (about .07) and the rank-order of loadings and correlations was very similar (correlation between sets of about .94). Due to a lack of research, it is difficult to say how informative this test really is, but it appears to lend additional support to the taxonic conjecture.

Harris et al. also employed a less-known CCK procedure, which Meehl and Yonce (1996) named SQUABAC, but the authors referred to as the Parabolic Function Method. Two SQUABAC analyses were performed, one with the PCL-R total score as the input variable and criminal recidivism as the output variable, and another with adult criminal history and recidivism as input and output variables, respectively. Recidivism history was paired with the two potential taxon indicators because it is a conceptually related but distinct variable. It is expected to be a valid indicator of the taxon, but it is not redundant with other indicators, thus nuisance correlations should not be a problem.

The PCL-R analysis yielded a clear parabolic shape with the minimum around a total score of 19. The adult criminal history analysis produced a uniformly increasing curve, which is inconsistent with the existence of a high base rate taxon. Once again, adult criminal history failed to show evidence of taxonicity, while psychopathy did. To ensure that the taxonic results were not due to the presence of a schizotypy or psychotic taxon, the authors removed all cases that met criteria for a diagnosis of a psychotic disorder ($N = 192$) and repeated the SQUABAC analyses. The pattern of findings did not change.

Finally, the base rate estimates were consistent across these four methods (two variants of Golden's procedure, SSMAXCOV and SQUABAC), ranging between .44 and .46. Unfortunately, no indexes of internal (within-method) consistency were reported, so it is difficult to determine the strength of each individual piece of evidence. Also, all methods consistently indicated that the hitmax in this sample, and hence the cutoff with the lowest overall rate of misclassification, was between the PCL-R total scores of 18 and 20, which is considerably lower than the conventional cutoff of 30. The implications of this finding remain to be explored. One concern regarding the accuracy of the cutoff is that it was derived with dichotomous PCL-R items. Further studies should attempt to derive the empirical cutoff using the standard three-point scoring scheme in large representative samples.

Findings of Harris et al. were replicated in a follow-up study by Skilling, Harris, Rice, and Quinsey (2002). Skilling et al. used the same indicators and essentially the same sample ($N = 684$, overlap with the Harris et al. sample was greater than 80%), but applied somewhat different taxometric procedures. Also, Skilling et al. evaluated the latent structure of antisocial personality disorder and conduct disorder, which were not examined in the previous study. Antisocial personality disorder criteria were coded from the files. Of the seven criteria, one symptom was impossible to code from the existing data and three symptoms were coded from PCL-R items. The authors faced a challenge of operationalizing Criterion B (history of conduct disorder). This is a necessary criterion and thus is different from other symptoms of antisocial personality disorder. In chapter 4, we recommend operationalizing such criteria as screeners. The authors instead chose to use Criterion B in their analyses as one of the indicators (without any "special privileges") and it did not change their findings.

Skilling et al. performed SSMAXCOV on six coded antisocial personality disorder symptoms, eight PCL-R items (the item selection procedure was not described), and the CATS items. The input was not standardized and MRIN was not specified. The resulting three average unsmoothed curves were clearly taxonic, but base rate estimates and their variability were not reported. Next, the authors performed MAMBAC analyses on three indicators of antisocial personality, the sum of CATS items, the sum of antisocial personality disorder symptoms, and the sum of CD symptoms (15 items). The resulting six MAMBAC plots were taxonic: four had clear peaks and two had pronounced right-end cusps. The report did not specify why CD was not examined with SSMAXCOV and PCL-R was not examined with MAMBAC. Skilling et al. also computed a Goodness of Fit Index (GFI) for antisocial personality disorder and CATS—the report did not specify how it was done—and it was found to be acceptably high (GFI = .93). Next, they used Golden's procedure with all of the consistency tests to compute Bayesian membership probabilities for antisocial personality disorder symptoms and PCL-R items. This resulted in a high level of agreement between the two classification procedures (kappa = .82).

It is unclear whether we should interpret this as evidence suggesting the existence of four semi-independent taxa (psychopathy, antisocial personality disorder, CATS, and conduct disorder), or one overarching antisocial personality taxon. This issue can be addressed by computing Bayesian probabilities for each taxon and examining the overlap between taxon memberships. Unfortunately, this comparison was conducted only for psychopathy and antisocial personality disorder, and a very high overlap between them suggests the presence of a single entity, although the agreement was probably inflated by the overlapping content of the two sets of items.

Skilling et al. interpreted their findings as suggesting the existence of a single taxon. They created a composite taxon membership variable in which a case received a positive score if it received a high Bayesian probability of being a taxon member according to both the PCL-R and the antisocial personality disorder symptoms. Next, the authors performed a forward regression that allowed them to identify 12 items from a joint set of PCL-R, CATS, antisocial personality disorder, and conduct disorder indicators that together were able to predict composite taxon membership with 98.4% accuracy. The resulting 12-item scale appears promising because it offers a simple and straightforward approximation of taxon membership. Unfortunately, the authors did not examine the psychometric properties and construct validity of this scale or of the identified taxon.

The Skilling et al. investigation advanced our knowledge of the psychopathy taxon, particularly in regard to the structure of antisocial personality disorder and conduct disorder, but the contribution of the study is limited because it was not independent from the Harris et al. report (1994). The first, largely independent replication of the psychopathy taxon was conducted by Skilling, Quinsey, and Craig (2001). Participants in this study were 1,111 boys in grades four through eight who were recruited from schools in a large urban area. The boys were assessed on a variety of self-report measures, but the battery did not include any instruments examined in the previous studies. Nevertheless, the authors reviewed the available measures and rationally selected items to match putative indicators of the psychopathy taxon. They were able to find matches for 7 out of 8 CATS items, 14 out of 15 conduct disorder symptoms, and 13 out of 18 PCL-YV (Youth Version) criteria. All data, including items matched to PCL-YV, were dichotomized. Reliabilities of the resulting indicators were a bit low, but probably acceptable (most of them had alphas in the .70–.80 range). Eight items with high item-whole correlations but modest inter-item correlations were selected from both the conduct disorder item set as well as the PCL-YV item set. Interestingly, five of the eight PCL-YV items were from Factor 1. To provide a comparison to analyses of psychopathy items, Skilling et al. also examined somatization, which they hypothesized to be continuous. Somatization was operationalized with eight self-report somatic complaints items from the Youth Self-Report (Achenbach, 1991).

SSMAXCOV analyses—performed without standardization of the input—of the selected conduct disorder, CATS, and PCL-YV items produced clearly peaked curves, although the highest covariances of these plots were between .03 and .04, which is below the threshold. Taxon base rate estimates and their variability were not reported. The somatic complaints graph had a peak (highest covariance of .04), but this peak was obscured by a right-end cusp. The authors took this as evidence of the dimensional structure of somatization. On the other hand, if the cusp was removed, one would probably conclude that the picture is taxonic. Furthermore, it is possible that the cusp was due to the high unreliability of covariance estimates in the most extreme interval, which resulted from the small number of cases that were allocated there. This issue is impossible to evaluate, since MRIN was not reported.

MAMBAC was performed on the total scores of the three sets of items. All the plots were consistent with the taxonic conjecture. These plots can be contrasted with two MAMBAC plots generated by combining the conduct disorder scale and somatic complaints scale. These two plots showed a right-end cusp, but they were clearly different in shape from the six "antisocial" plots, and the cusp was probably due to the high skew of the indicators. The GFI between PCL-YV and CATS items was acceptably high (.95). Finally, Skilling et al. performed Golden's procedure without consistency tests and found remarkably consistent base rate estimates. The average estimate was .08 for conduct disorder items (range .07 to .09), .10 for PCL-YV items (range .08 to .12), and .10 for CATS items (range .08 to .09). Moreover, the three methods were very consistent in identifying taxon members (96% agreement). This cross-measure consistency is truly remarkable and lends strong support for the existence of a single psychopathy taxon. Unfortunately, indicator validities and nuisance correlations were not reported.

The consistency of different taxometric methods was not directly examined in the Skilling et al. (2001) study, but two studies of the psychopathy taxon in adults (described above) found high cross-method consistency. On the other hand, within-method consistency (e.g., base rate variability) was neglected in these investigations and should be reported in future studies. Another limitation of this literature is that all of these investigations were based on file review and matching items from available instruments. Future studies should test the taxonic conjecture with standard measures, such as structured diagnostic interviews, that are specifically selected for taxometric analyses. One puzzling finding in the literature is that Factor 1 of PCL-R shows taxonicity in some studies (Skilling et al., 2001), but not others (Harris et al., 1994). This is particularly puzzling given that affective and interpersonal features are considered central to the phenomenon. However, the negative finding may be a methodological artifact. Another issue is whether the various manifestations of psychopathy examined in these studies reflect one or several latent entities. Nonoverlapping assessments of these constructs and careful examination of the resulting taxon memberships are necessary to answer this question. Finally, the studies suggested that the cutoff for a diagnosis of conduct disorder (3 out of 15 symptoms) is too low, and the conventional PCL-R cutoff for psychopathy (30 out of 40) is too high. These cutoffs should be further evaluated and refined in large representative samples.

SUMMARY

In this chapter, we reviewed taxometric investigations of schizotypy, dissociation, and psychopathy, the psychopathology domains where taxometric research is becoming more established. Despite the fact that relatively few taxometric studies have been completed and that available studies often suffer from one or more weaknesses, it is possible to offer some remarks about the taxonic status of these three forms of psychopathology.

The studies consistently indicate that each of these domains is taxonic. The existence of schizotypy, dissociation, and psychopathy taxa can be considered reasonably well established; however, the level of understanding of these entities varies considerably. The psychopathy literature still has to resolve several methodological problems and determine how many distinct taxa are encompassed by this domain. The dissociation literature faces fewer methodological concerns; however, procedures for the identification of taxon members require refinement, and the construct validity of the taxon needs to be investigated further. These issues also need to be addressed in the schizotypy literature, but understanding of the schizotypy taxon is sufficiently advanced to create the need for studies that link the descriptive taxon to underlying pathological processes. None of these literatures should terminate with establishing the existence of a taxon. Taxometric procedures need to be integrated with other methods of psychopathology research.

6

TAXOMETRIC STUDIES OF PSYCHOPATHOLOGY: FUTURE DIRECTIONS

When you know a thing, to hold that you know it; and when you do not
know a thing, to allow that you do not know it—this is knowledge.
— Confucius, *The Confucian Analects*

In this final chapter, we examine four psychopathology domains that
have received limited attention from taxometricians: eating disorders, depression, anxiety, and personality disorders. Due perhaps to the novelty of
the research, these areas are highly controversial, with taxometric investigations yielding seemingly conflicting results. Thus, discussion of some of these
areas will be divided in two sections: one section that reviews evidence for
dimensionality and another that reviews evidence for taxonicity. The issue
of comorbidity is not limited to any particular domain of psychopathology, as
it applies to all mental disorders. It was recently proposed that taxometrics
can address the problem of comorbidity, and we briefly consider this
taxometric frontier at the end of the chapter.

EATING DISORDERS

The *DSM–IV* includes two primary eating disorder diagnoses: Anorexia Nervosa (AN) and Bulimia Nervosa (BN). The *DSM* also includes a

diagnosis of Eating Disorder Not Otherwise Specified (EDNOS), essentially a catchall category, as well as a provisional diagnosis of Binge Eating Disorder (BED) that is under consideration to be included as a formal diagnosis. The central features of BED include frequent binge eating *without* purging behaviors. Both AN and BN are characterized by a dramatic overconcern about weight and body shape that typically results in dietary restriction, eating binges, purging behaviors, and in the case of AN, significant weight loss. Many patients with AN will also receive a BN diagnosis at some point. Despite the severity of AN, it has received relatively little systematic study. BN is a more prevalent condition and has received greater empirical attention. Theoretical models of eating pathology tend to posit continuity (Drewnowski, Yee, Kurth, & Krahn, 1994; Polivy & Herman, 1987; Stice, Ziemba, Margolis, & Flick, 1996), though some have suggested a discontinuity between eating disorders and typical weight concerns (Bruch, 1973). Taxometric tests of this issue produced evidence supporting both categorical and continuous models, although evidence for taxonicity is stronger and we will review the taxonic findings first.

Evidence of Taxonicity

Gleaves, Lowe, Snow, Green, and Murphy-Eberenz (2000) completed the first taxometric study of eating disorders. This investigation was specifically focused on BN. A total of 613 women participated in the study; 201 were recruited from an eating disorders clinic and had a diagnosis of BN, and the remaining 412 were undergraduate students recruited from an introductory psychology course. Two of the more widely used self-report measures of eating disorders were administered to participants: (a) the Bulimia Test-Revised (BULIT-R; Thelen, Farmer, Wonderlich, & Smith, 1991), a 36-item measure of bulimic behaviors and attitudes rated on a five-point scale; and (b) the Eating Attitudes Test-26 (EAT-26; Garner, Olmsted, Bohr, & Garfinkel, 1982), a 26-item multidimensional measure of anorexic thoughts and behaviors rated on a four-point scale (although each EAT-26 item has six response options, they are scored 0, 0, 0, 1, 2, 3, thus resulting in a four-point scale). The indicators were not dichotomized, which most likely enhanced the reliability of the analyses.

The authors selected items for taxometric analyses in a three-step procedure. First, they chose items that discriminated the clinical from nonclinical group by at least 1.5 SD. Nine BULIT-R items and three EAT-26 items met this requirement. Second, the authors tested items for a high association with the BULIT-R total score. All twelve had correlations of .70 or higher. Finally, items with inter-item correlations of .50 or higher in the clinical group were aggregated to lower nuisance correlations. This reduced the indicator set to one four-item parcel, two two-item parcels, and two single items. To supplement this empirical indicator selection, Gleaves et al. (2000) also created a set of indicators based on purely conceptual considerations. It included four rationally derived parcels (each consisting of at least six items) that tap binge-eating, purging, restrictive behavior, and body dissatisfaction.

The first series of taxometric analyses was conducted in a mixed sample of clinical and nonclinical subjects ($N = 418$, 209 participants in each group). The clinical group included 201 women diagnosed with BN, as well as eight undergraduates who scored 104 or higher on the BULIT-R, which is an established cutoff for BN (Thelen et al., 1991). MAMBAC analyses yielded 20 plots for the empirical indicators and 12 graphs for the theoretical indicators. All the plots were rated as taxonic. SSMAXCOV yielded 10 (out of a possible 10) taxonic plots for the empirical indicators and five taxonic curves (the sixth plot was ambiguous) for the theoretical indicators. Each MAMBAC and SSMAXCOV graph was rated by two individuals on a three-point scale (nontaxonic, ambiguous, and taxonic) and the raters showed an overall 90.7% agreement (kappa = .67). MAMBAC's average base rate estimate was .51 (SD = .04) for the empirical and .49 (SD = .07) for the theoretical indicators. The average SSMAXCOV base rate was .47 (SD = .07) derived from individual plots for empirical and theoretical indicators. SSMAXCOV plots were smoothed and the input was standardized, but the MRIN and the interval size were not reported.

It is important to note that the base rate estimates were very close to .50, suggesting that the results could have simply reflected sample selection. One way to rule out this type of possibility is to compute Bayesian probabilities and show that not all taxon members come from the clinical group. Bayesian probabilities cannot be computed with SSMAXCOV, but MAXCOV can do it. The empirical indicators were probably too short for MAXCOV, but it may have worked with the theoretical indicators, as they are much longer. Unfortunately this analysis was not performed.

The authors decided to show instead that the taxon is not a product of sample selection by replicating the original finding in the pure college sample ($n = 412$). This sample partially overlapped with the mixed sample and included eight individuals who scored above the BULIT-R cutoff. SSMAXCOV analyses of empirical indicators produced seven graphs with complete peaks (albeit substantially shifted to the right) and three graphs with cusps. Base rate estimates for the cusping plots were not computed, as these estimates are not expected to be accurate. The mean taxon base rate estimate for the seven complete graphs was .27, but the estimates were highly variable (SD = .19). Also, we expect the true taxon base rate to be lower, as cusping is usually associated with base rates less than .10 and base rate estimates for those three plots were not included in the average. For the theoretical indicators, three SSMAXCOV plots were incomplete and three had peaks, with the average base rate of .26 (SD = .06) for the complete plots.

MAMBAC analysis of the empirical indicators produced taxonic curves in every case. The average taxon base rate estimate was .15, but the variability of these estimates was rather high (SD = .15), providing only weak evidence in support of the taxonic conjecture. MAMBAC analyses of the theoretical indicators produced 11 taxonic plots and one nontaxonic plot. The average base rate estimate for the 11 taxonic plots was .25 (SD = .08). However, the indicators had a high positive skew in this sample, which may have produced spurious, taxonic-looking plots.

To determine whether the skew was responsible for the taxonic findings, Gleaves et al. transformed the data using a square root or log transformation and were successful at reducing the skew of all but one indicator to less than 1.0. This is a fairly conservative test of the taxonic conjecture, because data transformation not only reduces indicator skew, but it can also reduce indicator validities, and hence produce a nontaxonic result. Yet, this did not happen in this study. All but one plot originally rated as taxonic were still rated as taxonic after the transformation. MAMBAC base rate estimates were .19 (SD = .18) for transformed empirical indicators, and .24 (SD = .06) for transformed theoretical indicators. Nevertheless, these estimates are probably not as reliable as the original estimates because of the possible reduction in validity, which is likely to lower the precision of the estimates.

In addition, the authors generated a continuous simulated data set. All data points were drawn from the same distribution that matched the transformed data set on distributional characteristics, indicator means, skew, kurtosis, and intercorrelations. MAMBAC analysis of this simulated data produced mostly nontaxonic plots; some had a right-end increase, but none were rated as unambiguously taxonic.

Overall, this study supports the existence of an eating disorder taxon. However, the evidence is not particularly strong. The consistency of the mixed-sample analyses is fairly high (acceptably low base rate variability), but the sample composition confounds the interpretation of these findings. To resolve this issue, the authors performed analyses in the student-only sample and found evidence of taxonicity, but some of these analyses were not consistent. Interestingly, the high base rate variability was mostly a problem for analyses using the empirical indicators, which consisted of only a few items and hence were probably less reliable than theoretical indicators. The observed inconsistency may be due to low reliability of the empirical indicators.

A larger issue with the student-only analyses is that the taxon base rate was much higher than expected. Base rate estimates were probably inflated, but even if the true base rate was as low as .10, it would be potentially inconsistent with the findings in the mixed sample. The base rate of about .50 in the mixed sample suggests that all individuals with BN diagnoses were members of the taxon and all students were not (except for the eight who scored above the cutoff). Thus, the taxon base rate in the student-only sample should be very small. There are two interpretations for this inconsistency: either there is no taxon, or some of the individuals with BN are not taxon members, they are misdiagnosed. In fact, for the two sets of analyses to be consistent, the rate of misdiagnoses should equal the taxon base rate in the student-only sample. This question can be addressed by relating Bayesian probabilities to the diagnostic status. This issue again highlights the need for construct validation of the taxon. At this point, we don't know anything about the nature of the identified entity and cannot say that it is definitely a BN taxon; it may reflect a more general eating pathology, or some other related dysfunction.

A study by Williamson et al. (2002) attempts to address validity issues by separately examining the taxonicity of DSM eating disorders. The sample was a mixture of nonclinical undergraduates ($n = 116$), obese individuals ($n = 24$), and individuals diagnosed with an eating disorder ($n = 190$). The clinical group was recruited from an outpatient eating disorder treatment program and included 45 individuals with BN, 35 individuals with AN, 43 individuals with BED, and 67 individuals with EDNOS. The participants were assessed with the Interview for the Diagnosis of Eating Disorders-IV (Kutlesic, Williamson, Gleaves, Barbin, & Murphy-Eberenz, 1998), which is a semi-structured interview of DSM–IV eating disorder symptoms. Each symptom is rated on a five-point scale. An exploratory factor analysis of the interview in the total sample yielded three factors: binge eating (seven items), compensatory behaviors–fear of fatness (six items), and drive for thinness (three items). These three factor scores were used as indicators in the taxometric analyses. The first two factors were fairly reliable (alpha = .95 and alpha = .81), but factor three was only marginally reliable (alpha = .67). The compensatory behaviors factor was moderately correlated with binge eating and drive for thinness, but the two were unrelated to each other. The fourth indicator was the body mass index calculated from the participant's body weight and height measured in the lab. Mean scores were computed for three of the diagnostic groups (BN, AN, BED) on the four indicators, which allowed the authors to identify combinations of three indicators that distinguished each group from the control group. BN was defined by indicators other than BMI, AN was defined by indicators other than binge eating, and BED was defined by indicators other than drive for thinness.

Taxometric analyses were performed in the full sample using all four indicators to test for the existence of a general eating disorder taxon. MAMBAC produced eight taxonic plots, two ambiguous plots, and two nontaxonic plots, and thus cleared the most conservative cutoff (for a discussion of cutoffs see chap. 3). MAXCOV yielded six taxonic plots, one ambiguous plot, and five nontaxonic plots, and thus barely cleared the most liberal cutoff. The mean MAXCOV base rate estimate was .55 (SD = .08), and the MAMBAC base rate estimate was not reported. MRIN, interval size, indicator validities, and nuisance correlations were not reported either. The prevalence of eating disorders in this sample was 58% and the estimated base rate came out suspiciously close to this value. Unfortunately, Bayesian probabilities were not computed. Instead, Williamson et al. repeated the analyses in the clinical sample (n = 190), as it is presumably "natural," that is, was not created by combining predefined groups. In the clinical sample, eight MAMBAC analyses were taxonic, two were ambiguous, and two were nontaxonic, thus passing the most stringent cutoff. Eight MAXCOV analyses were taxonic and four were nontaxonic, thus passing the middle-of-the-road 2:1 cutoff. These findings strengthen the case for the taxonicity of eating disorders. However, it is impossible to understand the meaning of these findings because no base rate information was reported.

The authors also conducted secondary analyses in three subsamples consisting of nonclinical controls and members of a target diagnostic group, in order to test the taxonic status of these groups. The selection of indicators varied, depending on the diagnostic group in question (the combinations are described above). The subsamples were rather small (n between 151 and 161), so the probability of erroneous results—particularly false rejections of taxonicity—was high and the findings should be interpreted with caution. In the BN sample, MAMBAC analysis produced six taxonic plots (out of a possible six); MAXCOV yielded one taxonic and one nontaxonic graph (out of a possible three); and the third indicator did not have enough cases in the extreme intervals to serve as an input variable. In the AN sample, both MAMBAC and MAXCOV produced an equal number of taxonic, ambiguous, and nontaxonic graphs. In the BED sample, all six MAMBAC plots were taxonic, and one MAXCOV plot was taxonic (the other two curves could not be computed). None of the analyses yielded clear nontaxonic results, but evidence for the AN taxon was least supportive of taxonicity. Small sample sizes and incomplete reporting of the analyses do not allow us to reach a strong conclusion. The possibility that these results were influenced by selection factors is an important concern, especially because base rate estimates were not reported and it cannot be determined how close they were to values expected to emerge from sample selection.

Despite its many limitations, this study is an admirable, rare attempt to directly test the taxonicity of DSM syndromes. Use of a diagnostic interview, patient populations, and psychometrically sound indicators derived with factor analysis are all strong features of this study. Moreover, operationalizations of the syndromes under study were validated against the diagnostic status of participants, although more validation is required. This investigation should be followed up with studies that are similar in design, but that employ larger samples and report results more comprehensively.

Evidence of Dimensionality

The studies reviewed above focused on constructs that closely relate to DSM syndromes. However, the field of eating disorders is more complex. For example, Tylka and Subich (2003) emphasized a distinction between behavioral or symptomatic indicators, such as binging and purging, and nonbehavioral or psychological markers, such as body dissatisfaction and pressure for thinness. Tylka and Subich have further suggested that most DSM eating disorder criteria are behavioral, although it may be important to examine nonbehavioral variables. The authors argued that the application of taxometric methods to indicators that relate strongly to symptoms of eating disorders would create criterion contamination. Criterion contamination arises when the predictor and the criterion are defined in such a way that they overlap conceptually and an association between the constructs is thus expected by definition. This problem can complicate interpretation of the findings; the question is whether the constructs would still be related if the definitions were not overlapping. Criterion contamination is an important concern in relational research, but it is largely irrelevant to taxometrics as the primary goal of taxometrics is to determine the latent structure of a given construct, rather than to relate two ostensibly different constructs.

The review of the literature by Tylka and Subich (2003) indicated that nontaxometric methods tend to support the existence of a continuum in nonbehavioral indicators and discontinuity in measures of symptomatology. Gleaves et al. (2000) and Williamson et al. (2002) supported the validity of the first observation using taxometric methods. Tylka and Subich decided to test the second observation by applying taxometric procedures to a set of nonbehavioral indicators of eating psychopathology.

Specifically, the authors evaluated five measures of psychological constructs implicated in eating psychopathology (body dissatisfaction, internalization of thin–ideal stereotype, perception of the pressure for thinness, poor interoceptive awareness, and neuroticism) to a nonselected sample of 532 college women. All of these constructs were measured with standard self-report instruments, and the psychometric properties of the indicators appear to be adequate. However, inclusion of neuroticism in the indicator set could be problematic, as neuroticism is associated with a wide range of psychopathology and is not specific to eating disorders. In other words, neuroticism is not a valid marker of eating disorders relative to other forms of psychopathology. This lack of specificity may result in nontaxonic results for analyses that include neuroticism, even if other measures are valid indicators of the taxon. On the other hand, the indicator set included measures that assess conceptually distinct contributors to eating psychopathology, including psychological and sociocultural aspects of the dysfunction. This diversity is a notable strength of indicator selection.

To further test indicator properties, Tylka and Subich (2003) performed a taxometric power analysis. They used a self-report diagnostic measure to sort cases into two groups: those with significant eating psychopathology and those without it. According to this measure, the base rate of eating problems in the sample was 18%, estimated indicator validities ranged from 2 to 3 SD, and nuisance correlations on average were .23 (eating disorder group) and .32 (noneating disorder group). It was concluded that the data are appropriate for detection of a taxon if it exists. Next, the authors performed a MAXCOV analysis; interval size and MRIN were not reported. Three raters evaluated MAXCOV curves and concluded that seven curves were taxonic and 23 were nontaxonic. The interrater agreement was high (97%), but no plots were presented in the articles. The taxon base rate was .29 and it varied considerably (SD = .14), although as discussed in chapter 3 this level of variability does not necessarily indicate the absence of taxonicity. The high base rate estimate is of greater concern, however, as a taxon with a 29% base rate in a college population is unlikely to be clinically relevant. Tylka and Subich also performed MAXCOV analyses on a simulated taxonic and nontaxonic data set, and the research data was found to be more similar to nontaxonic than taxonic data in terms of base rate variability and GFI. However, the simulated data were generated using estimates derived in the initial MAXCOV analysis rather than in the taxometric power analysis, and the latter is a more meaningful reference point.

The authors also performed L-mode analyses of actual and simulated data sets. The L-mode plots for research data showed a plateau rather than a complete peak observable in simulated taxonic data. The authors interpreted this as evidence of dimensionality. On the other hand, the L-mode base rate estimate was quite similar to the MAXCOV estimate (P = .34). The reason for this consistency is unclear; perhaps the plateau hides a latent discontinuity. Another concern is that it is unclear from the description of the study how the raters interpreted cusped curves; they may have been rated as nontaxonic. A taxon with a base rate of about .30 would not produce cusped curves, but a smaller base rate taxon might. Despite these issues, the sum of evidence indicates that the given indicator set does not define a taxon, at least not in a sample of college-age females.

Summary

Taxometric studies replicated the initial nontaxometric findings of discontinuity in symptoms of eating disorder and continuity in measures of the underlying psychopathology. In our opinion, this pattern of findings does not suggest a problem with behavioral measures (i.e., criterion contamination), but rather affirms the validity of the DSM's operationalization of eating psychopathology as a collection of categorical syndromes. We should note that not all eating disorders have been identified as taxa. Currently, a BN taxon and a general eating disorder taxon have the strongest support, while the taxonic status of other eating disorders is unclear. There is also the question of whether the general eating disorder taxon and the BN taxon are two distinct entities.

DEPRESSION

Depression is a familiar experience and clinical forms of depression represent extremely prevalent psychiatric conditions. Is the day-to-day waxing and waning of mood qualitatively similar to pathological forms of depression? In their review in *Psychological Bulletin*, Flett, Vredenburg, and Krames (1997) suggested that the continuity question has been one of the most contentious issues in the depression literature. In this literature, questions regarding continuity arose from concerns about the use of nonclinical, so-called "analogue" college student samples. In many studies, depression was evaluated using college students with elevated scores on the Beck Depression Inventory (BDI; Beck et al., 1988), but some have suggested that these studies are not representative of true, clinical depression (Depue & Monroe, 1978). Flett et al. suggest a number of different tests of continuity, including psychometric–taxometric types of analyses. Unfortunately, their review is far from definitive. While they suggest that most of the available evidence is consistent with the continuity hypothesis, they propose a model of depression that allows for both continuities and discontinuities.

Unfortunately, taxometric investigations of the controversy have also produced conflicting findings. We will first review studies consistent with the continuity hypothesis and then evaluate investigations that found evidence of taxonicity. Finally, we attempt to integrate these findings and account for the discrepancies.

Evidence of Dimensionality

A study by Ruscio and Ruscio (2000) was the first to provide support for the dimensional model. The authors examined data from 996 male military veterans who received a psychological evaluation at the National Center for Post-Traumatic Stress Disorder. This sample was selected because depression is fairly common in outpatients with posttraumatic stress disorder. In fact, diagnostic assessment of a representative subsample of this group (n = 376) suggested a 63% prevalence of current major depression, which offers nearly ideal conditions for taxometric analyses. In other words, the authors examined the taxonic conjecture in a large sample with an expected base rate of about .50 without having to artificially create one. Nine hundred participants completed the BDI and 587 of them also completed the Zung Self-Rating Depression Scale (SDS; Zung, 1965), hence, the analyses that involved the SDS had a smaller n. The SDS includes 20 items scored on a four-point scale.

The BDI and the SDS were used to create five sets of indicators. The first set was composed of eight BDI items with the highest item-whole correlations that were not redundant with each other. The second set was analogously constructed from SDS items. The third set included four pairs of BDI items, and thus included four 7-level indicators. These eight items were chosen to (a) have high correlations with the total BDI score, and (b) correlate more highly with the paired item than with any other BDI item. The fourth set was analogously constructed from SDS items. The fifth set consisted of rationally created cross-measure composites. Each *DSM–IV* symptom of major depressive disorder was matched to BDI and SDS items, but some symptoms did not have good coverage in the measures. As a result, symptoms matching three or fewer items were combined, which resulted in a set of four relatively long, theoretical indicators (two tapping cognitive symptoms and two tapping somatic symptoms). Many indicator sets were partially overlapping, so the analyses do not provide truly independent tests of taxonicity. However, having different sets of markers allowed the authors to use both SSMAXCOV (with the single indicators) and MAXCOV (with the paired and theoretical indicators). Reliability is a concern with single items but is less of a problem for paired and theoretical indicators. Unfortunately, indicator alphas were not reported, so we do not know whether the use of composite indicators completely alleviated the reliability concerns.

The authors tried to ensure the adequacy of the markers by estimating their validities and nuisance correlations. As discussed in chapter 3, these estimates can be easily computed after Coherent Cut Kinetics (CCK) procedures have been run to yield information necessary for group assignment (e.g., Bayesian probabilities). However, Ruscio and Ruscio (2000) did not find a taxon (see below), so this option was closed for them; they did a taxometric power analysis instead. The authors used the top and bottom quartiles of the distribution of indicator set scores—the sum of all indicators in the set—for estimation of nuisance correlations in the taxon and nontaxon groups and used these estimates to approximate indicator validities. For each of the five indicator sets, nuisance correlations were low (ranging from .07 to .19) and validities were high (SD ranging from 1.31 to 2.25). These estimates of nuisance correlations seem extremely low given that all of the indicators were self-report measures with somewhat overlapping content and subject to the same report biases. However, the quartile approach used here can underestimate nuisance correlations and consequently lead to an overestimation of indicator validities. Thus, although taxometric power analysis suggested that the indicators were perfectly capable of detecting taxonicity, we cannot discount the possibility of inadequate measurement.

SSMAXCOV analyses were performed with the two sets of single indicators. Extreme values of the input indicators were combined in a single interval until there were at least 50 cases present in each interval, effectively setting MRIN at 50. MAXCOV was applied to the two sets of paired indicators with an interval size being set to "one" in raw score units; that is, each interval corresponded to a specific raw score. MAXCOV was also applied to the theoretical indicators, and instead of using the same interval size (e.g., .25 SD) for all indicators, each marker was divided into ten equal intervals. This deviation from standard procedures does not seem to pose any obvious problems, but it has not been tested in simulation studies, so this particular set of findings should be interpreted with caution. MRINs were not reported for either of the MAXCOV analyses.

The authors reported that only a handful of individual graphs were taxonic in each analysis. The plots were averaged without standardizing the input, and smoothed. Two were clearly flat, two clearly peaking, and one ambiguous. Ruscio and Ruscio concluded that the peaking curves were not taxonic because the ends of the curves did not go down to zero, which is inconsistent with the low nuisance correlations suggested by taxometric power analysis. Alternatively, this inconsistency can be interpreted as suggesting that true nuisance correlations are higher than estimated, rather than indicating a nontaxonic shape. The authors reported averages and standard deviations of individual base rate estimates. Means varied widely between indicator sets (from .47 to .71) and all SDs were .19 or higher. This lack of consistency suggests that neither indicator set was able to detect a taxon.

MAMBAC analyses were conducted as well. For individual and paired indicators, Ruscio and Ruscio rotated through each marker as the output variable with the sum of remaining markers as the input. This allowed for eight MAMBAC analyses with individual indicators and four MAMBAC analyses with paired indicators. Theoretical composites were analyzed using standard MAMBAC procedures. The vast majority of curves did not have a peak. There were quite a few plots with left-end cusps, but this implies an extremely high taxon base rate in the sample, which is inconsistent with theoretical expectations. Across indicator sets, the mean base rate estimates fell consistently between .52 and .64, and showed stability within analyses (SDs ranged between .05 and .12). However, this sort of consistency should not be taken as evidence of taxonicity, since MAMBAC analyses of dimensional data tend to produce base rate estimates in the neighborhood of .50. Overall, some MAXCOV graphs looked taxonic, but the inconsistency of base rate estimates leads us to conclude that it was not evidence of taxonicity. On the other hand, MAMBAC base rate estimates were consistent, but the shapes of the plots did not suggest taxonicity. This set of findings highlights the importance of using multiple consistency tests.

In the same article, Ruscio and Ruscio report a conceptual replication of the study using items from MMPI scale 2 (Depression). The data was obtained from the Hathaway data bank and included all of the MMPIs completed at the University of Minnesota Hospitals between 1940 and 1976. The data set was narrowed using several exclusionary criteria (e.g., all nonpatients were excluded) to 13,707 cases. This data set can be considered well suited for taxometric purposes. The prevalence of depression is fairly high in outpatient samples, and in fact, 40% of cases in the data set had an elevation on the depression scale. Because the gender difference in depression is substantial, the data were first analyzed for the entire sample and then separately for males and females. MMPI items are dichotomous and can be used in SSMAXCOV, but the authors wanted to use more reliable indicators so they created a set of theoretical indicators following the same procedure used in Study 1. This approach yielded three composite indicators, each having at least six levels. Taxometric power analysis estimated the nuisance correlations to be .23 with an average validity of 1.78 SD.

MAXCOV analyses were again performed in a nonstandard way—each input variable was cut in 20 intervals. There were more intervals than scale levels, which means that some cases with the same score on an input indicator were arbitrarily assigned to different intervals. It is unclear what impact this procedure had on the analyses. Out of nine possible plots (three total, three for men, and three for women), only four looked clearly nontaxonic and the rest can be judged either as ambiguous or taxonic. However, the base rates were inconsistent within each sample (SDs of about .13) and across samples (ranging from .27 to .52). MAMBAC analyses were conducted using the total Scale 2 score as the input and the three indicators as the outputs. It is also not typical to use variables that were not identified as taxon indicators as an input variable, but a larger problem is that the input variable (Scale 2) included items also used in the output variables. Nothing is currently known about the possible effects of indicator overlap, but it is plausible that this can distort the performance of the procedure and should be avoided. At any rate, all of the MAMBAC curves had right-end cusps, which was inconsistent with the expected base rate. Base rate estimates, on the other hand, consistently clustered around .37.

The results were not completely consistent, but these findings seem to favor a dimensional model of depression. However, this may reflect inadequate indicator selection. Taxometric power analysis suggests this is not the case, but the power analyses may have presented an overly optimistic view of indicator quality. In addition, the construct validity of the indicators used in this study is unknown. The validity of the BDI and the MMPI Scale 2 are well established, but the authors used indicators derived from these instruments, not the scales themselves. We cannot assume that the indicators assessed depression as accurately as the original scales. In fact, we don't know whether the derived scales are reliable. It is possible that the indicators actually did not tap syndromal depression, but instead they tapped a closely related factor such as negative affect, and thus are largely irrelevant to the question about the taxonicity of depression per se.

This last issue was addressed in another study by Franklin, Strong, and Greene (2002). In this report, the taxon indicators included three validated MMPI-2 subscales assessing depression. Specifically, this study used the 57-item Scale 2, the 33-item Content Depression scale (DEP), and the 34-item Introversion–Low Positive Emotionality scale (INTR). Unfortunately, these three MMPI-2 subscales have considerable item overlap, ranging from 15% to 38% of the scale's content. As mentioned above, content overlap could negatively impact the taxometric analyses—for example, overlap will certainly increase nuisance correlations. Franklin et al. could have eliminated overlap by removing shared items from the indicators, but this would have produced indicators with unknown validity, so the authors decided against it. The sample consisted of 1,000 men and 1,000 women randomly drawn from a large data set of psychiatric inpatients and outpatients with valid MMPI-2s. Data from men and women were analyzed separately.

MAMBAC did not yield any complete peaks, but all the graphs showed a gradual increase that was potentially indicative of a low base rate taxon. However, a low base rate is inconsistent with theoretical expectations, so the increase was probably due to indicator skew. The MAMBAC base rate estimates, on the other hand, consistently clustered around .31 for men and .40 for women. Out of the six possible MAXCOV plots (three for men and three for women), four were clearly nontaxonic, but two curves that had INTR as the input variable had a notable hump in the middle of the graph and these graphs could be interpreted as taxonic. The base rate estimates for the two taxonic plots were .40 in men and .49 in women (the other four estimates were much lower). These base rate estimates were consistent with theoretical expectations and, as predicted, the base rate was higher in women.

On the whole, the findings support the dimensional model, but there were some glimpses of taxonicity. The implicit assumption of this study is that the three selected scales together defined a coherent construct and all three scales measured this construct fairly well. If this were not the case—for example, if INTR was not a very valid measure of syndromal depression—we might get a mixed picture, where analyses involving the INTR look nontaxonic and analyses that don't use this indicator look taxonic. Our experiences with MAXCOV lead us to believe that the input variable influences the results of the procedure less than the output variables. The role of the input variable is to order the data in a more or less increasing fashion, but the real action is in the correlations. We are not aware of a simulation study testing this hypothesis, but it is consistent with the observed pattern of findings in this report suggesting that plots using the INTR as the input variable—which possibly had less influence on the results—were taxonic.

The authors did not attempt to address this issue. Although construct validity is important, it does not guarantee taxometric validity, so both issues must be examined, especially in the case of null finding. For example, Franklin et al. could have performed a principal component analysis and examined loadings of the three indicators on the first unrotated component. As mentioned previously, these loadings can give a sense of indicator validity, and if the INTR failed to load sufficiently, this would indicate a measurement problem.

While Franklin et al. (2002) replicated the MMPI findings of Ruscio and Ruscio (2000), Ruscio and Ruscio (2002) attempted a replication of the original BDI findings in a new sample of 2,260 introductory psychology students. This investigation had the specific goal of testing an assumption implicit in many studies of analogue depression, that a certain cutoff on the BDI demarcates a boundary between two qualitatively different forms of depression. Studies of so-called analogue depression have used a range of cutoffs from 9 to 16 and sometimes even as high as 24, but the authors geared their investigation to the most frequently used cutoff of 10. To select indicators with sufficient validity, Ruscio and Ruscio (2002) split their sample into high (BDI score of 10 and above) and low (BDI between 0 and 9) groups. Ten BDI items produced a separation of at least 1.25 SD between the groups. Nuisance correlations were estimated using the same groups, which is arguably a conservative approach as these groups are likely to contain a mixture of taxon and nontaxon members, and so the estimated correlations were probably inflated. Even with this overly stringent approach, the average estimates were well below .30.

To facilitate interpretation of the outputs, the authors also created two simulation data sets with identical distributional properties (number of indicators, number of levels, indicator intercorrelations, skew and kurtosis): one taxonic set and one dimensional set. The taxonic data set was created to have a base rate of .23, which corresponds to the proportion of cases falling at or above a BDI threshold of 10 in the undergraduate data set. Ruscio and Ruscio tried to ensure that indicator validities and nuisance correlations matched the estimated parameters of the real indicators, but they did not indicate how successful this was.

MAMBAC analyses were conducted using the modified protocol, where one indicator serves as an output variable and the remainder are summed into an input variable. The simulated taxonic curves exhibited clear peaks, albeit shifted greatly to the right. The average base rate estimate was .20, reassuringly close to the actual base rate of .23. The analyses of actual data yielded right-end cusps and base rate estimates that consistently clustered around .15 (SD = .05). The analyses of the simulated nontaxonic data yielded similar plots and the same average base rate. This, however, could have been an artifact of the graphs not showing complete peaks. Consider that skewed nontaxonic data and low base rate taxon data would both show a cusp. If we look beyond the range of data presented in the plots, we see that a nontaxonic curve keeps on increasing, while a low base rate taxon curve forms a peak. The similarity of base rate estimates just reflects the fact that both curves were cut off at the same point. In sum, we cannot separate a low base rate taxon from a nontaxon with this analysis; we need a longer scale to do it.

MAXEIG is quite good at detecting low base rate taxa. Given a sufficiently large number of windows, which is only limited by the number of cases in the data set, it can produce peaks even for very low base rate taxa. MAXEIG was performed by Ruscio and Ruscio using 10 selected items as output variables and the sum of the remaining 11 BDI items as the input, to get a sufficiently fine scale on the sorting (input) variable. However, the authors only went up to 60 windows with about 377 cases in each window, which definitely permits finer partitioning. At 60 windows, the simulated taxonic data yielded a clear peak, the simulated nontaxonic data yielded an evenly increasing curve, and the actual data yielded a shape that was generally similar to the nontaxonic data. However, the actual data curve exhibited a flattened pattern similar to a plateau at the extreme right, which is suggestive of a peak that only needs greater resolution to become more apparent.

Ruscio and Ruscio also used L-mode. This procedure combines the taxon indicators and optimally weights them to produce the most powerful indicator possible. It appears that this method offers the greatest payoff when applied to radically different measures by integrating a great deal of different types of information. This was not the case in this particular study. The ten BDI indicators arguably tapped very similar content, and the factor scores were not much more informative than the simple sum of the items, and we already know these do not show bimodality. Also, virtually nothing is known about the impact of nuisance correlations on the performance of the L-mode procedure. It seems likely, however, that high nuisance correlations can "highjack" the factor scores and severely distort the output (see a similar discussion in the antisocial personality section). Given the nature of the data (all self-report), nuisance correlations and their impact on L-mode is a concern.

The L-mode analysis of the simulated taxonic data produced a bimodal distribution, while analyses of the simulated nontaxonic data and the actual data revealed only one mode. What this means is unclear. It is possible that depression is actually taxonic, but the simulated taxonic data does not adequately reflect the structure of the actual data set. For example, higher nuisance correlations and lower indicator validities in the actual data may not have allowed a latent bimodality to emerge, even though this was detected in the simulated data. Another possibility, of course, is that the BDI items do not define a taxon.

The central issue to consider in interpreting these findings is the aptness of the simulated taxonic data set. The evidence is clear that if the taxon had a base rate of about .23 (i.e., a BDI cutoff of 10 had been appropriate for classifying groups), it would have been detected. However, this base rate seems much too high. Consider that the point prevalence of major depression is only about 3% (Joyce, 1994). Moreover, the cutoff of 10 is only one of several options. Many researchers use higher cutoffs (e.g., 16), which define much smaller groups. The use of these cutoffs is consistent with a low base rate taxon. The study tested the taxonic conjecture, but only in a narrow sense, because it evaluated evidence for the existence of a taxon with a base rate of about .23. The results were generally not inconsistent with the existence of a low base rate taxon, so we suggest that the broader question about the taxonicity of depression requires further investigation.

Evidence of Taxonicity

Support for a depression taxon comes primarily from subtyping studies. First, Haslam and Beck (1994) tested the taxonicity of several theoretical subtypes of depression in a sample of 531 outpatients with the primary diagnosis of major depression assessed at the Center for Cognitive Therapy in Philadelphia between 1983 and 1991. All participants were administered the BDI and the Sociotropy-Autonomy Scale (SAS; Beck, Epstein, Harrison, & Emery, 1983). The authors used various BDI items and SAS subscales to operationalize five subtypes of depression: endogenous–melancholic (defined in the *DSM*); autonomous (proposed by Beck et al., 1983); sociotropic (also proposed by Beck et al., 1983); self-critical (proposed by Blatt & Homann, 1992); and hopelessness (proposed by Abramson, Metalsky, & Alloy, 1989). The BDI items were used in operationalizing each subtype, and the SAS subscales were used only in defining the autonomous and sociotropic subtypes. Each subtype was defined by at least five or six indicators. Some of the indicator sets had item overlap, but the overall level of overlap was modest.

Haslam and Beck (1994) dichotomized all the indicators in two ways: (a) indicators were dichotomized by a median split (raw scores), and (b) indicators were dichotomized relative to the average level of endorsement for a given person (relative scores). To compute the relative scores, all the indicators were standardized, an average of these standard scores was calculated for each person, and finally, each person was assigned a 1 for all indicators for which his or her score was above the average standard score (the participant got 0 on all other indicators). These relative scores allowed the authors to control interindicator correlations, that is, to control for depression severity. Haslam and Beck were concerned that if there is a general depression severity taxon, the various indicator sets may show spurious taxonicity. Analyses of the relative scores allow an investigator to determine whether markers of a subtype covary beyond the effects of depression severity. Use of relative scores appears to be a sound practice. However, we don't believe that it is necessary to dichotomize either the relative scores or the raw data. SSMAXCOV can handle nondichotomous indicators, and any arbitrary dichotomization leads to a loss of information and an increase in error, which can be quite substantial (Cohen & Cohen, 1983). When faced with indicators of various lengths, like the combination BDI items and SAS scales, a researcher can use standard scores instead of raw scores and can obtain relative scores by subtracting the person's average standard score from the person's standard score on each indicator.

The SSMAXCOV analyses of the raw data produced the clearest peak with the endogenous indicator set (although it had a covariance of just under .05). The autonomous set showed a distinct peak as well. The other graphs were either flat or ambiguous. The SSMAXCOV analyses of relative data yielded essentially the same curves, but they were somewhat shifted downward, which is likely to represent a consistent reduction of covariance across all levels of the constructs. The base rate estimates were not reported.

The authors also applied Golden's consistency testing procedures to each indicator set. All the sets lost some items in the consistency tests, but the endogenous set lost the least. On this basis, the authors concluded that only the endogenous subtype is taxonic. This inference was hardly warranted. The purpose of Golden's consistency tests is to select the best indicators of a putative taxon. The finding that many indicators were lost in the consistency tests only indicates a weakness in the operationalization and cannot be used as evidence against taxonicity. If anything, such a finding would weaken our confidence in the ability of SSMAXCOV to reject the taxonic conjecture. In other words, under such circumstances, a flat SSMAXCOV plot cannot be interpreted as strong evidence, but a peaking plot is still indicative of taxonicity. Haslam and Beck used Golden's procedure to estimate the base rate of the endogenous subtype and found a mean taxon base rate of .42 (SD = .04). They did not report base rate estimates for other syndromes, which is unfortunate because it would have been informative to examine the consistency of these estimates.

A study by Whisman and Pinto (1997) sought to re-evaluate the taxonicity of hopelessness depression in a different age group. They recruited 160 depressed adolescents (mean age 15.2 years) who met DSM–III–R (American Psyciatric Association, 1987) criteria for major depressive disorder or dysthymic disorder. Participants were administered the BDI and the Hopelessness Scale for Children (HSC; Kazdin, Rodgers, & Colbus, 1986). BDI items were rationally matched to six symptoms hypothesized to be characteristic of hopelessness depression, and this resulted in a set of three individual items and three item composites (sums of items matched to the same symptom). The authors then correlated these symptom measures to the HSC and eliminated one marker because it did not show a significant association with hopelessness. Instead of using individual symptom measures as indicators, Whisman and Pinto summed the remaining five markers and used this composite and the HSC total score as two indicators.

The indicators were not tested for their suitability for taxometric analyses, but the authors reported that the composite was reasonably reliable (alpha = .76). Whisman and Pinto performed a MAMBAC analysis, and both curves had a clear peak (although it was substantially shifted to the right), indicating a taxon with the base rate of about .25. The actual base rate estimate was .44, but the inconsistency between the shape and the estimate was probably due to high nuisance correlations. The authors, however, concluded that the inconsistency indicated dimensionality and did not pursue the issue further. It appears that this conclusion is mistaken. Although the plots are somewhat ambiguous, and there are only two of them, no firm inference can be drawn from this study.

A more rigorous investigation of the taxonicity of adolescent depression was reported by Ambrosini, Bennett, Cleland, and Haslam (2002). This study included 378 adolescents (mean age of 15.7 years), most of whom (n = 358) were outpatients referred to a child and adolescent depression clinic; the remaining 20 were inpatients. Participants were assessed with the BDI and the Schedule for Affective Disorders and Schizophrenia for school-age children (K-SADS; Ambrosini, 2000), a structured interview that covers 17 symptoms of depression rated on a six-point scale. A clinician interviewed the adolescents and their mothers and then integrated all of the available information to make the severity ratings.

The authors wanted to select indicators that specifically tap melancholic depression. To evaluate this construct, a principal components analysis of the joint pool of K-SADS and BDI items was performed. Two independent statistical tests suggested a two-component solution, but the resulting components appeared to reflect method factors, rather than substantive factors. Specifically, all of the BDI items loaded on the first component (except for three items that did not load on either component) and nearly all of the K-SADS items loaded on the second component. In fact, the first component correlated .98 with the BDI and the second component correlated .93 with the K-SADS. Ambrosini et al., however, concluded that the first component reflected depression severity and the second component reflected melancholic depression. This interpretation was somewhat at odds with the data. Specifically, the second component included some K-SADS items that did not tap symptoms of melancholia (e.g., irritability and anger) and did not include some BDI items that measure symptoms of melancholia (e.g., loss of appetite).

Ambrosini et al. next created four indicators from the available 38 items (BDI and K-SADS). They weighted items by their loading on the "melancholic" component. Next, they ordered items by the magnitude of their loading on that component, and finally they assigned every fourth item from this ordered list to a corresponding indicator. For example, items 1, 5, 9, and so forth were assigned to indicator 1; items 2, 6, 10, and so forth were assigned to indicator 2, and so on. This indicator creation procedure seems reasonable. The weighting of scores allowed Ambrosini et al. to refine the data and focus it on the construct of interest, and they were thus able to use the entire item pool. Indicators were created in an unbiased manner to be of sufficient length and to have approximately equal validities, though the component loading is just an approximation of the indicator's validity. The only issue regarding the appropriateness of this procedure is whether the resulting indicator pool truly tapped melancholia or a more general construct of clinical depression. This question cannot be answered without additional construct validation, which was not conducted in this study.

The authors conducted MAMBAC and MAXCOV analyses. MRIN was set at 20 with an interval size of .25 SD. Somewhat at odds with convention, the MAMBAC input variable was also cut in .25 intervals, instead of making a cut after each case, but this appears to be an acceptable practice. MAMBAC mostly yielded peaking curves, but the positions of the peaks varied considerably. The mean base rate estimate was .43 and the variance of individual estimates was quite high (SD = .09), though this level was probably acceptable. All the MAXCOV plots showed peaks. The mean base rate estimate was .39 and the individual estimates were fairly consistent (SD = .05). A GFI computed with MAXCOV was .98, which was very high and suggests that the parameter estimates were accurate. Finally, Ambrosini et al. performed a mixture analysis to test whether the findings were consistent across procedures. The authors compared the fit of the taxonic model, defined as two latent normal distributions, to the fit of two, dimensional models: a single latent normal distribution and a single latent skewed distribution. The taxonic model fit the data better than either of the dimensional models. The estimated taxon base rate was .37, which was highly consistent with the MAXCOV and MAMBAC estimates.

Overall, these findings lend strong support for the taxonicity of the construct. One non-CCK and two CCK procedures consistently indicated the existence of a taxon. The level of agreement between and within procedures was excellent, except for some inconsistencies in the MAMBAC subanalyses. Interestingly, these findings are also consistent with the findings of Haslam and Beck (1994), who estimated a taxon base rate of .40. This represents remarkable agreement with previous research, despite the fact that very different samples were used in the two studies. We want to emphasize that this study also had a strong design. The sample was unselected, sufficiently large, and possessed an expected taxon base rate of about .50. The indicators were created using an empirically sound procedure and were primarily based on a clinical interview. The consistency of the findings was examined between CCK procedures, as well as between CCK and non-CCK procedures. On the negative side, the study did not provide other researchers with the means for scoring or approximating the identified taxon. In addition, the construct validity of the taxon was not examined, and there is some question as to whether this represents a true melancholia taxon.

In summary, taxometric investigations of depression have yielded mixed results, with some studies finding a taxon and others finding a continuum. What does this pattern mean? Beach and Amir (2003) suggested that popular measures of depression (e.g., the BDI), which were used to operationalize depression in most of the previous studies, primarily assess subjective distress or misery (e.g., sad affect) and include only a few items that tap symptoms unique to diagnosable depression (e.g., loss of libido). Subjective distress is present in nearly all mental disorders; therefore, measures that are laden with distress are too nonspecific to define a depression taxon. On the other hand, if an investigation focuses on features unique to depression, it is more likely to detect a taxon. This may be the reason subtyping studies were more successful at finding taxa than were analyses of general depression severity, as subtyping studies tended to evaluate symptoms that are fairly specific to depression.

Beach and Amir tested this idea by evaluating taxonicity of two sets of BDI items: depression specific and nonspecific. The authors used Gilbert's

(2000) evolutionary theory, which conceptualizes clinical depression as the involuntary defeat syndrome, to identify the specific markers. The involuntary defeat syndrome primarily manifests as homeostatic deregulation, thus the first indicator set included items tapping sleep disturbance, loss of appetite, weight loss, health concern, loss of sex drive, and withdrawal. Beach and Amir used items identified by Ruscio and Ruscio (2000) as the nonspecific set, because it included many distress items such as feelings of discouragement, dissatisfaction, punishment, and low self-regard.

The BDI was administered to 3,936 undergraduates, and the authors judged the sample as sufficiently large to be split into four subsamples of 984 and analyzed separately. First, SSMAXCOV was performed on the distress indicators; only one of the four average curves (one for each subsample) showed a somewhat taxonic pattern, and the rest were clearly flat. The authors did not report results of internal consistency tests, but base rate estimates were highly discrepant across subsamples, ranging from .15 to .45. SSMAXCOV analysis of the IDS indicators produced three cusping curves and one curve with a fairly complete peak. Base rate estimates were reasonably consistent across the subsamples, ranging from .11 to .18. It is important to note that SSMAXCOV inputs were standardized before averaging and indicator size was set at .50 SD, allowing for seven intervals with the sufficient number of cases for reliable estimation of covariance (MRIN was not reported, however). SSMAXCOV analysis of the IDS was also performed in a full sample with an interval size of .25 SD and an MRIN of 50, which again allowed for seven intervals. The average plot was cusped, and the base rate was estimated at .14.

Next, Beach and Amir created two-indicator composites from the IDS set, resulting in three seven-point indicators. The procedure for pairing items was not described. A SSMAXCOV was also performed on these indicators in a full sample with an interval size of .50 SD and an MRIN of 50. The average curve was cusping, and the base rate estimate was .12. Furthermore, these data were submitted to MAXEIG, which was conducted with 20 windows and produced a cusping average curve; the base rate estimate was .10. Averaging MAXEIG curves is not a standard procedure and precludes consistency testing. Moreover, the small number of overlapping windows did not permit the emergence of a full peak; given the sample size the authors could have safely used up to 1,000 windows. MAMBAC was also applied to these data and yielded a cusping average plot with a hint of a peak at the extreme right; the MAMBAC base rate estimate was .11.

There was a notable consistency across the methods both in terms of shapes of the plots and base rate estimates. However, this consistency is undermined by the fact that the graphs formed cusps rather than complete peaks. Cusps do not lend very strong support for taxonicity, as skewed data can produce cusping MAXEIG and MAMBAC plots; only complete peaks are unambiguous markers of taxonicity. At the very least, cusping may have led to inflation of base rate estimates. The cusps probably could have been turned into peaks by shortening interval sizes and lowering the MRIN. This, of course, would introduce sampling error and noise in the plots, but cusping is a larger problem. Another limitation of the study is the neglect of internal consistency tests. Averaging graphs and computing a single base rate estimate, instead of evaluating and comparing subanalyses, greatly limits the scope and utility of possible consistency tests. Nevertheless, the cross-method consistency found in this study is impressive. Also, utilization of cross-sample consistency is an important and fairly novel contribution of the study.

Beach and Amir have demonstrated that with a given sample using the same procedures, some markers of depression may define a taxon, while others do not. In other words, both continuous and taxonic forms of depression exist. However, questions remain about the nature of the identified taxon. Is it really a depression taxon or has the exclusive focus on vegetative symptoms changed the nature of the construct? Interestingly, certain somatic symptoms, such as sleep and appetite disturbance, are common in many disorders and can be considered the physical component of nonspecific distress (Clark & Watson, 1991). Thus, perhaps the identified taxon is not a depression taxon at all and actually reflects general somatic complaints. Only construct validation can address these concerns.

Summary

This review indicates that three studies found no support for the taxonicity of depression, but four other investigations did. What is the meaning of these mixed results? First, there are some methodological concerns about these studies. Although the first three investigations generally came out in favor of the dimensional model, there are some glimpses of taxonicity in their results. On the other hand, among the studies that supported the taxonic conjecture, two were methodologically weak and fairly limited. Second, investigations that supported the dimensional model focused on a more general depression construct, but studies that supported the taxonic conjecture examined more tightly defined constructs, such as the involuntary defeat syndrome. It is possible that the general construct of depression is dimensional, while certain types of depression are categorical. Why might self-report measures of depression severity fail to adequately detect taxonicity? One possibility is that more than one taxon exists at the high end of the depression continuum, and CCK procedures produce null findings because they are not designed to handle such situations. Another possibility is that the measures are not valid enough to discriminate categorical forms of depression from dimensional depression and non-depression. This is consistent with the argument made by Beach and Amir (2003) that indicator sets used in some previous studies tap subjective distress, which apparently is dimensional.

The conclusion seems to be that depression is a very broad, heterogeneous construct and a general depression taxon probably does not exist. However, taxa may be found in this domain if the researchers carefully select indicators to evaluate distinct constructs, such as melancholia. It is important to note that use of specific markers may permit clearer differentiation of the target taxon from other psychiatric problems and from other depression taxa, if they exist. The taxometrics of depression is a complex and interesting area that requires well-defined questions accompanied by careful research.

ANXIETY

Anxiety is an experience that is common to most people, but this phenomenon continues to elude precise definition. Many define anxiety as involving the perception of threat that typically includes somatic symptoms such as cardiopulmonary arousal; cognitive symptoms such as threatening thoughts regarding physical, social, or psychological disaster; and behavioral symptoms such as avoidance (Barlow, 1988). Within the *DSM*, a number of presumably discrete conditions are listed under the general heading of anxiety disorders (e.g., panic disorder, generalized anxiety disorder, posttraumatic stress disorder). The categorical organization of the *DSM* suggests that there is something about anxiety symptoms associated with each of these conditions that separates anxiety disorders from normative experience of anxiety.

In contrast to the depression literature, there has been little discussion of the taxonic structure of anxiety disorders. Consequently, taxometricians have paid considerably less attention to anxiety, though a few studies have very recently been conducted in this area. In this literature, there is evidence favoring both categorical and continuous models, and we start by reviewing the nontaxonic findings.

Evidence of Dimensionality

In the first study published in this area, Ruscio, Borkovec, and Ruscio (2001) examined the taxonicity of worry, a psychological phenomenon central to generalized anxiety disorder. A large sample of introductory psychology undergraduates ($N = 1,588$) was administered the Penn State Worry Questionnaire (PSWQ; Meyer, Miller, Metzger, & Borkovec, 1990), a widely used 16-item self-report measure of chronic worry rated on a five-point scale; and the Generalized Anxiety Disorder Questionnaire (GAD-Q-IV; Newman, Zuellig, Kachin, & Constantino, 1997), a 15-item self-report measure of *DSM–IV* generalized anxiety disorder symptoms.

The authors used these measures to construct three indicator sets. First, eight nonredundant PSWQ items were selected to have high correlations with the PSWQ total score. Second, a set of four item pairs was created by selecting eight PSWQ items that (a) had high correlations with the total score, and (b) correlated more strongly with the paired item than any other PSWQ item. Third, sixteen PSWQ items and five GAD-Q-IV items specific to worry were combined in one item pool. The five selected GAD-Q-IV items were dichotomous, so the PSWQ items were dichotomized as well. Specifically, the two highest responses (scores of 4 or 5) were classified as "present" and the other three responses were classified as "absent." This cutoff was chosen because the median of the item means in this sample was 3, so this cutoff was somewhat similar to a median split. The three sets overlapped significantly (e.g., set one and two shared five items), so they only provide semi-independent tests of the taxonic hypothesis. Ruscio et al. also generated several simulated data sets (10 taxonic and 10 dimensional) to serve as comparisons for the third indicator set. The authors mentioned that the parameters of the artificial data sets matched real data, but they did not describe this in detail. For example, the base rate of the simulated taxonic data was not specified. It is possible that the simulated taxonic data were more ideal than real data, and therefore taxonicity could have been more readily detectable.

Next, Ruscio et al. conducted a taxometric power analysis using the top and bottom quartiles. This approach is somewhat problematic in this sample given that only seven percent of participants met diagnostic criteria according to the GAD-Q-IV. In the absence of direct taxonic evidence, we assume that the base rate of the taxon (if one exists) is about seven percent. This means that the top quartile included a mixture of taxonic and nontaxonic cases (with a proportion of about 1:3) and likely leads to a gross overestimation of the nuisance correlations in the taxon group. On the other hand, the use of a bottom quartile probably underestimated the nuisance correlations in the nontaxon group. Interestingly, the average of the nuisance correlations for each indicator set did not exceed .16. This alone can be taken as evidence against the presence of a low base rate taxon (unless the correlations in the top quartile were high and positive and correlations in the bottom quartile were moderate and negative, yielding a low positive average). Unfortunately, the authors did not report the nuisance correlations in sufficient detail to determine if this was the case. Estimates of indicator validities were all acceptable with at least an average separation of 1.75 SD.

MAMBAC was performed using a modified protocol where one indicator is used as the input variable and the sum of the remaining indicators is used as the output variable. This procedure was applied to the individual PSWQ indicators and to the paired indicators (MAMBAC does not work well with dichotomous indicators, so the third indicator set was not used). The authors reported that all of the resulting curves were dish-shaped, but only two of the averaged curves were presented. Interestingly, the average curve for the paired indicators showed a complete peak on the extreme right. On the other hand, the base rate estimates were inconsistent with the existence of a low base rate taxon (the average estimate was about .46). Overall, MAMBAC did not support the taxonic conjecture, but keep in mind that these results may be misleading given that MAMBAC is likely to fail under the highly unfavorable conditions that can be expected in a general population sample (e.g., very low base rate).

MAXCOV, on the other hand, is a more robust procedure, and Ruscio et al. applied it to the same two indicator sets. They used an interval size of .25 and an MRIN of 20 (extreme values were combined until there were at least 20 cases in the most extreme interval). The authors reported that the smoothed plots did not exhibit a clear taxonic pattern. However, they also did not provide an exact count of the number of taxonic and nontaxonic curves. Base rate estimates were implausibly high for both indicator sets (.53 and .43) and they were inconsistent (the corresponding SDs of the base rate estimates were .25 and .21). SSMAXCOV was applied to the third (dichotomous) indictor set. The average curve was flat and the highest covariance was only .03. The simulated nontaxonic data looked very similar to the actual data, whereas the simulated taxonic data produced a clear peak.

In summary, this study found no evidence of a worry taxon. However, there are a few concerns, including the effects of indicator unreliability and a very small base rate on the procedures employed. This investigation should be replicated with continuous markers of established reliability and validity, preferably in a sample in which taxon base rate is expected to be above .10.

In the second study, Ruscio, Ruscio, and Keane (2002) examined the taxonicity of PTSD in a large sample of male combat veterans ($N = 1,230$), who were seen at the Behavioral Sciences Division of the Veterans Affairs Boston Healthcare System's National Center for posttraumatic stress disorder between 1985 and 2000. All the participants completed the Mississippi scale (Keane, Caddell, & Taylor, 1988), a 35-item measure of combat-related posttraumatic stress disorder symptoms rated on a five-point scale; a subset of this sample ($n = 841$) was assessed with the Clinician Administered Posttraumatic Stress Disorder Scale (CAPS), an interview measure of posttraumatic stress disorder symptoms that a clinician rates on a five-point scale. According to the CAPS, 68% of the sample qualified for a posttraumatic stress disorder diagnosis.

The authors created three indicator sets. The first set included six item pairs drawn from the Mississippi scale. The second set was composed of four subscales of the Mississippi scale derived in previous factor analyses. The reliability of the subscales ranged from alpha of .71 to .84, with two indicators failing to clear the .80 threshold. The third set consisted of four factor-analytically derived subscales of the CAPS. The reliabilities of these scales were rather low (alpha range from .59 to .77). Ruscio et al. performed a taxometric power analysis using the upper and lower quartiles. The resulting average estimates of nuisance correlations were under .15 and average estimates of the indicator validities were over 1.5 SD. It is important to keep in mind, however, that these estimates might have been overly optimistic. The authors also created two simulated comparison data sets (one taxonic and one nontaxonic). These data sets were similar to the second and third indicator set, except that the simulated data was normally distributed and the actual data was somewhat skewed. In the simulated taxonic data set, the base rate was set at .68 and nuisance correlations were set at .10.

First, Ruscio et al. performed a MAMBAC analysis using a modified protocol and found generally U-shaped curves with somewhat elevated left sides, which may either reflect indicator skew or the presence of a high base rate taxon. On the other hand, the average base rate estimate was only about .70. The simulated taxonic data produced clearer plots (though most did not form a complete peak either), and yielded an expected base rate of .70. Next, MAXEIG was conducted. The authors varied the number of windows, but presented only the graphs using 75 windows. The majority of the MAXEIG plots were generally flat with an elevated left end. For MAMBAC, this output either reflects the presence of a high base rate taxon or indicator skew. However, some of these plots (especially the ones based on CAPS subscales) had complete left-sided peaks, suggesting a high base rate taxon. Interestingly, MAXEIG analyses of the CAPS indicators consistently estimated the taxon base rate to be .93. Finally, L-mode analyses yielded a clear bimodal distribution for the simulated taxonic data and a clear unimodal distribution for the nontaxonic data. Two of the three L-mode curves for the actual data suggested the presence of the second mode (which was especially evident in the CAPS data). Although this pattern did not emerge completely from the main distribution, that is, the graphs showed a plateau rather than a clear second peak, the plateaus were located around the standard score of −1, consistent with the presence of a high base rate taxon.

In summary, this study rejected the existence of a posttraumatic stress disorder taxon with a prevalence around 70%, but it could not rule out the existence of a taxon with a much higher base rate. There are some indications that such a taxon was present, but the measures used in this study have limited validity for capturing it. The CAPS appeared to be more valid than the Mississippi scale, which is interesting given that it was designed to reflect the *DSM*'s definition of posttraumatic stress disorder. MAXEIG appears to be the best technique for detecting this taxon, but future studies should use finer intervals (more windows). Finally, the use of factor-analytically derived indicators is a definite strength of the study. However, some indicators had marginal reliability, which may have obscured the results. Further studies should strive to utilize more reliable indicators.

Evidence of Taxonicity

While these two studies generally failed to support the existence of anxiety taxa associated with specific anxiety disorders, an unpublished study by Kotov, Schmidt, Lerew, Joiner, and Ialongo (2004) found support for a general anxiety taxon. In this investigation, anxiety was operationalized using a measure of anxious cognitive style (Vulnerability Scale; Schmidt, Joiner, Young, & Telch, 1995); a measure of anxiety-related impairment (Anxiety Impairment Scale; Lerew, Schmidt, & Jackson, 1999); and two factor-analytically derived subscales of the Beck Anxiety Inventory (BAI; Beck, Epstein, Brown, & Steer, 1988), a widely used 21-item self-report measure of anxiety symptoms. One of the BAI subscales taps into subjective anxiety and the other one measures physiological arousal. The Vulnerability Scale (VS) and the Anxiety Impairment Scale (AIS) are not widely known, but the authors decided to include them, as the only other alternative was analysis of individual BAI items. The reason for this decision was that while psychometric properties of the VS and the AIS are not well established, the same can be said about individual BAI items and item composites (e.g., the item pairs identified in Ruscio, Borkovec, & Ruscio, 2001). Moreover, individual items tend to be unreliable, while the four selected indicators all had alphas above .80. The sample consisted of first-year, Air Force cadets ($N = 1,215$) assessed during basic training on a variety of measures, including the four indicators.

MAXCOV analyses were performed with various intervals sizes (ranging from .15 SD to .30 SD). The most interpretable plots were obtained for an interval size of .18 SD. Seven of the 12 graphs were clearly taxonic, indicating that this analysis cleared only the minimal cutoff on the nose count consistency test. The base rate estimates were consistent (mean = .16, SD = .04) but the fit was rather low (GFI = .82), suggesting high nuisance correlations. In fact, the estimated nuisance correlations were acceptable in the taxon group (average correlation = .13), but they were too high in the nontaxon group (.42). Estimates of indicator validities, on the other hand, were satisfactory (average validity = 1.89 SD).

To resolve these ambiguities, the authors created two simulated data sets, taxonic and nontaxonic, with distributional parameters identical to the parameters in the actual data. Since Kotov et al. (2004) did not have an a priori hypothesis about the parameters of the taxon, they matched the latent parameters of the simulated taxonic data (e.g., base rate, indicator validities, nuisance correlations, etc.) to estimates obtained in the MAXCOV analysis. Analysis of the simulated taxonic data yielded findings that were similar to those produced by the actual data, while the analysis of simulated nontaxonic data produced only two taxonic graphs with highly variable base rate estimates (mean = .20, SD = .10). These comparisons were somewhat limited because the taxonic data set was modeled exactly after the actual data set. This only allowed the authors to show that the original MAXCOV results can be recreated, and that a taxon with parameters estimated in that analysis can be reliably identified by MAXCOV. However, the comparisons between the actual and simulated nontaxonic data sets indicated that the actual data set is not continuous, and thus the other comparison tests are not really necessary.

Next, the MAXCOV analyses were repeated with smoothed plots (using Tukey's 3RH twice procedure; Tukey, 1977). The general shape of the taxonic plots did not change, but the peaks shifted and the base rate estimates lost their cohesion (SD = .10). It is notable that smoothing had this effect. This would suggest that smoothing can aid in the interpretation of the curves, but the precise estimation of the taxon base rate and location of hitmaxes may be sacrificed.

Kotov et al. also tested the consistency of the MAXCOV results using MAXEIG and Bayesian Normal Mixture Modeling (BNMM; Brooks & Gelman, 1998). BNMM is a form of mixture modeling that estimates the parameters of distributions using Bayesian statistics. Three of the four MAXEIG plots were clearly taxonic with an estimated taxon base rate of .06, which is quite a bit lower than the MAXCOV estimate, but as discussed in chapter 3, MAXEIG base rate estimation is inexact and should not be weighted very heavily. The BNMM analyses revealed a superior fit for the taxonic solution and estimated the taxon base rate to be .15, which is perfectly consistent with MAXCOV.

High nuisance correlations probably significantly distorted the estimates in the original MAXCOV analysis. To obtain more precise estimates of latent parameters, the authors performed truncation by dropping the low-scoring half of the sample. In the truncated sample, MAXCOV yielded clearer results. Ten out of twelve plots were now taxonic, which clears even the most conservative threshold, and the average nuisance correlations were less than .10. Unfortunately, the indicator validity estimates decreased as well (average validity = 1.6 SD), but they were still well within the limits of tolerance. The base rate estimates also decreased (mean = .07, SD = .03). Note that these values are given as proportions of the full sample, which was done by dividing the estimates by two, because the truncated sample is half the size of the full sample. We suspect that the dramatic reduction of nuisance correlations in the nontaxon group probably was inflating the original estimates.

Two more comparison data sets were generated using the logic described above. Again, the MAXCOV analysis of the simulated taxonic data closely resembled the actual data; however, the analysis of the nontaxonic data yielded very different findings and failed most of the consistency tests. Sample truncation is an experimental procedure and its impact on taxometric procedures is not well understood; however, in this study, truncation had the desired effect and performed as expected. We should be cautious, though, in interpreting findings in the truncated sample.

Although there are weaknesses in the findings, we can conclude that the taxonic conjecture successfully passed several internal and external consistency tests. An important aspect of this is that the CCK findings were replicated with a fundamentally different method (BNMM). However, questions about the nature of the identified taxon remain. To address this, the authors performed construct validation. First, they examined correlations between dichotomous taxon membership (based on Bayesian probabilities) and other measures administered at the beginning of basic training: four taxon indicators; two measures of depression (the Beck Depression Inventory and the Beck Hopelessness Scale); one measure of current anxiety (State-Trait Anxiety Inventory, state version); two measures of vulnerability to anxiety (the Anxiety Sensitivity Index and the Body Sensations Questionnaire); and one measure of pain and discomfort sensitivity (Discomfort Intolerance Scale; Fitzpatrick & Schmidt, 2000).

The construct validation findings generally followed the expected pattern: the four indicators were highly correlated with the taxon ($r = .38$ to $.50$); measures of depression, anxiety, and anxiety vulnerability had somewhat lower correlations ($r = .30$ to $.39$); and pain sensitivity was largely unrelated to the taxon ($r = .18$). The one surprising finding was that the taxon correlated with the BDI more strongly ($r = .51$) than it correlated with either of the taxon indicators. This anomaly led the authors to reconceptualize the identified entity as a general distress taxon that reflects a pathology common to both anxiety and depression, rather than to consider this to be a pure anxiety taxon. This dramatic shift highlights the importance of construct validation.

Kotov et al. (2004) also examined the predictive validity of taxon membership by correlating it to measures that were administered at the end of basic training. The general pattern of association remained the same, although there was a substantial reduction in correlations, most of which now ranged between .20 and .32. Thus, taxon membership appears to have limited predictive validity. Furthermore, the authors sought to examine utility of the taxon. Specifically, they assessed the incremental validity of taxon membership in predicting future psychopathology after controlling for scores on each of the four taxon indicators. This is a stringent test indeed, but the authors found that taxon membership predicted BDI scores at the end of basic training above and beyond the predictive validity of the continuous indicators that it was derived from (partial correlation of .08). This finding lends strong support to the taxonic conjecture.

Another study by Schmidt, Kotov, Lerew, Joiner, and Ialongo (in press) found support for a specific taxon that reflects a cognitive vulnerability to panic attacks. The data was drawn from the same Air Force sample, although fewer participants ($N = 1,029$) had complete data on three measures of cognitive vulnerability used as taxon indicators: the Anxiety Sensitivity Inventory (ASI; Peterson & Reiss, 1987), the Body Sensations Questionnaire (BSQ; Chambless, Caputo, Bright, & Gallagher, 1984), and the Body Vigilance Questionnaire (BVQ; Schmidt, Lerew, & Trakowski, 1997). All the measures had acceptable reliability (alphas above .80). There is extensive evidence supporting the validity of the ASI and the BSQ, but relatively little is known about the validity of the BVQ. However, conceptually body vigilance is an important component of vulnerability to panic attacks (Schmidt et al., 1997).

The MAXCOV analysis yielded three clearly taxonic plots. The base rate estimates were somewhat variable, but generally consistent and suggested a taxon with a base rate of .19 (SD = .08). Indicator validities were acceptable (average of 1.74 SD), but the nuisance correlations were somewhat elevated in the nontaxon group (average $r = .34$), resulting in a relatively low GFI (.88) and probably an overestimation of the taxon base rate. MAXEIG was performed as an external consistency test and analyses suggested the existence of a taxon with base rate of .16. It is notable that MAXEIG did not produce a complete peak, with fewer than 50 windows indicating that even relatively prevalent taxa require a fairly large number of windows to emerge. MAXEIG provides only a weak consistency test for MAXCOV, as the two procedures are so similar, which is particularly problematic when there are only three indicators. However, the authors did not perform any further taxometric analyses.

Schmidt et al. did some initial evaluation of construct validity of the taxon, but focused on only one of its many components: predictive validity. The taxon was derived from data at the beginning of basic training and it was related to the number of panic attacks that occurred during basic training. Dichotomous taxon membership was a significant predictor of panic attacks, but it did not outperform continuous measures of anxiety sensitivity. This may mean that taxon membership reflects an underlying pathological process, while the frequency of panic attacks is a superficial, descriptive measure, and the association between underlying pathology and observed symptoms is not sufficiently strong for taxon membership to be highly predictive. If this hypothesis is correct, taxon membership should outperform continuous vulnerability measures in predicting the results of tests that specifically target the underlying dysfunction, which is unclear at this point. Another possibility is that the identified taxon is related to a broader range of anxiety pathology, and although taxon membership is not very predictive of panic attacks, it may be useful at predicting other anxiety symptoms. However, additional taxometric work remains to be done before the existence of the purported vulnerability taxon is completely established.

Summary

We are aware of two studies that suggest the presence of taxa in the domain of anxiety and two studies that failed to find anxiety taxa. What can be learned from this discrepancy? One obvious consideration is that anxiety pathology is heterogeneous and these four studies examined different constructs. Perhaps some forms of anxiety pathology are taxonic, while others are not. Another consideration is that if anxiety taxa exist, they may not correspond neatly to our current conceptions of anxiety disorders and anxiety constructs. The failures to detect taxonicity may not imply the complete absence of anxiety taxa but may suggest that we have not operationalized anxiety pathology in a way that allows for the detection of latent taxonicity. The selection of appropriate indicators is critically important for the ability of taxometric procedures to find an underlying category; it may take many trials to determine these indicators and identify the corresponding taxa. Current evidence supporting the existence of any anxiety taxa is very weak, and we should not yet abandon the hypothesis that anxiety phenomena are actually continuous.

PERSONALITY DISORDER

The debate over the categorical versus continuous structure of mental disorders has been going on for a number of years (Nathan & Lagenbucher, 1999), but the controversy is especially intense in the domain of personality disorders (Clark & Watson, 1999). The *DSM–IV* defines a personality disorder as an enduring, inflexible, and pervasive pattern of maladaptation and proposes a taxonomy that consists of ten specific categories, plus the residual class of personality disorder not otherwise specified (American Psychiatric Association, 1994). Critics of the categorical approach, on the other hand, tend to view personality pathology as an extreme form of normal personality traits and do not assume a qualitative distinction between normal and disordered personality. There is some disagreement about the best type of continuous taxonomy for capturing personality disorder, but arguably the most popular approach is to describe personality pathology in terms of five general personality factors—the "Big Five" (Widiger & Frances, 2002). Another approach is to depict personality disorders with a larger number of specific personality traits (Clark, Livesley, Schroeder, & Irish, 1996).

A number of investigations have found that personality disorders are not very distinct from each other (on both conceptual and empirical levels) or from normal personality (Clark & Watson, 1999). The lack of distinctiveness from normal personality presents a fundamental challenge to the categorical approach. However, most of this evidence is indirect (e.g., lack of clear bimodality in the distribution of scores on personality disorder criteria). Taxometrics is unique in its potential to provide direct empirical evidence that can help resolve the discontinuity question. Surprisingly, only one taxometric study has been conducted on this topic to date.

Trull, Widiger, and Guthrie (1990) examined the latent structure of the *DSM–III–R* (American Psychiatric Association, 1987) criteria for borderline personality disorder, as well as criteria for dysthymia. Dysthymia is not classified as a personality disorder in the *DSM*, but it tends to be chronic and is quite similar to personality disorders in this respect. To assist in the interpretation of the borderline personality disorder analyses, dysthymia was evaluated because it was expected to serve as a nontaxonic benchmark. Also, eight indicators of male gender were included in the study to serve as a standard for taxonic findings.

The borderline personality disorder and dysthymia criteria were scored from records of 409 adult psychiatric inpatients evaluated at acute admission units of a state psychiatric hospital. This population was chosen because borderline personality disorder is fairly prevalent among inpatients; in fact, 28% of the sample met *DSM–III–R* criteria for borderline personality disorder. Male gender criteria were scored from charts of 244 inpatients (59% of these were from men). Each of the three data sets included eight dichotomously scored indicators. Approximately ten percent of the charts were re-reviewed to check for reliability. Agreement was very high for the male gender criteria (average kappa of .95), but reliability was not impressive for the dysthymia criteria (average kappa of .67), and was even lower for borderline criteria (average kappa of .60, with one criterion having a kappa of .37).

The authors performed SSMAXCOV analyses on the three indicator sets, averaged the results without standardization, and smoothed the plots. The curve for male gender had a clear peak (highest covariance of .20) that was centrally located. The base rate estimate was not provided. The curve for dysthymia was perfectly flat and the curve for borderline personality disorder showed a clear right-end cusp (highest covariance of .20) and clearly passes the .05 cutoff. Trull et al., however, erroneously concluded that the borderline personality disorder plot is nontaxonic. It seems that finding a cusp, rather than a full peak, misled the authors. A complete peak probably failed to emerge because the input scale was too short. A *DSM–III–R* diagnosis of borderline personality disorder requires meeting five out of eight criteria, and if this definition is accurate, SSMAXCOV should have produced a full peak with the hitmax in the next-to-last interval. As a complete peak was not observed, we conclude that a more conservative cutoff—perhaps six out of eight criteria—should be required for the diagnosis.

Of course it is premature to draw definitive conclusions from the Trull et al. (1990) study. In this investigation, we only see the first glimpse of taxonicity. The taxonic conjecture should be tested much more thoroughly, using multiple consistency tests, multiple taxometric procedures, and multiple samples. In addition, this particular study can be criticized on the grounds that the criteria ratings were not very reliable. Generally, this is a valid concern, as low reliability can deflate correlations and make the taxonic graphs appear flat; however, it is not as much of a problem in this particular case because the SSMAXCOV graph of borderline personality disorder criteria showed a clear cusp despite low reliability. The nontaxonic finding for dysthymia is notable, but this should not be over-interpreted. A more thorough investigation of dysthymia is necessary—and should include some kind of assessment of indicator suitability—before a firm conclusion can be made.

COMORBIDITY

The comorbidity, or higher than chance co-occurrence, of mental disorders became a focus of research attention in the last two decades. Dramatically high rates of comorbidity have been observed between many disorders (Krueger, 2002). For example, lifetime comorbidities between Major Depressive Disorder and some anxiety disorders are as high as 60% (Mineka, Watson, & Clark, 1998), which is three to six times greater than expected by chance. Also, in the Epidemiological Catchment Area Study, 60% of participants who had a psychiatric disorder also had at least one other disorder in their lifetime (Robins, Locke, Regier, 1991). The issue of comorbidity is particularly important because it challenges the validity of the current classification system. Some researchers argue that high rates of comorbidity suggest that the *DSM–III, DSM–III–R,* and *DSM–IV* make too many fine distinctions; that is, they split a small number of real psychopathological categories into many arbitrary ones (Nathan & Lagenbucher, 1999). Other psychologists go further and interpret high comorbidity as indicating that all psychopathological phenomena are continuous and any attempt to fit them in a categorical system will fail due to such problems (Nathan & Langenbucher, 1999).

Can taxometrics help resolve the problem of comorbidity? Initially, an argument was made that only investigations of underlying pathology and etiology can advance this issue (Lilienfeld, Waldman, & Israel, 1994). Lilienfeld et al. even suggested that the concept of comorbidity is meaningless on a purely descriptive, syndromal level, which is where taxometric investigations are usually confined. However, Meehl (2001) rejected this view and outlined an approach in which taxometrics can address comorbidity. Meehl's central argument is that the comorbidity of two arbitrary syndromes is uninformative, but the overlap of two empirically derived taxa is informative about the underlying processes as it can be associated with practical considerations such as prognosis, resistance to treatment, and so forth.

We also believe taxometrics can be helpful in addressing issues associated with comorbidity, but we emphasize that this enterprise is somewhat distinct and more complicated than the process of establishing the taxonicity of individual constructs. Nearly all the studies we reviewed so far were primarily concerned with separating the disordered from the nondisordered, while a taxometric investigation of comorbidity is primarily concerned with separating one type of disorder from another. There are many implications of this shift in orientation, including (a) sample selection (a diagnostically homogeneous patient sample may be preferable to a general population sample); (b) indicator selection (indicators may need to be specific, free of general psychopathology factors such as distress); (c) design of analyses (two parallel analyses may be necessary); and many others. Clearly, taxometric modeling of comorbidity is a complicated issue as many more latent structures are possible relative to only one or two underlying distributions. Meehl's description of these models (2001) only scratched the surface, and unfortunately we cannot go into a discussion of these issues because this topic warrants its own separate treatment. Moreover, virtually nothing is known about the pragmatic considerations and problems associated with taxometrics of comorbid models, because no investigations of this issue using simulated or real data have been published to date. We are aware of only one unpublished study that considered taxonic comorbidity, but because it is not fully completed, we will describe it only briefly.

Kotov and Watson (2004) examined the comorbidity of schizotypy (operationalized with measures of cognitive slippage) and dissociative taxa in a large sample of undergraduates ($N = 955$). They used at least three continuous and reliable indicators to define each entity. MAXCOV and MAMBAC analyses replicated previous findings and identified a schizotypy taxon with the base rate of .065 and a dissociation taxon with the base rate of .084. Nearly half of the schizotypy taxon members (47%) were also members of the dissociation taxon, which is six times greater than expected by chance. The authors also examined the construct validity of the resulting three groups (pure schizotypy, pure dissociation, and the comorbid group) by relating them to "Big Five" traits of personality, measures of obsessive-compulsive symptoms, and a few others, and found essentially identical profiles for the groups. The authors concluded that it is likely that the identified taxa reflect the same underlying abnormality, but they did not test this hypothesis formally.

One possible test of this hypothesis is to remove the cases that belong to one taxon (e.g., schizotypy) and examine indicators of another taxon (dissociation) for evidence of taxonicity. If the results are still taxonic, it can be concluded that the taxa are at least partially independent. If the results are nontaxonic, it can be presumed that the two identified taxa reflect the same underlying abnormality and removal of comorbid cases left only marginal taxon members and misclassified cases that cannot (and should not) be detected by taxometric procedures. However, removal of the comorbid cases may make the taxon too small to be detectable. This confound can be tested by dropping only pure cases and keeping comorbid cases, which would make the taxon just as small, and performing taxometric analyses on this sample. If the taxon is identified, we can conclude that a small number of cases is not really a problem.

CONCLUSIONS

In this chapter we reviewed taxometric studies in domains of psychopathology that only recently attracted the attention of taxometricians: eating disorders, depression, anxiety, personality disorder, and issues surrounding comorbidity. In all these areas the findings are mixed, and it is impossible to offer a verdict about the taxonic status of any of these forms of psychopathology. Perhaps the reason for these inconsistencies is the heterogeneity of the constructs. In the domain of eating disorders, there is some evidence supporting the taxonicity of bulimia, whereas the taxonic status of anorexia is unclear; psychological processes underlying eating disorders seem to be continuous. It appears that a general depression taxon does not exist, but there is emerging evidence that certain subtypes of depression may be taxonic. Anxiety remains relatively neglected, with initial investigations suggesting that generalized anxiety disorder and posttraumatic stress disorder are not taxa. There is some indication, however, that a general anxiety taxon may exist. Personality disorders are virtually untested, and the only published study in this domain suggests that borderline personality disorder is taxonic. These findings as well as results of studies reviewed in the previous chapter are summarized in Table 6.1.

The summary suggests that a number of psychopathology taxa have been identified to date and some forms of psychopathology were found to be continuous. However, support for many of these taxa and continua is rather weak and replications are desperately needed. In fact, at this point we cannot say that the taxonic status of any of the DSM disorders is known with certainty. Constructs where the structure has been consistently supported (e.g., schizotypy or depression severity) do not map clearly on the DSM. Only a handful of taxometric studies have directly evaluated DSM diagnoses, and multiple replications are needed before any firm conclusions can be drawn.

Nevertheless, it is clear to us that the field of psychopathology is undergoing a transformation. There have been dramatic advances in quantitative methods that allow researchers to evaluate the basic premise behind our nosological system. Thus far the implicit assumption of the DSM was that psychiatric disorders are well represented by categorical diagnoses. This assumption is not necessarily true and may be valid only for certain mental disorders. We believe that all DSM entities must be tested using taxometrics (with CCK or non-CCK procedures). If all diagnoses are tested, we are likely to find that many of them are best conceptualized as continua.

We believe that categorical and dimensional models can be integrated to provide richer and more useful descriptions of mental disorders. This is not only true for continuous forms of psychopathology but for taxonic disorders as well. Consider that taxa are almost never all-or-nothing entities. Dimensionality still can be observed within the nontaxon and the taxon groups and these gradations may be important. For example, a diagnosis of spinal meningitis is categorical (the infection either is or is not present in the spine), and it is an important determinant of treatment. However, a person with meningitis can have different degrees of fever, which is an important determinant of survival. Thus, degrees of severity are observed within the meningitis taxon, and knowing a patient's diagnosis does not provide critical information that a measurement of a continuous construct (body temperature) offers. This is why Waller and Meehl (1998) pointed out that it is a mistake

TABLE 6.1
Summary of Taxometric Research in Psychopathology

Construct	Status	Number of studies	Strength of evidence	Evidence of construct validity
Cognitive Slippage	Taxonic	5	Strong	Limited
Social Anhedonia	Taxonic	1	Fair	None
Dissociation	Taxonic	2	Strong	Fair
Antisocial Personality– Psychopathy	Taxonic	3	Fair to strong	None
Eating Disorder– Bulimia Nervosa	Taxonic	2	Fair	Limited
Dysfunctional Eating Attitudes	Nontaxonic	1	Limited	NA
General Depression Severity	Nontaxonic	3	Fair to strong	NA
Depression Subtypes (Melancholic & IDS)	Taxonic	4	Fair to strong	None
GAD	Nontaxonic	1	Fair	NA
PTSD	Nontaxonic	1	Limited to fair	NA
General Anxiety	Taxonic	1	Fair	Fair to strong
Anxiety Sensitivity	Taxonic	1	Fair	Fair
Borderline PD	Taxonic	1	Limited	NA

Note. IDS = Involuntary Defeat Syndrome.

to think about results of taxometric analyses simply in terms of taxa versus continua; rather, the results should be interpreted to indicate presence of a taxon and a continuum versus a continuum alone. The implication is that even if a substantial number of psychopathology taxa are found, dichotomous, qualitative diagnostics can be completed by dimensional assessment.

It also seems likely that some mental disorders (perhaps major depressive disorder) in their present form will fail to show evidence of taxonicity, but definitional refinement would help elucidate underlying taxa (e.g., melancholia). Thus, taxometrics may be able to serve as an impetus and a guide for revising the diagnostic system. Of course, taxometric methods alone are not sufficient to tackle this task and should be used in conjunction with dimensional methods, such as exploratory factor analysis. Dimensions provide the building blocks for construction of taxa, and research on the structure of psychopathology should integrate dimensional and taxometric methods.

Much of our discussion is based on the idea that a variety of forms of psychopathology are taxonic. The critical question is, "How common are these taxa?". The empirical base is currently too limited to answer this question, although it is reassuring that Table 6.1 includes nine taxonic versus four nontaxonic constructs. Instead, let us evaluate this question conceptually. First, notice that the notion of continuity easily translates into the idea of monotonous relations, such as linear, quadratic, exponential, and asymptotic effects. If a construct is dimensional, it should relate to other dimensional variables in an even fashion without any sudden jumps or threshold effects. In other words, nothing unusual can occur at any particular level of the construct; dimensional models cannot account for sudden changes in relations between variables. Thus, response to treatment should be a simple function of symptom severity, and impairment should grow proportionally to the number of symptoms present. It seems unlikely that these models fit many data perfectly; common sense suggests that there almost certainly are some abnormalities in the data. These irregularities are taxa. It seems plausible to us that quite a few taxa exist out there; otherwise, the world would be an extremely orderly place.

The real concern, however, is that at least some of these taxa are trivial or unimportant (Widiger, 2001). In other words, the fact that a taxon exists does not mean it is of any use to anyone. Perhaps not every psychopathology taxon should be made into a diagnosis. How can we tell whether a taxon should be included in the nosological system? Our answer is that the utility of an entity has to be shown empirically. We believe that a taxon should be validated before it is included in the diagnostic system: Its construct validity and utility need to be shown. This idea is not new and is required of *DSM* diagnoses as well. Unfortunately, as can be seen in Table 6.1, this aspect of taxometric work has been largely neglected. It is an imperative for future taxometric studies to evaluate construct validity of a taxon.

REFERENCES

Abramson, L., Metalsky, G. I., & Alloy, L. B. (1989). Hopelessness depression: A theory-based subtype of depression. *Journal of Abnormal Psychology, 96*, 358–372.

Achenbach, T. M. (1991). *Manual for the youth self-report and 1991 profile*. Burlington: University of Vermont, Department of Psychiatry.

Aldenderfer, M. S., & Blashfield, R. K. (1984). *Cluster analysis*. Beverly Hills, CA: Sage.

Allen, J. G., Fultz, J., Huntoon, J., & Brethour, J. R. (2002). Pathological dissociative taxon membership, absorption and reported childhood trauma in women with trauma-related disorders. *Journal of Trauma and Dissociation, 3*, 89–110.

Ambrosini, P. J. (2000). Historical development and present status of the Schedule for Affective Disorders and Schizophrenia for school-age children (K-SADS). *Journal of the American Academy of Child and Adolescent Psychiatry, 39*, 49–58.

Ambrosini, P., Bennett, D. S., Cleland, C. M., & Haslam, N. (2002). Taxonicity of adolescent melancholia: A categorical or dimensional construct? *Journal of Psychiatric Research, 36*, 247–256.

American Psychiatric Association. (1952). *Diagnostic and statistical manual of mental disorders*. Washington, DC: Author.

American Psychiatric Association. (1968). *Diagnostic and statistical manual of mental disorders* (2nd ed.). Washington, DC: Author.

American Psychiatric Association. (1980). *Diagnostic and statistical manual of mental disorders* (3rd ed.). Washington, DC: Author.

American Psychiatric Association. (1987). *Diagnostic and statistical manual of mental disorders* (3rd ed., rev.). Washington, DC: Author.

American Psychiatric Association. (1994). *Diagnostic and statistical manual of mental disorders* (4th ed.). Washington, DC: Author.

American Psychiatric Association. (2000). *Diagnostic and statistical manual of mental disorders* (4th ed., text rev.). Washington, DC: Author.

Amering, M., & Katschnig, H. (1990). Panic attacks and panic disorder in cross-cultural perspective. *Psychiatric Annals, 20,* 511–516.

Amir, N. (2001). *Taxometrics.* Retrieved January 30, 2004, from University of Georgia, Center for Understanding and Treating Anxiety Web site: http://nas.psy.uga.edu/TAX.html

Barlow, D. H. (1988). *Anxiety and its disorders.* New York: Guilford.

Barlow, D. H. (2002). *Anxiety and its disorders* (2nd ed.). New York: Guilford.

Beach, S. R. H., & Amir, N. (2003). Is depression taxonic, dimensional, or both? *Journal of Abnormal Psychology, 112,* 228–236.

Beauchaine, T. P., & Beauchaine, R. J. (2002). A comparison of maximum covariance and k-means cluster analysis in classifying cases into known taxon groups. *Psychological Methods, 7,* 245–261.

Beck, A. T., Epstein, N., Brown, G., & Steer, R. A. (1988). An inventory for measuring clinical anxiety: Psychometric properties. *Journal of Consulting and Clinical Psychology, 56,* 893–897.

Beck, A. T., Epstein, N., Harrison, R. P., & Emery, G. (1983). *Development of the Sociotropy-Autonomy Scale: A measure of personality factors in psychopathology.* Unpublished manuscript, University of Pennsylvania, Philadelphia.

Bem, S. L. (1974). The measurement of psychological androgyny. *Journal of Consulting and Clinical Psychology, 47,* 155–162.

Bernstein-Carlson, E., & Putnam, F. W. (1986). Development, reliability, and validity of a dissociation scale. *The Journal of Nervous and Mental Disease, 174,* 727–735.

Beutler, L., & Malik, M. L. (2002). *Rethinking the DSM: A psychological perspective.* Washington, DC: American Psychological Association.

Blanchard, J. J., Gangestad, S. W., Brown, S. A., & Horan, W. P. (2000). Hedonic capacity and schizotypy revisited: A taxometric analysis of social anhedonia. *Journal of Abnormal Psychology, 109,* 87–95.

Blashfield, R. K. (1976). Mixture model tests of cluster analysis: Accuracy of four agglomerative hierarchical methods. *Psychological Bulletin, 83,* 377–388.

Blashfield, R. K. (1986). Structural approaches to classification. In T. Millon & G. L. Klerman (Eds.), *Contemporary directions in psychopathology: Toward the DSM–IV* (pp. 363–379). New York: Guilford.

Blashfield, R. K., Sprock, J., & Fuller, A. K. (1990). Suggested guidelines for including or excluding categories in the *DSM–IV. Comprehensive Psychiatry, 31,* 15–19.

Blatt, S. J., & Homann, E. (1992). Parent–child interaction in the etiology of dependent and self-critical depression. *Clinical Psychology Review, 12,* 47–91.

Brooks, S. P., & Gelman, A. (1998). Alternative methods for monitoring convergence of iterative simulations. *Journal of Computational and Graphical Statistics, 7,* 434–455.

Bruch, H. (1973). *Eating disorders*. New York: Basic Books.

Carlson, E. B., Putnam, F. W., Ross, C. A., Torem, M., Coons, P., Dill, D., et al. (1993). Validity of the Dissociative Experiences Scale in screening for multiple personality disorder: A multi-center study. *American Journal of Psychiatry, 150,* 1030–1036.

Carpenter, W. T., Strauss, J. S., & Bartko, J. J. (1973). Flexible system for the diagnosis of schizophrenia: Report from the WHO International Pilot Study of Schizophrenia. *Science, 182,* 1275–1277.

Carson, R. C. (1991). Dilemmas in the pathway of DSM–IV. *Journal of Abnormal Psychology, 100,* 302–307.

Carson, R. C. (1996). Aristotle, Galileo, and the DSM taxonomy: The case of schizophrenia. *Journal of Consulting and Clinical Psychology, 64,* 1132–1139.

Chambless, D. L., Caputo, G. C., Bright, P., & Gallagher, R. (1984). Assessment of fear of fear in agoraphobics: The body sensations questionnaire and the agoraphobic cognitions questionnaire. *Journal of Consulting and Clinical Psychology, 52,* 1090–1097.

Chapman, J. P., Chapman, L. J., & Kwapil, T. R. (1995). Scales for the measurement of schizotypy. In A. Raine, T. Lencz, et al. (Eds.), *Schizotypal personality* (pp. 79–106). New York: Cambridge University Press.

Chapman, L. J., Chapman, J. P., & Raulin, M. L. (1976). Scales for physical and social anhedonia. *Journal of Abnormal Psychology, 85,* 374–382.

Chapman, L. J., Chapman, J. P., & Raulin, M. L. (1978). Body-image aberration in schizophrenia. *Journal of Abnormal Psychology, 87,* 399–407.

Clark, D. M. (1986). A cognitive approach to panic. *Behaviour Research and Therapy, 24,* 461–470.

Clark, L. A., Livesley, W. J., & Morey, L. (1997). Personality disorder assessment: The challenge of construct validity. *Journal of Personality Disorders, 11,* 205–231.

Clark, L. A., Livesley, W. J., Schroeder, M. L., & Irish, S. L. (1996). Convergence of two systems for assessing specific traits of personality disorders. *Psychological Assessment, 8,* 294–303.

Clark, L. A., & Watson, D. (1991). Tripartite model of anxiety and depression: Psychometric evidence and taxonomic implications. *Journal of Abnormal Psychology, 100,* 316–336.

Clark, L. A., & Watson, D. (1995). Constructing validity: Basic issues in objective scale development. *Psychological Assessment, 7,* 309–319.

Clark, L. A., & Watson, D. (1999). Personality, disorder, and personality disorder: Toward a more rational conceptualization. *Journal of Personality Disorders, 13,* 142–151.

Cleckley, H. (1941). *The mask of sanity*. Augusta, GA: C. V. Mosby.

Cleland, C., Rothschild, L., & Haslam, N. (2000). Detecting latent taxa: Monte Carlo comparison of taxometric, mixture model, and clustering procedures. *Psychological Reports, 87,* 37–47.

Clogg, C. C. (1995). Latent class models. In G. Arminger, C. C. Clogg, & M. E. Sobel (Eds.), *Handbook of statistical modeling for the social and behavioral sciences* (pp. 311–359). New York: Plenum.

Cohen, J. (1988). *Statistical power analysis for the behavioral sciences* (2nd ed.). Hillsdale, NJ: Erlbaum.

Cohen, J., & Cohen, P. (1983). *Applied multiple regression–correlation analysis for the behavioral sciences* (2nd ed.). Hillsdale, NJ: Erlbaum.

Coyne, J. C. (1994). Self-reported distress: Analog or ersatz depression? *Psychological Bulletin, 116,* 29–45.

Cronbach, L. J., & Meehl, P. E. (1955). Construct validity in psychological tests. *Psychological Bulletin, 52,* 281–302.

DeAngelis, T. (1993). Controversial diagnosis is voted into latest DSM. *Monitor on Psychology, 24,* 32–33.

Depue, R. A., & Monroe, S. M. (1978). Learned helplessness in the perspective of the depressed disorders: Conceptual and definitional issues. *Journal of Abnormal Psychology, 87,* 3–20.

Drewnowski, A., Yee, D. K., Kurth, C. L., & Krahn, D. D. (1994). Eating pathology and the *DSM–III–R* bulimia nervosa: A continuum of behavior. *American Journal of Psychiatry, 151,* 1217–1219.

Eckblad, M. L., & Chapman, L. J. (1983). Magical ideation as an indicator of schizotypy. *Journal of Consulting and Clinical Psychology, 51,* 215–225.

Eckblad, M. L., Chapman, L. J., Chapman, J. P., & Mishlove, M. (1982). *The Revised Social Anhedonia Scale.* Unpublished test, University of Wisconsin, Madison.

Fabrigar, L. R., Wegener, D. T., MacCallum, R. C., & Strahan, E. J. (1999). Evaluating the use of exploratory factor analysis in psychological research. *Psychological Methods, 4,* 272–299.

Faust, D., & Miner, R. A. (1986). The empiricist and his new clothes: *DSM–III* in perspective. *American Journal of Psychiatry, 143,* 962–967.

First, M. B., Spitzer, R. L., Gibbon, M., & Williams, J. B. (1994). *Structured clinical interview for DSM–IV-patient edition.* (SCID-I/P, Version 2.0). New York: Biometrics Research Department.

Fitzpatrick, K. K., & Schmidt, N. B. (2000, November). *The Discomfort Intolerance Scale (DIS): Psychometric properties and clinical utility in patients with panic disorder.* Poster session presented at the annual meeting of the Association for Advancement of Behavior Therapy, New Orleans, LA.

Flett, G. L., Vredenburg, K., & Krames, L. (1997). The continuity of depression in clinical and nonclinical samples. *Psychological Bulletin, 121,* 395–416.

Follette, W. C., & Houts, A. C. (1996). Models of scientific progress and the role of theory in taxonomy development: A case study of the DSM. *Journal of Consulting and Clinical Psychology, 64,* 1120–1132.

Fossati, A., Maffei, C., Battaglia, M., Bagnato, M., Donati, D., Donini, M., et al. (2001). Latent class analysis of the *DSM–IV* schizotypal personality disorder criteria in psychiatric patients. *Schizophrenia Bulletin, 27,* 59–71.

Franklin, L. C., Strong, D. R., & Greene, R. (2002). A taxometric analysis of the MMPI-2 Depression Scales. *Journal of Personality Assessment, 79,* 110–121.

Frischholz, E. J., Braun, B. G., Sachs, R. G., & Schwartz, D. R. (1991). Construct validity of the Dissociative Experiences Scale (DES): I. The relationship between the DES and other self-report measures of DES. *Dissociation: Progress in the Dissociative Disorders, 4,* 185–188.

Gangestad, S., & Snyder, M. (1985). To carve nature at its joints: On the existence of discrete classes in personality. *Psychological Review, 92,* 317–349.

Garner, D. M., Olmsted, M. P., Bohr, Y., & Garfinkel, P. E. (1982). The Eating Attitudes Test: Psychometric features and clinical correlates. *Psychological Medicine, 12,* 871–878.

Gilbert, P. (2000). Varieties of submissive behavior as forms of social defense: Their evolution and role in depression. In L. Sloman & P. Gilbert (Eds.), *Subordination and defeat: An evolutionary approach to mood disorders and their therapy* (pp. 3–45). Mahwah, NJ: Erlbaum.

Gleaves, D., Lowe, M., Green, B., Cororve, M., & Williams, T. (in press). Do anorexia and bulimia nervosa occur on a continuum? A taxometric analysis. *Behavior Therapy.*

Gleaves, D., Lowe, M., Snow, A. C., Green, B., & Murphy-Eberenz, K. P. (2000). Continuity and discontinuity models of bulimia nervosa: A taxometric investigation. *Journal of Abnormal Psychology, 109,* 56–68.

Golden, R. R. (1982). A taxometric model for the detection of a conjectured latent taxon. *Multivariate Behavioral Research, 17,* 389–416.

Golden, R. R., & Meehl, P. E. (1979). Detection of the schizoid taxon with MMPI indicators. *Journal of Abnormal Psychology, 88,* 217–233.

Gorenstein, E. E. (1984). Debating mental illness: Implications for science, medicine, and social policy. *American Psychologist, 39,* 50–56.

Gottesman, I. I. (1991). *Schizophrenia genesis. The origins of madness.* New York: Freeman.

Gould, S. J. (1996). *Full house.* New York: Three Rivers Press.

Green, B. F. (1951). A general solution for the latent class model of latent structure analysis. *Psychometrika, 16,* 151–166.

Green, B. F. (1952). Latent structure class analysis and its relation to factor analysis. *Journal of American Statistical Association, 47,* 71–76.

Grove, W. M., & Meehl, P. E. (1993). Simple regression-based procedures for taxometric investigations. *Psychological Reports, 73,* 707–737.

Harding, J. P. (1949). The use of probability paper for the graphical analysis of polymodal frequency distributions. *Journal of the Marine Biological Association, 28,* 141–153.

Hare, R. D. (1991). *The Psychopathy Checklist–Revised.* Toronto, Ontario, Canada: Multi-Health Systems.

Hare, R. D., Harpur, T. J., Hakstian, A. R., Forth, A. E., Hart, S. D., & Newman, J. P. (1990). The revised psychopathology checklist: Reliability and factor structure. *Psychological Assessment, 2*, 338–341.

Harpur, T. J., Hart, S., & Hare, R. D. (1994). Personality of the psychopath. In P. T. Costa & T. A. Widiger (Eds.), *Personality disorders and the five-factor model of personality* (pp. 149–173). Washington, DC: American Psychological Association.

Harris, G. T., Rice, M. E., & Quinsey, V. L. (1994). Psychopathy as a taxon: Evidence that psychopaths are a discrete class. *Journal of Consulting and Clinical Psychology, 62*, 387–397.

Haslam, N., & Beck, A. T. (1994). Subtyping major depression: A taxometric analysis. *Journal of Abnormal Psychology, 103*, 686–692.

Haslam, N., & Kim, H. C. (2002). Categories and continua: A review of taxometric research [Monograph]. *Genetic, Social, and General Psychology Monographs, 128*, 271–320.

Hayes, S. C., Wilson, K. G., Gifford, E. V., Follette, V. M., & Strosahl, K. (1996). Experiential avoidance and behavioral disorders: A functional dimensional approach to diagnosis and treatment. *Journal of Consulting and Clinical Psychology, 64*, 1152–1168.

Hempel, C. G. (1965). *Aspects of scientific explanation.* New York: Free Press.

Holden, C. (1986). Proposed new psychiatric diagnoses raise charges of gender bias. *Science, 231*, 327–328.

Joiner, T., & Schmidt, N. B. (2002). Taxometrics can do diagnostics right (and it isn't quite as hard as you think). In L. Beutler & M. L. Malik (Eds.), *Rethinking the DSM: A psychological perspective* (pp. 107–120). Washington, DC: American Psychological Association.

Jöreskog, K. G., & Sörbom, D. (1988). *LISREL 7: A guide to the program and applications.* Chicago: SPSS.

Joyce, P. R. (1994). The epidemiology of depression and anxiety. In J. A. den Boer & J. M. A. Sitsen (Eds.), *Handbook of depression and anxiety* (pp. 57–69). New York: Marcel Dekker.

Kazdin, A. E., Rodgers, A., & Colbus, D. (1986). The Hopelessness Scale for Children: Psychometric characteristics and concurrent validity. *Journal of Consulting and Clinical Psychology, 54*, 241–255.

Keane, T. M., Caddell, J. M., & Taylor, K. L. (1998). Mississippi Scale for Combat-Related Posttraumatic Stress Disorder: Three studies in reliability and validity. *Journal of Consulting and Clinical Psychology, 56*, 85–90.

Kessler, R. C., Stein, M. B., & Berglund, P. (1998). Social phobia subtypes in the National Comorbidity Survey. *American Journal of Psychiatry, 155*, 613–619.

Klein, D. F. (1993). False suffocation alarms, spontaneous panics, and related conditions: An integrative hypothesis. *Archives of General Psychiatry, 50*, 306–317.

Korfine, L., & Lenzenweger, M. F. (1995). The taxonicity of schizotypy: A replication. *Journal of Abnormal Psychology, 104*, 26–31.

Kotov, R., Schmidt, N. B., Lerew, D. R., Joiner, T. E., & Ialongo, N. S. (2004). *Latent structure of anxiety: Taxometric exploration and construct validation*. Manuscript submitted for publication.

Kotov, R., & Watson, D. (2004). *The comorbidity of the schizotypy and dissociative taxa*. Unpublished manuscript, University of Iowa, Iowa City.

Kraepelin, E. (1899). *Psychiatrie: Ein lehrbuch fur studierende und aerzte* (6th ed.) [Psychiatry: A textbook for studying and practitioners]. Leipzig, Germany: Barth.

Krueger, R. F. (2002). Psychometric perspectives on comorbidity. In J. E. Helzer & J. J. Hudziak (Eds.), *Defining psychopathology in the 21st century: DSM–V and beyond* (pp. 41–54). Washington, DC: American Psychiatric Press.

Kutlesic, V., Williamson, D. A., Gleaves, D. H., Barbin, J. M., & Murphy-Eberenz, K. P. (1998). The interview for the Diagnosis of Eating Disorders-IV: Application to *DSM–IV* diagnostic criteria. *Psychological Assessment, 10*, 41–48.

Landy, D. (1985). Pibloktoq [hysteria] and Inuit nutrition: Possible implication of hypervitaminosis A. *Social Science and Medicine, 21*, 173–185.

Lazarfeld, P. F., & Henry, N. W. (1968). *Latent structure analysis*. Boston: Houghton Mifflin.

Leavitt, F. (1999). Dissociative experiences scale taxon and measurement of dissociative pathology: Does the taxon add to an understanding of dissociation and its associated pathologies? *Journal of Clinical Psychology in Medical Settings, 6*, 427–440.

Lenzenweger, M. F. (1993). Explorations in schizotypy and the psychometric high-risk paradigm. In L. J. Chapman, J. P. Chapman, & D. Fowles (Eds.), *Progress in experimental personality and psychopathology research* (Vol. 16, pp. 66–116). New York: Springer.

Lenzenweger, M. F. (1999). Deeper into the schizotypy taxon: On the robust nature of maximum covariance analysis. *Journal of Abnormal Psychology, 108*, 182–187.

Lenzenweger, M. F., Bennett, M. E., & Lilenfeld, L. R. (1997). The Referential Thinking Scale as a measure of schizotopy: Scale development and initial construct validation. *Psychological Assessment, 9*, 452–463.

Lenzenweger, M., & Korfine, L. (1992). Confirming the latent structure and base rate of schizotypy: A taxometric analysis. *Journal of Abnormal Psychology, 101*, 567–571.

Lerew, D. R., Schmidt, N. B., & Jackson, R. J. (1999). Evaluation of psychological risk factors: Prospective prediction of psychopathology during basic training. *Military Medicine, 164*, 509–513.

Lilienfeld, S. O., & Marino, L. (1995). Mental disorder as a Roschian concept: A critique of Wakefield's "harmful dysfunction" analysis. *Journal of Abnormal Psychology, 104*, 411–420.

Lilienfeld, S. O., Waldman, I. D., & Israel, A. C. (1994). A critical examination of the use of the term and concept of comorbidity in psychopathology research. *Clinical Psychology-Science and Practice, 1*, 71–83.

Macfarlane, R. M. (1997). Taxometric analysis of schizotypy. *Dissertation Abstracts International: Section B: The Sciences & Engineering, 57*, 7735.

Maser, J. D., Kaelber, C., & Weise, R. E. (1991). International use and attitudes toward *DSM–III* and *DSM–III–R*: Growing consensus in psychiatric classification. *Journal of Abnormal Psychology, 100*, 271–279.

McCutcheon, A. L. (1987). *Latent class analysis.* Newbury Park, CA: Sage.

McLachlan, G. J. (1988). *Mixture models: Inference and applications to clustering.* New York: Marcel Dekker.

McNally, R. J. (1994). *Panic disorder: A critical analysis.* New York: Guilford.

Medin, D. L., & Shoben, E. J. (1988). Context and structure in conceptual combination. *Cognitive Psychology, 20*, 158–190.

Meehl, P. E. (1962). Schizotaxia, schizotypy, schizophrenia. *American Psychologist, 17*, 827–838.

Meehl, P. E. (1965). *Detecting latent clinical taxa by fallible quantitative indicators lacking an accepted criterion* (Rep. No. PR–65–2). Minneapolis: University of Minnesota, Research Laboratories of the Department of Psychiatry.

Meehl, P. E. (1973). MAXCOV-HITMAX: A taxonomic search method for loose genetic syndromes. In P. E. Meehl (Ed.), *Psychodiagnosis: Selected papers* (pp. 200–224). Minneapolis: University of Minnesota Press.

Meehl, P. E. (1977). Specific etiology and other forms of strong inference. *The Journal of Medicine and Philosophy, 2*, 33–53.

Meehl, P. E. (1978). Theoretical risks and tabular asterisks: Sir Karl, Sir Ronald, and the slow progress of soft psychology. *Journal of Consulting and Clinical Psychology, 46*, 806–834.

Meehl, P. E. (1979). A funny thing happened to us on the way to the latent entities. *Journal of Personality Assessment, 43*, 563–581.

Meehl, P. E. (1986). Diagnostic taxa as open concepts: Meta-theoretical and statistical questions about reliability and construct validity in the grand strategy of nosological revision. In T. Millon & G. L. Klerman (Eds.), *Contemporary directions in psychopathology: Toward the DSM–IV* (pp. 215–231). New York: Guilford.

Meehl, P. E. (1990). Toward an integrated theory of schizotaxia, schizotypy, and schizophrenia. *Journal of Personality Disorders, 4*, 1–99.

Meehl, P. E. (1992). Factors and taxa, traits and types, differences of degree and differences of kind. *Journal of Personality, 60*, 117–174.

Meehl, P. E. (1995a). Bootstrap taxometrics. *American Psychologist, 50*, 266–275.

Meehl, P. E. (1995b). Extension of the MAXCOV-HITMAX taxometric procedure to situations of sizeable nuisance covariance. In D. Lubinski & R. V. Dawis (Eds.), *Assessing individual differences in human behavior: new concepts, methods, and findings* (pp. 81–92). Palo Alto, CA: Davies-Black.

Meehl, P. E. (1997). Credentialed persons, credentialed knowledge. *Clinical Psychology: Science & Practice, 4*, 91–98.

Meehl, P. E. (1999). Clarifications about taxometric method. *Applied and Preventive Psychology, 8,* 165–174.

Meehl, P. E. (2001). Comorbidity and taxometrics. *Clinical Psychology: Research and Practice, 8,* 507–519.

Meehl, P. E., & Golden, R. (1982). Taxometric methods. In P. Kendall & J. Butcher (Eds.), *Handbook of research methods in clinical psychology* (pp. 127–181). New York: Wiley.

Meehl, P. E., & Yonce, L. J. (1994). Taxometric analysis: I. Detecting taxonicity with two quantitative indicators using means above and below a sliding cut (MAMBAC procedure). *Psychological Reports, 74,* 1059–1274.

Meehl, P. E., & Yonce, L. J. (1996). Taxometric analysis: II. Detecting taxonicity using covariance of two quantitative indicators in successive intervals of a third indicator (MAXCOV procedure). *Psychological Reports, 78,* 1091–1227.

Meyer, T. J., & Keller, F. (2001). Exploring the latent structure of the Perceptual Aberration, Magical Ideation and Physical Anhedonia Scales in a German sample. *Journal of Personality Disorders, 15,* 521–535.

Meyer, T. J., Miller, M. L., Metzger, R. L., & Borkovec, T. D. (1990). Development and validation of the Penn State Worry Questionnaire. *Behaviour Research and Therapy, 28,* 487–495.

Miller, M. B. (1996). Limitations of Meehl's MAXCOV-HITMAX procedure. *American Psychologist, 51,* 554–556.

Mineka, S., Watson, D., & Clark, L. A. (1998). Comorbidity of anxiety and unipolar mood disorders. *Annual Review of Psychology, 49,* 377–412.

Nathan, P. E., & Lagenbucher, J. W. (1999). Psychopathology: Description and classification. *Annual Review of Psychology, 50,* 79–107.

Nelson, E., & Rice, J. (1997). Stability of diagnosis of obsessive-compulsive disorder in the Epidemiologic Catchment Area Study. *American Journal of Psychiatry, 154,* 826–831.

Newman, M. G., Zuellig, A. R., Kachin, K. E., & Constantino, M. J. (1997, November). *Examination of the reliability and validity of the GAD-Q-IV: A revised self-report measure of generalized anxiety disorder.* Poster session presented at the annual meeting of the Association for Advancement of Behavior Therapy, Miami, FL.

Perry, C. (1992). Problems and considerations in the valid assessment of personality disorders. *American Journal of Psychiatry, 149,* 1645–1653.

Peterson, R. A., & Reiss, S. (1987). *Anxiety sensitivity manual.* Worthington, OH: International Diagnostic Systems.

Pfohl, B., Blum, N., & Zimmerman, M. (1997). *Structured interview for DSM–IV personality (SIDP–IV).* Washington, DC: American Psychiatric Press.

Plomin, R., DeFries, J. C., McClearn, G. E., & Rutter, M. (1997). *Behavioral genetics* (3rd ed.). New York: Freeman.

Polivy, J., & Herman, C. P. (1987). Diagnosis and treatment of normal eating. *Journal of Consulting and Clinical Psychology, 55,* 635–644.

Popper, K. R. (1959). *The logic of scientific discovery*. New York: Basic Books.

Putnam, F. (1989). *Diagnosis and treatment of multiple personality disorder*. New York: Guilford Press.

Robins, L. N., Locke, B. Z., & Regier, D. A. (1991). An overview of psychiatric disorders in America. In L. N. Robins & D. A. Regier (Eds.), *Psychiatric disorders in America: The Epidemiologic Catchment Area Study* (pp. 328–366). New York: Free Press.

Robinson, M. D., & Clore, G. L. (2002). Episodic and semantic knowledge in emotional self-report: Evidence for two judgment processes. *Journal of Personality and Social Psychology, 83*, 198–215.

Rosch, E. R. (1973). Natural categories. *Cognitive Psychology, 4*, 328–350.

Rosenhan, D. L. (1973). On being sane in insane places. *Science, 179*, 250–258.

Ross, C. A. (1996). Epidemiology of dissociation in children and adolescents: Extrapolations and speculations. *Child & Adolescent Psychiatric Clinics of North America, 5*, 273–284.

Ross, C. A., Joshi, S., & Currie, R. (1991). Dissociative experiences in general population: A factor analysis. *Hospital and Community Psychiatry, 42*, 297–301.

Ruscio, A. M., Borkovec, T. D., & Ruscio, J. (2001). A taxometric investigation of the latent structure of worry. *Journal of Abnormal Psychology, 110*, 413–422.

Ruscio, A. M., & Ruscio, J. (2002). The latent structure of analogue depression: Should the Beck Depression Inventory be used to classify groups? *Psychological Assessment, 14*, 135–145.

Ruscio, A. M., Ruscio, J., & Keane, T. M. (2002). The latent structure of posttraumatic stress disorder: A taxometric investigation of reactions to extreme stress. *Journal of Abnormal Psychology, 111*, 290–301.

Ruscio, J. (2000). Taxometric analysis with dichotomous indicators: The modified MAXCOV procedure and a case-removal consistency test. *Psychological Reports, 87*, 929–939.

Ruscio, J. (2004). *Taxometric programs in the R language*. Retrieved January 30, 2004, from Elizabethtown College, Psychology Department Web site: http://www.etown.edu/psychology/Faculty/Ruscio.htm

Ruscio, J., & Ruscio, A. M. (2000). Informing the continuity controversy: A taxometric analysis of depression. *Journal of Abnormal Psychology, 109*, 473–487.

Ruscio, J., & Ruscio, A. M. (2002). A structure-based approach to psychological measurement: Matching measurement models to latent structure. *Assessment, 9*, 4–16.

Schmidt, N. B., Joiner, T. E., Young, J., & Telch, M. J. (1995). The Schema Questionnaire: Investigation of psychometric properties and the hierarchical structure of a measure of early maladaptive schemas. *Cognitive Therapy and Research, 19*, 295–321.

Schmidt, N. B., Kotov, R., Lerew, D. R., Joiner, T. E., & Ialongo, N. S. (in press). Evaluating latent discontinuity in cognitive vulnerability to panic: A taxometric investigation. *Cognitive therapy and research.*

Schmidt, N. B., Lerew, D., & Trakowski, J. J. (1997). Body vigilance in panic disorder: Evaluating attention to bodily perturbations. *Journal of Consulting and Clinical Psychology, 65*, 214–220.

Seedat, S., Stein, M. B., & Forde, D. R. (2003). Prevalence of dissociative experiences in a community sample: Relationship to gender, ethnicity, and substance use. *Journal of Nervous & Mental Disease, 191*, 115–120.

Sheehan, D. V. (1983). *The anxiety disease.* New York: Scribners.

Simpson, G. G. (1961). *Principles of animal taxonomy.* New York: Columbia University Press.

Skilling, T. A., Quinsey, V. L., & Craig, W. M. (2001). Serious antisocial behavior in boys: Evidence of an underlying taxon. *Criminal Justice and Behavior, 28*, 450–470.

Skilling, T. A., Harris, G. T., Rice, M. E., & Quinsey, V. L. (2002). Identifying persistently antisocial offenders using the Hare Psychopathy Checklist and DSM antisocial personality disorder criteria. *Psychological Assessment, 14*, 27–38.

Spitzer, R. L. (1973). A proposal about homosexuality and the APA nomenclature: Homosexuality as an irregular form of sexual behavior and sexual orientation disturbance as a psychiatric disorder. *American Journal of Psychiatry, 130*, 1214–1216.

Spitzer, R. L. (1975). On pseudoscience in science, logic in remission, and psychiatric diagnosis: A critique of Rosenhan's "On being sane in insane places." *Journal of Abnormal Psychology, 84*, 442–452.

Spitzer, R. L. (1991). An outsider–insider's views about revising the DSMs. *Journal of Abnormal Psychology, 100*, 294–296.

Spitzer, R. L., Forman, J. B., & Nee, J. (1979). DSM–III field trials: I. Initial interrater diagnostic reliability. *American Journal of Psychiatry, 136*, 815–817.

Stice, E., Ziemba, C., Margolis, J., & Flick, P. (1996). The dual pathway model differentiates bulimics, subclinical bulimics, and controls: Testing the continuity hypothesis. *Behavior Therapy, 27*, 531–550.

Sullivan, P. F., Prescott, C. A., & Kendler, K. S. (2002). The subtypes of major depression in a twin registry. *Journal of Affective Disorders, 69*, 273–284.

Tellegen, A., Ben-Porath, Y. S., McNulty, J. L., Arbisi, P. A., & Graham, J. R. (2003). *The MMPI-2 Restructured Clinical (RC) Scales: Development, validation, and interpretation.* Minneapolis: University of Minnesota Press.

Thelen, M. H., Farmer, J., Wonderlich, S., & Smith, M. (1991). A revision of the Bulimia Test: The BULIT-R. *Psychological Assessment, 3*, 119–124.

Trull, T. J., Widiger, T. A., & Guthrie, P. (1990). Categorical versus dimensional status of borderline personality disorder. *Journal of Abnormal Psychology, 99*, 40–48.

Tukey, J. W. (1977). *Exploratory data analysis.* Reading, MA: Addison Wesley.

Tylka, T. L., & Subich, L. M. (2003). Revisiting the latent structure of eating disorders: Taxometric analyses with nonbehavioral indicators. *Journal of Counseling Psychology, 50*, 276–286.

Tyrka, A. R., Cannon, T. D., Haslam, N., Mednick, S. A., Schulsinger, F., Schulsinger, H., & Parnas, J. (1995). The latent structure of schizotypy: I. Premorbid indicators of a taxon of individuals at risk for schizophrenia–spectrum disorders. *Journal of Abnormal Psychology, 104,* 173–183.

van den Brink, W., Schoos, C., Hanhart, M., Rouwendael, J., & Koeter, M. (1986, May). *Joint and test–retest reliability of DSM–III Axis II disorders.* Paper presented at the meeting of the American Psychiatric Association, Washington, DC.

Vredenburg, K., Flett, G. L., & Krames, L. (1993). Analogue versus clinical depression: A critical appraisal. *Psychological Bulletin, 113,* 327–344.

Wakefield, J. C. (1992). Disorder as harmful dysfunction: A conceptual critique of *DSM–III–R's* definition of mental disorder. *Psychological Review, 99,* 232–247.

Waldo, T. G., & Merritt, R. D. (2000). Fantasy proneness, dissociation, and *DSM–IV* Axis II symptomatology. *Journal of Abnormal Psychology, 109,* 555–558.

Waller, N. G. (2004). *The taxometrics home page.* Retrieved January 30, 2004, from Peabody College at Vanderbilt University, Psychology and Human Development Web site: http://peabody.vanderbilt.edu/depts/psych_and_hd/faculty/wallern/tx.html

Waller, N. G., & Meehl, P. E. (1998). *Multivariate taxometric procedures.* Thousand Oaks, CA: Sage.

Waller, N. G., Putnam, F. W., & Carlson, E. B. (1996). Types of dissociation and dissociative types: A taxometric analysis of dissociative experiences. *Psychological Methods, 1,* 300–321.

Waller, N. G., & Ross, C. A. (1997). The prevalence and biometric structure of pathological dissociation in the general population: Taxometric and behavior genetic findings. *Journal of Abnormal Psychology, 106,* 499–510.

Watson, D. (2003). Investigating the construct validity of the dissociative taxon: Stability analyses of normal and pathological dissociation. *Journal of Abnormal Psychology, 112,* 298–305.

Wechsler, D. (1997). *Wechsler Adult Intelligence Scale–III.* San Antonio, TX: The Psychological Corporation.

Whisman, M. A., & Pinto, A. (1997). Hopelessness depression in depressed inpatient adolescents. *Cognitive Therapy and Research, 21,* 345–358.

Widiger, T. A. (2001). What can be learned from taxometric analyses? *Clinical Psychology: Science and Practice, 8,* 528–533.

Widiger, T. A., & Frances, A. J. (2002). Toward a dimensional model for the personality disorders. In P. T. Costa & T. A. Widiger (Eds.), *Personality disorders and the five-factor model of personality* (pp. 23–44). Washington, DC: American Psychological Association.

Widiger, T. A., & Rogers, J. H. (1989). Prevalence and comorbidity of personality disorders. *Psychiatric Annals, 19,* 132–136.

Williams, J. B. W., Hyler, S. E., & Spitzer, R. L. (1982). Reliability in the *DSM–III* field trials: Interview versus case summary. *Archives of General Psychiatry, 39,* 1275–1278.

Williamson, D. A., Womble, L. G., Smeets, M. A. M., Netemeyer, R. G., Thaw, J. M., Kutlesic, V., et al. (2002). Latent structure of eating disorder symptoms: A factor analytic and taxometric investigation. *American Journal of Psychiatry, 159,* 412–418.

World Health Organization. (1992). *International Statistical Classification of Diseases and Related Health Problems* (Rev. ed.). Geneva, Switzerland: Author.

Zimmerman, M. (1988). Why are we rushing to publish *DSM–IV? Archives of General Psychiatry, 45,* 1135–1138.

Zung, W. W. K. (1965). A self-rating depression scale. *Archives of General Psychiatry, 12,* 63–70.

INDEX

ABOUT THE AUTHORS

Norman B. Schmidt received his PhD in 1991 in clinical psychology from the University of Texas at Austin. He completed his clinical internship at Brown University Medical Center as well as a National Institutes of Health postdoctoral fellowship at the University of Texas at Austin. Currently, he is a professor of psychology at Florida State University, where he directs the Anxiety and Behavioral Health Clinic. Dr. Schmidt's work primarily focuses on the nature and treatment of anxiety disorders. He conducts experimental psychopathology research as well as prevention and treatment trials for anxiety disorders. Dr. Schmidt has published over 80 articles and book chapters as well as a recent book, also published by the American Psychological Association, on combined treatments for mental disorders. Most of these articles focus on the nature, causes, and treatment of anxiety problems as well as the medical or health consequences of pathological anxiety. He currently serves on the editorial boards of many of the leading psychopathology journals. His research has been funded by the National Institute of Mental Health, the U.S. Department of Defense, Ohio State University, Ameritech Corporation, and the Ohio Department of Mental Health. For his research, Dr. Schmidt has received numerous awards including the American Psychological Association's Distinguished Scientific Award for Early Career Contribution to Psychology in the Area of Applied Research.

Roman Kotov studied physics at the Moscow State University. He received a double BS in physics and psychology from Ohio State University in 2000. He is currently a PhD candidate in clinical psychology at the University of Iowa. Mr. Kotov's research interests include taxometrics, individual differences in psychopathology, and cross-cultural studies. He has authored or co-authored several articles evaluating the taxonicity of constructs related to anxiety.

Thomas E. Joiner Jr. received his PhD in clinical psychology in 1993 from the University of Texas at Austin. He is the Bright-Burton Professor and Director of the University Psychology Clinic in the Department of Psychology at Florida State University. Dr. Joiner's recent papers on the psychology, neurobiology, and treatment of depression, suicidal behavior, anxiety, and eating disorders have established him as a leading international expert in these areas. He has authored or edited 6 books and published close to 200 peer-reviewed publications. Dr. Joiner was associate editor of the journal *Behavior Therapy* and currently sits on many editorial boards. Dr. Joiner has received numerous awards for his work, including a Guggenheim Fellowship as well as the Distinguished Scientific Award for Early Career Contribution to Psychology from the American Psychological Association in the area of psychopathology. His work has been supported by research grants from the National Institute of Mental Health and various other foundations.